# Internet Finance in China

This book is about Internet finance, a concept coined by the authors in 2012. Internet finance deals specifically with the impacts of Internet-based technologies, such as mobile payments, social networks, search engines, cloud computation, and big data, on the financial sector. Major types of Internet finance include third-party payments and mobile payments, Internet currency, P2P lending, crowdfunding, and the use of big data in financial activities.

Internet finance is highly popular and heavily discussed in China. Chinese Premier Li Keqiang made the healthy development of Internet finance a policy priority in 2014 state-of-union address. This book, as a detailed report on Internet finance in China, will help readers understand the status quo and development of China's financial system and will serve as a guide for readers doing financial businesses in China.

**Dr. Ping XIE** has been executive vice president of China Investment Corporation since 2007. He is responsible for private equity and direct investment. He is currently the Vice Chairman of CF40 Executive Council. From 2005–2007, he served as the President of Central Huijin Investment Corporation, which is now the domestic arm of CIC. He played an important role in the reform of China's big five state owned banks. Prior to that, he worked at the People's Bank of China for 20 years, where he held a number of senior positions, including the Head of the Financial Stability Department and Head of the Research Department. He has conducted extensive research in monetary theory and policy, comparative studies of financial systems, financial markets, rural finance, and financial regulation. He is a three-time winner of the Sun Ye Fang Economic Prize (1995, 2000, and 2005).

**Dr. Chuanwei ZOU** works at China Investment Corporation. He received his BS in statistics and MA in economics from Peking University, and his PhD in economics from the Graduate School of People's Bank of China (now PBC School of Finance, Tsinghua University). His research work is focused on credit markets, risk management, and financial regulation.

**Dr. Haier LIU** currently works at Guangdong University of Finance. He received his MA and PhD in economics from Southwestern University of Finance and Economics. His research work is focused on mobile banking and rural finance.

## The Editorial Board

The "New Finance Book Series" was created by the Shanghai Finance Institute (SFI). The book series traces developments in new finance, explores new trends, pursues solutions to novel problems, and inspires new knowledge.

Founded on July 14, 2011, the Shanghai Finance Institute (SFI) is a leading non-governmental, non-profit institute dedicated to professional academic financial research. SFI is operated by the China Finance 40 Forum (CF40) and has a strategic cooperation with the Shanghai Huangpu District government.

# Internet Finance in China

Introduction and Practical Approaches

**Ping Xie**
**Chuanwei Zou**
**Haier Liu**

Routledge
Taylor & Francis Group

LONDON AND NEW YORK

First published 2016
by Routledge

2 Park Square, Milton Park, Abingdon, Oxfordshire OX14 4RN
52 Vanderbilt Avenue, New York, NY 10017

*Routledge is an imprint of the Taylor & Francis Group, an informa business*

First issued in paperback 2020

*British Library Cataloguing in Publication Data*
A catalogue record for this book is available from the British Library

*Library of Congress Cataloging in Publication Data*
Xie, Ping, 1955- | Zou, Chuanwei. | Liu, Haier.
Internet finance in China : introduction and practical approaches /
Ping Xie, Chuanwei Zou, Haier Liu.
Description: 1 Edition. | New York, NY : Routledge, 2016.
Identifiers: LCCN 2015037695 | ISBN 9781138195080 (hardcover : alk. paper) |
ISBN 9781315637921 (ebk)
Subjects: LCSH: Internet banking—China. | Mobile commerce—China. | Big
data—China.
Classification: LCC HG1708.7 X54 2016 | DDC 332.0285/4678—dc23
LC record available at http://lccn.loc.gov/2015037695

ISBN: 978-1-138-19508-0 (hbk)
ISBN: 978-0-367-51580-5 (pbk)

Typeset in Bembo
by diacriTech, Chennai

# Contents

# List of figures

# List of tables

# 1   Introduction

SECTION 1: DEFINING INTERNET FINANCE

The concept of Internet finance originated in 2012. It includes all financial transactions and organizational structures under the influence of the Internet and ranges from traditional financial intermediaries and markets such as banks, securities, insurance, and exchanges all the way to those corresponding with Walrasian equilibrium.

## 1 Internet finance is a forward looking concept

It takes imagination to understand the concept of Internet finance. Today, all levels of institutions are involved. E-commerce companies, IT companies and mobile network operators now join the typical players such as banks, securities, insurance, and funds. The latter group is especially active in the evolution of various business models. This then blurs the line between the financial and non-financial industries.

Even so, at the time of writing, the development of Internet finance is far from complete. We optimistically estimate that it will take at least twenty years for Internet finance to fully develop. We draw this conclusion mainly based on the following two considerations. First, the speed of Internet finance's development largely depends on that of Internet technology, rather than that of finance itself. We predict that in twenty years, Internet technology will further decrease transaction costs and information asymmetry in financial transactions. Second, after twenty years, a generation that has grown up with the Internet will be the pillar of our society. Their habit of Internet use will influence financial transactions and organizational structures across the economy.

In such circumstances, academic research must look forward to examine future prospects. Internet finance is not merely a summary of history or the current situation; it is a forward-looking concept that emphasizes the future. It embodies three "rational anchors." First, Internet finance is grounded in reality. Forms of Internet finance that have already arisen serve as a starting point for our consideration. Second, Internet finance corresponds with basic principles of economics and finance, just like moving objects follow basic physical principles. We believe that the present theories of economics and finance provide sufficient analytical tools to explain forms already in existence and predict the prospects of Internet finance. This approach guides our thinking for this book. Third, the ultimate culmination of Internet finance research is the unintermediated market corresponding with Walras' General Equilibrium. Walras' General Equilibrium is a theoretical corner-stone of economics. It demonstrates that with a series of ideal assumptions, a per-fectly competitive market will reach an equilibrium state, in which supply of and demand for all commodities are equivalent and resource allocation is Pareto optimal (making someone better off without making anyone else worse off). In Walras' General Equilibrium, there are no financial intermediaries, and markets and cur-rency become unnecessary. Influential factors such as asymmetric information and transaction costs lead to the existence of financial intermediaries and markets in reality. Asymmetric information and transaction costs have markedly decreased due to the Internet. Internet finance will gradually reach an unintermediated state for finance and markets (Figure 1.1).

## 2 The changeable and unchangeable of Internet finance

### 2.1 The unchangeable

First, the core function of Internet finance is unchangeable. It allocates resources spatially and temporally in an uncertain environment and thus serves the real econ-omy. Specifically, it includes: payment and settlement, fund allocation, channels for transferring economic resources, risk management, information provision, and incentive management.

Second, the connotation of financial contracts such as equity rights, creditor rights, insurance, and trust funds is unchangeable. The nature of financial contracts is to specify rights and obligations, which mainly aims at the future cash flows of each party in an uncertain environment in the future. For example, equity rights denote residual claims or interests in the assets of all shareholders. Creditor rights permit creditors to charge principal and interest for a fixed period. Not long ago, financial contracts mainly existed in physical form (like the earliest A shares in China), but now are generally in electronic form. Moreover, it sets up a mechanism concerning trusteeships, transactions, and clearing. The connotation of financial contracts is unchangeable no matter the form. In Internet finance, all contracts are digitized and constitute the concept's foundations.

Third, the meaning of some concepts such as financial risk and externality are unchangeable. In Internet finance, risk means the possibility of suffering future loss. Concepts and analytical frameworks of market risk, credit risk, liquidity risk, operational risk, reputational risk, and legal compliance risk always apply. Problems such as misleading consumers, exaggerated advertising, and fraud also exist in Internet finance. Therefore, basic concepts for the regulation of Internet finance are unchangeable, and the main types of regulation like prudential regulation, behavio-ral regulation, and investor protection also apply. However, it differs from traditional finance for specific regulatory measures (see Chapter 10).

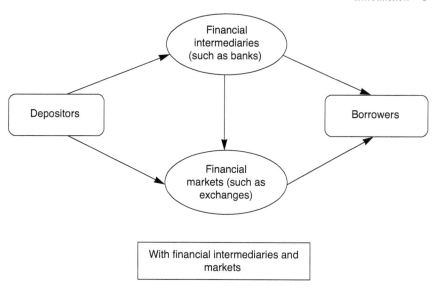

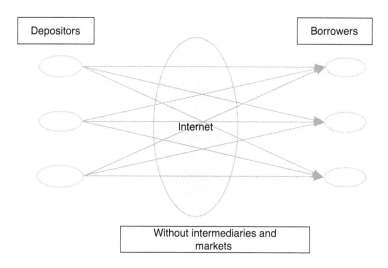

*Figure 1.1* How to understand a state without intermediaries and markets. Arrows denote
fund flows.

## 2.2 The changeable

The changes of Internet finance are mainly manifest in the penetration of the Internet
into finance. First, we have the influence of Internet technology, mobile and third-
party payments, big data, social networks, search engines, and cloud computing.

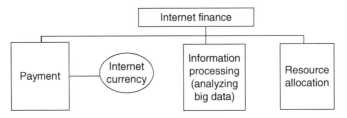

*Figure 1.2* Three pillars of Internet finance.

The Internet can significantly decrease transaction costs and asymmetric information, increase efficient management and pricing of risk, and expand the boundaries of possible transactions. It provides a platform for suppliers and demanders of capital to transact directly, which influences financial transactions and organizational forms.

Second, we have the influence of the Internet "spirit." The core of Internet spirit lies in openness, sharing, decentralization, equality, freedom of choice, usefulness, and democracy. On the other hand, traditional finance is more elitist. It stresses professional qualifications and entry thresholds, which manifest in the fact that not everyone can access financial services. Internet finance reflects the emergence of the individual organization and platform model in finance. Finance will be even more useful when financial distribution and specialization are weakened.

### 2.3 Three pillars of Internet finance (Figure 1.2)

The first pillar is payments. Payments are the infrastructure of finance and flow through all financial activities. In Internet finance, payments are based on mobile and third-party payments. It is out of the range of traditional payment and settlement systems, which are predominantly led by banks, and it reduces transaction costs. In Internet finance, payment links financial products, promoting richer business models (see Chapter 3 for the analysis of Yu'e Bao). Finally, due to the close connection of payment and currency, Internet currency has emerged.

The second pillar is information processing. Information is the core of finance. It constitutes the foundation for the allocation of financial resources. In Internet finance, big data is widely used in information processing (reflected in algorithms and automatic, high-speed calculations). It improves the pricing of risk and dramatically decreases asymmetric information. Internet finance's information processing method is the most significant difference between indirect finance through commercial banks and direct finance through capital markets.

The third pillar is resource allocation. Allocation of financial resources refers to the way they are transferred from suppliers to demanders. The fundamental goal of financial activities is resource allocation, thus the efficiency of resource allocation in Internet finance is the basis of its existence. In Internet finance, financial products are closely connected with the real economy. Boundaries for possible transactions are significantly expanded, and the supply and demand of funds can reach equilibrium without traditional financial intermediaries and markets, such as banks, securities companies, and exchanges.

We believe that any kind of financial transaction and contract form possessing at least one of the characteristics in the three pillars should be classified as Internet finance. This can be viewed as a constructive definition of Internet finance that can cover its main types. For example, if commercial banks use big data to conduct credit assessment and lending businesses, they are using Internet finance.

## SECTION 2: THE DEVELOPMENT OF INTERNET FINANCE

### 1 The rise of Internet finance

First, the Internet exerts its strongest influence on industries that do not need physical logistics, and finance is no exception. Over the past decade, it has exerted a revolutionary influence on industries such as telecommunication, journalism, books, publishing, television, music, and retail, followed by the film, education, and advertising industries. One clear example is that traditional handwritten letters have virtually disappeared after the rise of e-mail. Finance is essentially figures, (fixed assets account for a relatively low percentage of financial assets) and it has the same numerical characteristics as the Internet. All financial products can be viewed as a combination of figures and all financial activities as a movement of figures on the Internet.

Second, society is moving toward digitalization. About 70% of societal information has already been digitized. In the future, sensory equipment will be increasingly common. For example, smartphones integrate complicated sensors and programs. Activities such as shopping, consumption, reading, and others will move online. After the popularization of 3D printing, even manufacturing will move online. The Internet will bring about complicated new ways to communicate, cooperate, and divide labor. Under these conditions, it is possible that 90% of societal information could be digitized. This creates the conditions under which big data can be employed in finance. If individuals and companies put the majority of their information online, one could make accurate estimations of their credit quality and the outlook for their profitability (see Chapter 6 for a discussion of big data).

Third, risk-management tools and big data, which are accumulated by enterprises operating in the real economy, can also be applied in financial activities, typical cases of which are e-commerce companies like Alibaba and Jingdong. Internet finance thus naturally connects up with e-commerce and the sharing economy.

Fourth, some distortions and inefficient aspects of the Chinese financial system create space for the development of Internet finance.

- Formal finance has not always been able to meet the financial demands of small- and medium-sized enterprises (SMEs) and farmers, and private finance (or informal finance) has intrinsic limitation and risks.
- Economic restructuring has created spending and credit demands beyond those which can be met by formal finance.

- Banks are hugely profitable when the interest spreads between deposits and loans are protected, which is currently the case in China due to interest rate controls on deposits and lending. Capital thus has a strong incentive to enter the banking industry.
- The capped deposit interest rate, which has recently been at or below inflation, a stock market that has been weak for years and the recent restrictive policy on home purchases create barriers to effectively fulfilling the financial services demands of the population.
- Under the current IPO management system, channels for equity financing are impeded.
- Sales of securities, funds, and insurance are restricted to banks, so they are motivated to expand network sales.

In this context, Internet finance in China currently aims to meet the credit financing needs of individuals and SMEs, the equity financing needs of some creative projects, the investing and financing needs of ordinary people, and financial product sales through non-bank channels. It thus can also be considered inclusive finance. Internet finance will not have as large of an impact on big enterprises or big projects, but the share of such enterprises in the economy will decline over time. Moreover, financial resources in China have been allocated mostly to the central government and state-owned sectors for a long time. We predict that in the next ten years, large amounts of financial resources will be distributed from the central to local and state-owned to private sectors. This profound change in the distribution of financial resources will contribute to the development of Internet finance.

## 2 The scope of Internet finance

One typical example of the concept of spectrum is that of light. Sunlight can be divided into several continuous spectra according to their frequency. One end of the spectrum of Internet finance includes traditional financial intermediaries and markets such as banks, securities, insurance, and exchanges; the other end is a state without intermediaries or markets, corresponding to the Walrasia General Equilibrium. All other kinds of financial transactions and organizational forms between the two ends are on the range of Internet finance.

We divide Internet finance into six main types depending on the three pillars: payment, information processing, and resource allocation.

1   The internetization of finance
    Finance internetization reflects that the Internet is replacing manual provision of services by financial intermediaries and markets. This includes network and mobile banks, such as by ING Direct in Europe and M-Pesa in Kenya. It also comprises network stock exchanges, such as Charles Schwab in the United States. Network insurance companies such as Esurance provide insurance

products over the Internet, and network platforms such as SecondMarket, SharePost, and the Chinese Qianhai equity exchange handle financial transactions. Finally, network sales of financial products such as Yu'e Bao, Baidu Finance and Rong 360 are growing parts of the Internet finance landscape in China and elsewhere.

2   Mobile and third-party payments
    Mobile and third-party payments reflect the influence that the Internet has on the payments industry. The main players are Paypal in the USA, Alibaba, Caifutong, and Tencent's Wechat payment in China.

3   Internet currency
    Internet currency reflects the influence that Internet has on currency. It includes Bitcoin, Q-coin, and Amazon Coins.

4   Using big data for credit scoring and network loans
    Credit bureaus are key for loan provision, so we discuss credit investigation together with network loans. ZestFinance in the USA and Kreditech in Germany already do credit scoring based on big data, while Kabbage in the USA and Alibaba microcredit in China give out network loans based on big data.

5   Peer-to-Peer (P2P) network loans
    P2P network loans include personal debit and credit on the Internet, which is represented by Prosper, Lending Club, Zopa, Credit Ease, Lufax, Paipai Lending, and P2P Lending.

6   Crowdfunding
    Crowdfunding is financing over the Internet in which many investors are able to contribute small sums for a project or company. Current crowdfunding platforms include Kickstarter (which provides returns through means other than equity) and AngelCrunch.

We must clarify that there are no clear lines between so many different forms of Internet finance. They are all constantly changing. For example, usage-based insurance came into being in the insurance industry; equity research found that Twitter activity can predict future share prices; and the combination of big data with actuarial studies and portfolio investment will contribute to many new business models (see Chapter 12). Thus, the six main types of Internet finance in this book are neither mutually exclusive nor collectively exhaustive.

## 3 Governmental attitudes toward Internet finance

Generally speaking, the Chinese government has taken a positive attitude toward Internet finance. In April 2013, the Chinese State Council set up nineteen key financial projects, including "the development and regulation of Internet finance." The research group is composed of the People's Bank of China (PBoC), the China Banking Regulatory Commission (CBRC), the China Securities Regulatory

Commission (CSRC), the China Insurance Regulatory Commission (CIRC), the Ministry of Industry and Information Technology, the Ministry of Public Security, and the office of Legal Affairs. The results of this research will have far-reaching implications for the development of Internet finance in China.

In August 2013, Internet finance was written into two important State Council documents. In "Suggestions to Promote the Development of Small- and Medium-Sized Enterprises" by the State Council, the Council proposes making the most of new technologies and tools to create innovate network financial service models. In "Several Opinions on Promoting Information Consumption and Expanding Domestic Demand" by the State Council, the government proposes promoting Internet financial innovation and standardizing Internet financial services.

The PBoC gave a positive evaluation of Internet finance in its Q2 2013 executive report of currency policy. It deemed that Internet finance has advantages in its high transparency, inclusiveness, low transaction costs, convenient payments, rich credit information, and high efficiency of information processing. This was the first time that Internet finance has been written into such authoritative official documents.

In December, 2013, the Payment and Clearing Association of China established a specialized committee for Internet finance and introduced a self-regulatory system. Local governments are also very enthusiastic about Internet finance. For example, Zhongguancun and Shijingshan in Beijing and the Huangpu district in Shanghai all view Internet finance as an important emerging industry and have created incentives to promote the development of Internet finance in their jurisdictions.

## SECTION 3: STRUCTURE OF THIS BOOK

This book has 12 chapters divided into four parts. Figure 1.3 shows the structure.

1  Chapter 1 is a brief introduction of the book.
2  Chapters 2–10 is the main body of this book, discussing Internet finance.
   Chapter 2 discusses the principles of Internet finance.
   Chapters 3–9 discuss six main types of Internet finance: finance internetization (Chapter 3), mobile and third-party payments (Chapter 4), Internet currency (Chapter 5), credit bureaus and network loans based on big data (Chapter 7), P2P network loans (Chapter 8), and crowdfunding (Chapter 9). Before Chapter 7 (credit investigation and network loans based on big data), we will have a general discussion about big data to serve as a technical base. Chapters 4 and 5 mainly discuss the first pillar, Chapters 6 and 7 the second, and Chapters 8 and 9 the third. Chapter 10 discusses the regulation of Internet finance.
3  Chapter 11 discusses the Internet exchange economy.
4  Chapter 12 points out questions that need further research, mainly the application of big data for portfolio investment and actuarial studies.

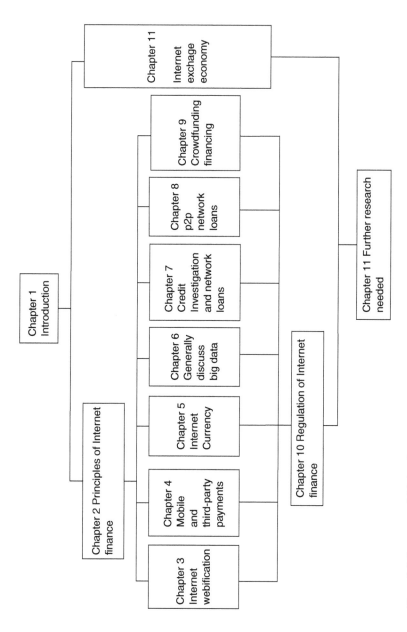

*Figure 1.3* Structure of this book.

# 2   The theory of Internet finance

## SECTION 1: INTRODUCTION

The basic function of a financial sector is to intermediate funds between those in need of money and those with extra money. However, financial intermediaries do not exist in the classic version of general equilibrium theory (Mas-Colell *et al.*). Mishkin suggests two reasons why financial intermediaries do exist in the real world.[1] First, financial intermediaries have special technologies and economies of scale to reduce transaction costs. Second, financial intermediaries process information to alleviate adverse selection and moral hazard caused by information asymmetry.

Traditionally, there are two types of financial intermediaries: commercial banks (indirect financing) and securities markets (direct financing). They play an important role in resource allocation and promote economic growth, but also incur large costs.

Internet-based technologies such as mobile payments, social networks, search engines, and cloud computing will lead to a paradigm shift in the financial sector. Beside indirect financing via commercial banks and direct financing through securities markets, a third way to conduct financial activities will emerge, which we call "Internet finance." Over the past ten years, similar paradigm shifts driven by the Internet have occurred in areas such as bookstores, music, and retail sales.[2]

Under Internet finance, mobile payments of individuals will be efficiently integrated with central payment systems managed by central banks. Information processing and risk assessment will be conducted on the Internet, and information will be highly transparent. Costs of maturity matching and risk sharing will be so low that financial intermediaries will be unnecessary, and the issuance and trading of stocks, bonds, and loans will be carried out smoothly. Markets will be so efficient that they highly resemble the world without financial intermediaries described by general equilibrium theory. Furthermore, Internet finance will be able to achieve the same allocative efficiency while greatly reducing transaction costs.

More importantly, under Internet finance, the division of labor of the modern financial industry will be obsolete and replaced by Internet-related technologies. Companies and ordinary people will be able to conduct financial transactions on the Internet. Complicated tasks such as risk sharing and maturity matching will be simpler and more user friendly. Financial services will be available to all, and everyone will enjoy the benefits. In this way, Internet finance is more democratic than a finance controlled by professional elites.

Internet finance is still in the nascent stage of development. Currently, the most prominent examples of Internet finance include mobile banking and peer-to-peer (P2P) lending. Internet finance will generate great opportunities and challenges. Governments can employ Internet finance to address the problem of small- and medium-sized enterprise (SME) financing, promote the transparency and safety of informal financing, and increase the availability of financial services. However, Internet finance will also bring about regulatory challenges.[3] For financial and IT companies, Internet finance will generate tremendous opportunities but also induce fierce competition. For academia, the payments revolution will shed new light on monetary policy.

We are the first to introduce the concept of Internet finance and present an in-depth analysis of this new concept based on case studies, economic modeling, sociological studies, and IT know-how. Our study focuses on three pillars of Internet finance. The first pillar is payment. Payment is the most important piece of the financial system's infrastructure and influences the form of financial activities. The second pillar is information processing. Information is at the heart of financial activities and lays the foundation for resource allocation. For Internet finance, information processing marks the greatest divergence from commercial banks and securities markets. The third pillar is resource allocation. Internet finance is justified by its allocative efficiency.

## SECTION 2: PAYMENT UNDER INTERNET FINANCE

Under Internet finance, money and securities will be transferred through mobile communication networks.

The foundation for mobile payments is the development of mobile communication technologies, especially the high penetration of smart phones and tablets. According to Goldman Sachs, the volume of mobile payments reached US$105.9 billion in 2011 and was expected to grow at 42% annually in the coming five years to reach US$616.9 billion by 2016. The share of mobile payments in the global payment market was 1% in 2011 and will reach 2.2% by 2015.[4]

Backed by Wi-Fi and 4G technologies, Internet and mobile communication networks are increasingly integrated, and cable telephone, radio, and TV networks will be incorporated in the near future. Mobile payments will then be further combined with credit cards, online banking, and e-payments to become more available, convenient, and user-friendly. With the development of security software such as identity authentication and digital signatures, mobile payments will be applied not only to small sum payments in daily life, but also to large payments between companies. It could completely replace payment instruments such as cash and checks.

Cloud computing ensures the storage and computing capabilities necessary for mobile payments. Despite becoming increasingly smart, mobile communication devices cannot match personal computers in terms of storage capacity and computing speed due to requirements for portability and size. Cloud computation can overcome such shortcomings through a transfer of storage and computation from mobile communication terminals to cloud computation servers.

Under Internet finance, the payment system will have the following characteristics. First, all individuals and institutions will open accounts at the payment center of their central bank for registration of deposits and securities. Second, transfers of money and securities will be conducted through mobile Internet networks. Third, payment and settlement will be electronic. The need for cash circulation will be greatly reduced. Fourth, the division of labor between commercial banks and central banks (or the two-tier banking system) will cease to exist. If deposit accounts are all located at central banks, the theory and practice of monetary policy will be fundamentally changed.[5] For instance, current deposits reserved for payment will diminish and the proportion of time deposits will increase. However, such a payment system will not challenge central banks' role in money supply. The relationship between money and price of goods will not fundamentally change either.

## SECTION 3: INFORMATION PROCESSING UNDER INTERNET FINANCE

### 1 General views

Information about capital suppliers and, more essentially, capital demanders, is imperative in financial activities. Mishkin points out that there are two types of information processing under direct and indirect financing.[6] The first type is the production and sale of information by private entities. Many specialized institutions produce information that can differentiate the quality of capital demanders, such as credit rating agencies and research teams at investment banks. Commercial banks are information producers and users at the same time, so they also belong to this category. The second type is information disclosure required or encouraged by governments, such as financial statements of listed companies.

Compared with commercial banks and securities markets, Internet finance will differ most in its information processing. First, social networks will generate and spread information, especially information without disclosure obligations. Second, search engines will structure, sequence, and index information to alleviate the overload problem. Third, cloud computation will ensure rapid processing capabilities for mass information. Thus, the overall picture is that, with the help of cloud computation, information from capital suppliers and demanders will be revealed and spread through social networks, concentrated and standardized by search engines to produce a dynamic information sequence. With such processed information, risk assessment of any capital demander will be carried out at a low cost. Thus information needs in financial activities will be satisfied in a way similar to the credit default swap (CDS) market. According to Xie and Zou, CDS creates a time series of default probability via transaction mechanisms similar to social networks and search engines.[7] It is even more effective than credit rating agencies. The following paragraphs discuss the roles of social networks, search engines, and cloud computation, respectively.

First, social networks digitize and map social relationships on the Internet and serve as platforms to release, spread, and share information. Social networks are based on two foundations. First, networking behaviors are intrinsic to human beings and characterized by the attributes of exchangeability,[8] consistency,[9] contagiousness,[10] and transmissibility.[11] Second, the development of the Internet and other communication technologies has reduced individuals' costs to release information and contact with strangers, leading to new types of collaboration such as Chinese phenomenon of "Cyber Manhunt" and editing of Wikipedia.[12] Social networks also contain lots of relational data, that is information about contact, connection, community attachment, and gathering.[13]

Second, from mass information, search engines can identify contents that best match the needs of information users. Integration between search engines and social networks is inevitable,[14] which is embodied in the development of social search.

Third, with the performance of integrated circuit (IC) approaching physical limits, cloud computation employs a large number of PCs to share computational tasks with great extendibility, fault tolerance and consistency of multiple backup data, producing huge computational capabilities and storage space. Cloud computation thus facilitates the processing of mass information and is instrumental in the development of search engines.[15] The financial sector, as one of the biggest users of computation power, will also be influenced by the development of cloud computation.

We use a simple example to demonstrate information processing under Internet finance. Individuals (or institution) have many stakeholders, who all have some information about their wealth, employment status, personality, and so on. If all stakeholders' information is released and pooled on social networks, and inaccurate information is disputed or filtered through social networks and search engines, we will get a reliable picture of their creditworthiness. Social networks also enable the accumulation of "social capital" among people, with which costs of financial activities will drop considerably and opportunistic behaviors will be constrained.

## 2 Model

### 2.1 Assumptions

Suppose there are $n$ persons who express their views on default probability of a person or entity ("reference entity") by trading a financial product similar to CDS. This financial product is essentially a two-period contract with two types of participants, sellers and buyers. For one unit of financial product, in the first period, the buyer pays to the seller a premium of $s$ (also the financial product's price); in the second period, if the reference entity defaults, the seller compensates the buyer an amount of $l$. Suppose $l$ is determined beforehand and $s$ by market equilibrium. Our target is to explore the information content of $s$.

Suppose all persons have an initial wealth in the first period, which exists in the form of risk-free bonds with zero risk-free rate. In the first period, every person decides whether to buy or sell the financial product and by what amount based on his information, wealth and risk preference. In the second period, if the reference entity defaults, compensation between buyers and sellers is triggered. Suppose that the utility of all persons is a CARA function of second-period wealth with absolute risk aversion coefficient $\alpha$, that is:

$$u(w) = -\alpha \exp(-\alpha \cdot w) \tag{2.1}$$

We use $Y$ to denote the fundamentals of the reference entity, such as credit record, income, liabilities, and so on. Suppose the default of the reference entity is characterized by a Logistic model. If $Y + e > 0$, default occurs; otherwise, there is no default. $e$ is random disturbance term and follows a Logit distribution with cumulative probability distribution function $F(e) = \dfrac{\exp(e)}{1 + \exp(e)}$. Hence, the default probability of the reference entity is:

$$P = \Pr(Y + e > 0) = 1 - \Pr(e \leq -Y) = \frac{\exp(Y)}{1 + \exp(Y)} \tag{2.2}$$

Suppose there are two types of information in $Y$. The first is public information, denoted by $X$. The second is private information acquired by every person, with private information of no. $i$ person denoted by $Z_i$. We introduce five assumptions on information structure:

1  $Y = X + \sum_{i=1}^{n} Z_i$, that is simple linear addition between public and private information;
2  For any $i$, $E(Z_i) = 0$;
3  For any $i \neq j$, $E(Z_j|Z_i) = 0$, that is private information of different persons is uncorrelated;
4  For any $i$, $E(Z_i|X) = 0$, that is public and private information is uncorrelated;
5  Assumptions I–IV are public knowledge.

## 2.2 Model solution

### 2.2.1 Representative person's utility maximization problem

Take person $i$ as an example. Based on his estimation of default probability, he decides how to buy or sell the financial product in the first period to maximize expected utility.

First, person $i$ has public information $X$ and private information $Z_i$ and his estimation of the fundamentals of the reference entity is $Y_i = E[Y|X, Z_i]$. Based on the above-mentioned assumptions, $Y_i = X + Z_i$, his estimation of default probability is:

$$P_i = \Pr(Y_i + e > 0) = \frac{\exp(X + Z_i)}{1 + \exp(X + Z_i)} \tag{2.3}$$

Second, we use $w_{i1}$ to denote the initial wealth of person $i$ and $\theta_i$ to denote the financial product bought in the first period, with $\theta_i > 0$ meaning a purchase and $\theta_i < 0$ meaning sales. Hence, second-period wealth is $w_{i2} = w_{i1} - \theta_i \cdot s + \theta_i \cdot l \cdot 1_{\{default\}}$, where $1_{\{default\}}$ indicates whether reference entity defaults.

Therefore, the utility maximization problem for person $i$ is:

$$\max_{\theta_i} \quad E_i\left[U\left(w_{i2}\right)\right] \qquad (2.4)$$

$$s.t. \quad w_{i2} = w_{i1} - \theta_i \cdot s + \theta_i \cdot l \cdot 1_{\{default\}}$$

where $E_i$ denotes conditional expectation based on the information set of person $i$.

FOC is :

$$P_i \cdot \exp\left(-\alpha\left(w_{i1} - \theta_i \cdot s + \theta_i \cdot l\right)\right) \cdot (l - s) - \left(1 - P_i\right) \cdot \exp\left(-\alpha\left(w_{i1} - \theta_i \cdot s\right)\right) \cdot s = 0,$$

thus

$$\theta_i = \frac{1}{\alpha l}\ln\left(\frac{P_i}{1 - P_i}\left(\frac{l}{s} - 1\right)\right) \qquad (2.5)$$

Monotonic increasing transformation $S = -\ln\left(\frac{l}{s} - 1\right)$ is introduced (or equivalently $s = l\dfrac{\exp(S)}{1 + \exp(S)}$. Since $S$ has the same information content as $s$,[16] we will focus on $S$ in the following analysis. Based on Equation (2.3), $\theta_i$ can be equivalently expressed as:

$$\theta_i = \frac{X + Z_i - S}{\alpha l} \qquad (2.6)$$

### 2.2.2 Model equilibrium

At equilibrium, the market clears, that is the buy and sell orders of the financial product offset each other.

$$\sum_{i=1}^{n}\theta_i = 0 \qquad (2.7)$$

Based on Equations (2.6) and (2.7), the equilibrium price of the financial product is:

$$S = X + \frac{1}{n}\sum_{i=1}^{n}Z_i \qquad (2.8)$$

*2.2.3 The information content of the equilibrium price*

The equilibrium price (Equation 2.8) embodies major attributes of information processing under Internet finance. First, private information is reflected and concentrated in the equilibrium price through the channel of $Z_i \rightarrow P_i \rightarrow \theta_i \rightarrow S$. Second, in the real world, much of private information may be classified as soft information and is difficult to transfer to others without distortion.[17] However, after every person converts his private information into the purchase or sale of the financial product, it is clear whether the information was positive or negative. Thus, soft information turns into hard information that is understandable to others. These two points mainly demonstrate the role of social networks in information processing.

Third, there is a relationship between the equilibrium price and the fundamentals of the reference entity: $Y = X + n(S - X)$. Clearly,[18]

$$E[Y|S,X] = Y \tag{2.9}$$

Therefore, the fundamentals of the reference entity can be correctly deduced based on public information and the equilibrium price, leading to accurate estimation of default probability based on Equation (2.2).[19] Hence, the equilibrium price can reflect all available information. This mainly demonstrates the role of search engines in information processing, which produce indicators that contain information in a condensed and effective way (like "sufficient statistics").

*2.2.4 The spread of information in social networks*

Suppose that during a certain period, the risk aversion coefficient and private and public information all remain constant. Consider the scenario that one person spreads private information in social networks. For simplicity, assume no. $i$ person spreads his private information $Z_i$.

Suppose that at a certain time $t$, the proportion of individuals who know $Z_i$ ("the informed") is $v_t \in (0,1)$ and who are unaware of $Z_i$ ("the uninformed") is $1 - v_t$. Suppose that during a short period of time with a length of $dt$, the informed increase by the following proportion:

$$dv_t = \lambda v_t(1 - v_t)dt \tag{2.10}$$

$\lambda$ reflects the interconnectedness of social networks. With other conditions constant, the higher interconnectedness of social networks is (higher value of $\lambda$), the faster information spreads. Based on Equation (2.10), we get

$$v_t = \frac{v_0 \exp(\lambda t)}{1 - v_0 + v_0 \exp(\lambda t)} \tag{2.11}$$

Where $v_0$ is the initial proportion of the informed. When $t \rightarrow \infty$, $v_t \rightarrow 1$, that is after a sufficiently long time, almost everyone will become informed.

Based on Equations (2.8) and (2.11), the relationship between equilibrium price and time is:

$$S_t = X + Z_i \cdot v_t + \frac{1}{n}\sum_{i=1}^{n} Z_i \tag{2.12}$$

Obviously, when $t \to \infty$, $S_t \to X + Z_i + \frac{1}{n}\sum_{i=1}^{n} Z_i$. So the spread of information is essentially a process of private information becoming public. This demonstrates the sharing and communication of information in social networks.

## SECTION 4: RESOURCE ALLOCATION UNDER INTERNET FINANCE

### 1 General views

Under Internet finance, capital supply and demand information will be released on the Internet and smoothly matched. Capital suppliers and demanders will contact each other directly and conduct transactions without the help of any financial intermediary.

An example is P2P lending such as Lending Club, which provides deposit and loan services similar to commercial banks. Lending Club is a US company founded in 2007. For qualified loan applications, Lending Club assigns internal credit ratings. Different ratings are associated with different loan interest rates. The lower the rating is, the higher the loan interest rate is. Lending Club refers to each loan as a note and publishes information of the loan and the borrower on its website for potential investors to select. For each note, the minimum amount an investor can buy is US$25, which is small enough to ensure risk diversification. Lending Club provides instruments for investors to construct loan portfolios and trade loans. Lending Club is also responsible for loan administration, such as receiving principal and interest payments from borrowers and transferring them to investors, handling payment delay or default, and so on.

Another example is crowdfunding such as Kickstarter, which functions similar to securities markets. Kickstarter is a US company founded in 2009. It helps creative projects to raise funds through an innovative online platform. Return to investors is in the form of project products, such as music CDs and movie posters. Investors can also recommend projects to their friends on Facebook. In April 2012, the United States passed the Jumpstart Our Business Startups Act (JOBS Act), allowing small companies to raise equity through crowdfunding.

To better explain resource allocation under Internet finance, we compare P2P lending represented by Lending Club with Rotating Savings and Credit Association (ROSCA) in the following paragraphs.

ROSCA is an informal financial organization that exists almost worldwide. Typically, an originator invites several friends or relatives to participate and meet every month or quarter for mutual assistance. For example, in coastal regions of southeast China, the number of participants is usually around 30. At every meeting, participants lend a certain amount of money to one person on a rotational basis. According to Zhang and Zou, ROSCA can be considered as a collection of P2P lending between participants who receive funds early and participants who receive funds later.[20] Although many researchers find that ROSCA plays an import role in promoting credit availability, crashes of ROSCA do occur. Zhang and Zou point out that ROSCA mainly relies on networks of acquaintances and has a safety frontier[21]. Once ROCSA expands beyond the circle of friends or relatives, it becomes very difficult to control participants' moral hazard, usually in the form of arbitrage among different ROSCAs. ROSCA has multiple rounds and it is almost impossible for participants to transfer their shares to others or withdraw early. When ROSCA encounters any problem, participants' utility maximizing behaviors usually lead to "fallacy of composition."

We can arrive at two conclusions. First, essentially both P2P lending and ROSCA are direct lending between two individuals. In fact, according to *SmartMoney Magazine*,[22] the founder of Prosper, the first P2P lending company, was inspired by ROSCA. Hence, P2P lending can be considered as an integration between Internet-based technologies and informal financial organizations.

Second, in P2P lending, an investor may extend loans as small as a few dozen dollars to hundreds of borrowers, which would be unimaginable in ROSCA. This is made possible by two factors. First, in P2P lending, borrowers' credit risk is evaluated by independent third parties. This greatly alleviates the information asymmetry problem and enables transactions between strangers. Second, investment and loan administration are carried out by modern technologies, which reduce transaction costs substantially.

By an extension of the above logic, we believe that, driven by Internet-based technologies such as mobile payments, social networks, search engines and cloud computing, direct financing among people (the oldest type of financial activities in human society) will reach beyond the traditional frontier of safety and commercial viability. With little information asymmetry and low transaction costs, Internet finance will generate a sufficiently large "transaction possibility set" where bilateral or multilateral transactions can be carried out simultaneously, quickly, and efficiently. Resource allocation under Internet finance will maximize social welfare and promote social equality. Everyone will have transparent and fair opportunities to invest or raise money. People who have never met will become acquaintances through Internet finance, which will facilitate their cooperation in other activities.

A key concept here is "transaction possibility set." Below is an explanation of this concept and how it is influenced by information asymmetry and transaction costs.

## 2 "Transaction possibility set"

We define "Transaction possibility set" as a set of one or multiple pairs of capital demander and supplier where among each pair, the highest funding cost affordable to the capital demander is higher than the minimum investment yield required by the capital supplier. "Transaction possibility set" emphasizes that based on the price of financing, the capital demander and supplier have the possibility to reach deals. But in the real world, capital suppliers usually have budgetary constraints and multiple investment opportunities. Whether a deal can be reached with a certain capital demander depends on complex conditions, which are not covered by "transaction possibility set."

### 2.1 Highest funding cost affordable to capital demander

Let's use $I$ to denote the set of capital demanders. Suppose all capital demanders are risk neutral and consider a representative capital demander $i \in I$. Assume he has an initial wealth of $E_i$ and needs a loan[23] of $L_i$ to start an investment project. The project has an expected yield of $\mu_i$, a success probability of $\theta_i$ and revenue in case of success $\dfrac{(1 + \mu_i)(E_i + L_i)}{\theta_i}$ and 0 in case of failure. Assume that when the capital demander does not apply for a loan, his wealth will stay at $E_i$. Let's use $f_i$ to denote loan interest rate and $l_i = \dfrac{L_i}{E_i}$ to denote the capital demander's debt-to-equity ratio.

Whenever the expected net profit of the project $(1 + \mu_i)(E_i + L_i) - \theta_i(1 + f_i)L_i$ exceeds $E_i$, the capital demander will apply for a loan. This is equivalent to:

$$1 + f_i \leq \frac{1 + \mu_i + \mu_i / l_i}{\theta_i} \tag{2.13}.$$

Equation (2.13) gives the highest funding cost affordable to the capital demander. The higher expected yield is (higher $\mu_i$), the higher project risk is (lower $\theta_i$) or the lower leverage ratio is (lower $l_i$), the higher funding cost the capital demander can afford.

### 2.2 Minimum investment yield required by capital supplier

We use $J$ to denote the set of capital suppliers. Assume that all capital suppliers are risk neutral and consider a representative capital supplier $j \in J$. Suppose his capital cost (or opportunity cost) is $r_j$. Assume that there exists transaction costs and information asymmetry between capital supplier $j$ and capital demander $i$. Assume transaction costs (credit assessment cost included) equal $c_{ij}$ times the loan amount, where $c_{ij} > 0$ and higher $c_{ij}$ indicates higher transaction costs. Assume that even after credit assessment, capital supplier $j$ still cannot accurately evaluate the success probability of capital demander $i$ and underestimate it to be $(1 - \lambda_{ij})\theta_i$, where $\lambda_{ij} \in (0,1)$ and higher $\lambda_{ij}$ indicates higher degree of information asymmetry.

The capital supplier's condition to extend a loan is that, loan yield (adjusted for possible loss caused by loan default) $(1 - \lambda_{ij})\theta_i(1 + f_i) - c_{ij}$ is higher than his opportunity cost, which is equivalent to:

$$1 + f_i \geq \frac{c_{ij} + 1 + r_j}{(1 - \lambda_{ij})\theta_i} \tag{2.14}$$

Equation (2.14) gives the minimum investment yield required by the capital supplier. It needs to compensate for capital cost, transaction costs, credit risk of the capital demander and information asymmetry.

### 2.3 Expression of "transaction possibility set"

The necessary condition for a pair of capital demander and supplier to reach a deal is that the highest funding cost affordable to the capital demander is higher than the minimum investment yield required by the capital supplier, which according to Equation (2.13) and (2.14) is equivalent to:

$$c_{ij} + (1 + \mu_i + \mu_i/l_i)\lambda_{ij} \leq \mu_i + \mu_i/l_i - r_j \qquad (2.15)$$

In Equation (2.15), only $c_{ij}$ and $\lambda_{ij}$ are determined by the relationship between the capital demander and supplier. With other parameters constant, the lower transaction costs are, or the lower the degree of information asymmetry becomes, Equation (2.15) is more likely to be satisfied. So the "transaction possibility set" is:

$$\left\{(i,j) \middle| i \in I, j \in J, c_{ij} + (1 + \mu_i + \mu_i/l_i)\ \lambda_{ij} \leq \mu_i + \mu_i/l_i\ - r_j\right\} \qquad (2.16)$$

The "transaction possibility set" has the following characteristics. First, it is determined by transaction costs and information asymmetry. Different levels of transaction costs or information asymmetry correspond to different "transaction possibility sets."

Second, with other conditions held constant, lower transaction costs or information asymmetry are associated with larger "transaction possibility sets." Under such circumstances, capital suppliers and demanders are more likely to reach deals, which is "financial deepening" in some sense.

Third, assuming transaction costs and information asymmetry cease to exist $(c_{ij} \rightarrow 0, \lambda_{ij} \rightarrow 0)$, the "transaction possibility set" will approach:

$$\left\{(i,j) \middle| i \in I, j \in J, \mu_i + \mu_i/l_i \geq r_j\right\} \qquad (2.17)$$

Under this scenario, as long as the expected return of a capital demander (adjusted for leverage) exceeds the opportunity cost of a capital supplier, a deal between them is possible.

### SECTION 5: CONCLUDING REMARKS

We have introduced the concept of Internet finance and discussed its payment, information processing and resource allocation. We believe that Internet finance can promote economic growth and generate considerable social benefits by increasing resource allocation efficiency, reducing transaction costs, and promoting availability of financial services.

Currently, China has made the following progresses in Internet finance. First, the central bank (People's Bank of China) issues third-party payment licenses to the top three mobile operators. Second, several P2P lending companies have been established. Third, some institutions such as Alibaba have employed information on social networks to facilitate SME financing. However, many problems have also emerged and the banking regulator (China Banking Regulatory Commission) alerted banks of P2P lending's risk in 2011.

We believe Internet finance will become more and more important in the future. It is inevitable that Internet finance will face many technological, commercial, and regulatory challenges in early stages of development. But we should never deny, overlook, or underestimate its potential.

## Notes

1 Mishkin, Frederic. 1995. "The Economics of Money, Banking, and Financial Markets," Harper Collins College Publishers.
2 For instance, physical bookstores such as Borders have gone bankrupt under competition from electronic books and online bookstores. MP3 and music sharing websites have reshaped the business model of music industry. Amazon and Taobao have seriously eroded the traditional retail industry.
3 Under Internet finance, prudential regulation on financial institutions (such as commercial banks, securities firms, and insurance firms) may cease to exist and is to an extent replaced by behavioral regulation and protection of financial consumers.
4 Goldman Sachs. 2012. "Mobile Monetization: Does the Shift in Traffic Pay?"
5 Xie, Ping, and Long Yin. 2001. "The Financial Theory and the Financial Governance Under Internet Economy." Journal of Economic Research, no. 4.
6 Mishkin, Frederic. 1995. "The Economics of Money, Banking, and Financial Markets," Harper Collins College Publishers.
7 Xie, Ping, and Chuanwei Zou. 2011. "The Irreplaceable Functions of CDS." Review of Financial Development, no. 1.
8 Conditions for people to establish relationships and access precious resources, that is the concepts, "courtesy demands reciprocity" and "return a favor with a favor."
9 People have the tendency to establish communication networks with others who have similar traits, that is "birds of a feather flock together."
10 How ideas, information, and views are exchanged among people in a communication network, that is "if you live with a lame person, you will learn to limp."
11 Monge, Peter R., and Noshir S. Contractor. 2003. "Theories of Communication Networks," Oxford University Press, Inc. If individual A has a relationship with individual B and individual B has a relationship with individual C, then individual A has a relationship with individual C, that is "a friend's friend is a friend and an enemy's enemy is a friend."
12 Shirky, Clay. 2008. "Here Comes Everybody: The Power of Organizing Without Organizations," Penguin Press.
13 Scott, John. 2000. "Social Network Analysis: A Handbook," Sage Publications, Inc.
14 Technically speaking, processing of relational data has always been a major component of search engines. For instance, the "crawler" algorithm for capturing web pages and link analysis method for web page sequencing have all employed the linkage between web pages that belong to relational data. Recently, Facebook has launched Graph Search.
15 For instance, real-time search involves a tremendous quantity of computation. Google is a forerunner in the development of cloud computation.

16 Strictly speaking, due to the one-to-one correspondence between S and s, σ-algebras induced by S and s are the same.
17 Petersen, Mitchell A. 2004. "Information: Hard and Soft," Working Paper, Kellogg School of Management.
18 Under current model setting, people may deduce others' private information from equilibrium price and adjust their estimation of default probability and trade decision, thus affecting market equilibrium. This scenario belongs to rational expected equilibrium.
19 Huang, Chi-fu, and Robert H. Litzenberger. 1988. "Foundations for Financial Economics," Elsevier Science Publishing Co., Inc.
20 Zhang, Xiang, and Chuanwei Zou. 2007. "The Mechanism of Systemic Bidding ROSCA Default." Journal of Financial Research, no. 11.
21 Zou, Chuanwei, and Xiang Zhang. 2011. "Arbitrage and Systemic Bidding ROSCA Default." Journal of Financial Research, no. 9.
22 "Global Lessons for Better Savings Habits," SmartMoney, Nov 18 2011.
23 In other words, financing takes the form of loans. However, similar logic also applies to other forms of financing such as preferred stocks, ordinary stocks, and convertible bonds.

# 3   The internetization of finance

## SECTION 1: THE INTERNETIZATION OF FINANCE

Internetization (financing activity moving online) is an unavoidable trend. More and more people are getting used to the Internet, and many no longer have the time to make it to a bank teller due to the accelerating pace of life. Thus, financial institutions are using the Internet to adapt to customers' needs. Additionally, the rapid development of Internet technology helps reduce these institutions' transaction costs. This chapter successively discusses network banking, mobile banking, network securities companies, network insurance companies, network financial trading platforms, and the online marketing of financial products.

## 1 Network banks

According to Yin Long,[1] network banking has two meanings. The first touches upon the meaning of the term and identifies the nature of network banking. "Network" has a meaning beyond Local Area Networks (LAN), the Internet, and other open electronic networks. It also includes internal bank networks, money transfer networks, payment and clearing networks, and even telecommunication networks. If it serves as a carrier for financial information, products, or services, it is seen as a new channel for the banking industry and fits under the scope of network banking. The second meaning touches upon the identification of the network banking business and the function of banking. Network banks are recognized as possessing an independent website used to provide certain customer services (here network means Internet). Network banking is not only an evolution in banks' business model; it is the internetization of banking itself.

The evolution of network banking has experienced three stages: business process digitization, business management digitization, and reengineering of the bank (see Table 3.1)

In the first stage, banks mainly use information and communication technologies to assist and support business development, such as data storage and centralized processing for transactions. In this stage, banks basically automated office processes, but at that time information communication technology was not mature. The bank information systems were dispersed and closed.

*Table 3.1* Information technology and commercial bank innovation[2]

| Time | Innovative themes | Related technologies |
| --- | --- | --- |
| 1950 | Credit cards | Magnetic stripe |
| Early-1960 | Autopay | Telephone |
| Early-1960 | Check processor | Magnets |
| 1969 | ATM | Mechatronics |
| 1970 | POS | Computer and Communications |
| 1970 | Credit scoring model | Database Technology |
| 1970 | CHIPS | Communication |
| 1973 | Automatic payment technology | Communications, computer |
| 1977 | SWIFT system | Communication |
| 1980 | Derivatives | High-speed operation of computer and information communication technology |
| 1982 | Household bank | Computer and information communication technology |
| Mid-1980 | Enterprise bank | Computer and information communication technology |
| 1988 | Electronic Data Interchange (EDI) | Communications, security control |
| 1990 | Customer relationship management (CRM) | Database Technology |
| 1990 | Credit separation model | Database Technology |
| 1990 | Credit scoring model | Information and communication technologies and the Internet |

In the second stage, the rapid development of information technology and the reduction of cost provided favorable conditions for the extensive application of information technology networks in banks. Banks widely use networked real-time trading, developed internal networks, and rolled out both point of sale (POS) and ATM machines.

The third stage is marked by the birth of the first network bank, Security First Network Bank, in October 1995. With this, a new service channel emerged. Network banking, telephone banking, mobile banking, and television banking helped customers get more convenient service. The innovation of this phase has revolutionized the banking business system, breaking the sub-sectoral restrictions of banking, insurance, and securities, thereby continuously integrating the financial sector. Business development in turn increased the demand for information and communication technology, which has been increasingly outsourced.

## 2 Mobile banks

Mobile banking refers to the use of mobile phones, PDAs and other mobile devices to connect customers and financial institutions. The first mobile bank was built in the Czech Republic in the late 1990s by the Expandia Bank and mobile operator Radiomobile. Since then mobile banking has appeared in a variety of modes and a lot of cases. In December 2013, Zhou Xiaochuan, the governor of the PBoC said, "We should learn from international experience through mobile banking to provide basic financial services to rural areas, remote areas and poor areas" in an interview with the Financial Times.

### *2.1 The main forms of mobile banking*

Table 3.2 summarizes four major mobile banking types. Most mobile banks are bank-led, so mobile operators only supply the operating platform. This model was the first to appear and is still the mainstream in developed countries.

Second, there have been a large number of mobile banking innovations in African countries, and non-bank institutions such as mobile operators and third-party payment companies play an important role. For example, Kenya's mobile banking M-PESA, which is owned by a mobile operator, has become the world's most used mobile payment system, and the remittance business of M-PESA has exceeded that of all other financial institutions in Kenya. African countries' financial

*Table 3.2* The forms of mobile banking

|  | *Bank based* | *Partnership business* | *Non-bank based* | *Non-bank-sponsored* |
|---|---|---|---|---|
| Who hold accounts or deposits | Bank | Bank | Bank | Operators or other non-bank institutions |
| Withdraw agency | Bank | Bank | Bank or agents | Operators or other institutions |
| Who executes payment instructions | Any operator | Specific operator | Specific operator | Specific operator |
| Typical examples | Most mobile banks | MTN Mobile Money, Smart | M-PESA, Wizzit | Globe, Celpay |

*Table 3.3* Overview of African national mobile banking[3]

|  | Celpay | M-PESA | MTN Mobile Money | Wizzit |
|---|---|---|---|---|
| Whether they target financial gaps | No | Yes | Yes | Yes |
| Security | Funds deposited in banks | Funds deposited in banks | Bank account required | Bank account required |
| Withdrawal method | Withdraw cash not allowed | Agent | ATM;bank branches | ATM;bank branches |
| Transfers allowed? | Yes | Yes | Yes, any bank account | Yes, any bank account |
| Special hardware requirements | Yes | No | 32k SIM | No |

systems are underdeveloped and find it difficult to meet basic needs for financial services, especially lacking physical outlets, which leads to a huge space for development of these emerging mobile banking models (see Table 3.3, analysis focused on the following cases).

### 2.2 Requirements for mobile banking

Mobile banking requires a specific infrastructure, such as mobile terminals and information communication technology. Economic conditions are even more important. Surprisingly, mobile banking mainly exists in less developed countries such as some African countries, but why? In the current circumstances, mobile banking acts more as a substitute than a complement for online banking and banking networks. Most African countries do not have access to basic financial services, yet they have strong financial needs. Mobile banking does not need a sales network, which grants access to basic financial services. Mobile banking providers also significantly reduce transaction costs in order to make profits. This provides the necessary conditions for mobile banking to solve the problem of financial inclusion. In addition, African countries' financial regulation allows mobile operators with a comparative advantage in providing mobile banking. In short, the matching of supply and demand are the basic conditions for the existence of mobile banking.

Why is the penetration rate of mobile banking in Europe and other developed countries not as high? This is due to the widespread availability of bank branches. People can get financial services at any time, and the small mobile phone screen makes them less likely to use their phones for mobile banking.

Why has mobile banking developed so slowly in rural China and other countries? The development of mobile banking in underdeveloped areas needs a "Coca-Cola method," namely to design a business model that can be promoted at a large scale to achieve low cost and high-density sales. The higher the marketization level of banks and mobile communication institutions, the more it can take the initiative to meet customer demand rather than make customers adapt to providers. However, if the provider is an absolute monopoly, there is no incentive to build and promote the Coca-Cola model.

Most people now believe security is the main obstacle to the promotion of mobile banking. For example, security concerns make mobile banking unpopular in developed countries, while people in underdeveloped countries may not be cognizant of the security problems of mobile banking. In fact, the poor are more concerned about safety, because deposits are essential to them. In the future, the financial model will change. There will be more branchless services and the supply and demand sides of funds through mobile phones and other mobile terminals can be directly matched. At that time, product pricing, risk management, and information processing can be completed in everyone's hand. There will be no need for bank intermediaries. At that time, mobile banking will replace physical financial institutions and gain popularity in both underdeveloped and developed regions.

### 2.3 Mobile banking case studies

### 2.3.1 M-PESA (Kenya)[4]

Safaricom, Vodafone's[5] partner in Kenya, launched M-PESA in 2007. Its initial purpose was to meet the remittance demands of the poor, but it later developed to complete services like transfers, remittances, cash withdrawal, prepaid recharges, bill payment, wage payment, and repayment of loans by phone. People can remit through M-PESA both home and abroad. One important factor in the success of M-PESA is to achieve access to cash businesses. M-PESA introduced the post office, pharmacy, supermarket, and others as agents to provide cash services under the aegis of M-PESA.

M-PESA charges transfer fees, but the account registration, deposits and prepaid recharge M-PESA are all free. M-PESA has also opened up channels between mobile operators and banks to transfer between M-PESA accounts and bank accounts, and M-PESA users can withdraw cash at bank ATMs (Table 3.4).

The design of M-PESA's virtual account means its bank activities do not fall under Kenyan banking laws. Therefore, Safaricom can choose agents according to its own business judgment and is not liable for agent misconduct. Other than ensuring that customer-stored value funds are not deposited into only one bank, there are no strict regulations for those branchless banking services dominated by the non-bank institutions such as M-PESA.

In the beginning, M-PESA only had 52,000 users, 355 agents. By the end of April 2011, M-PESA customers grew to about 14 million, and agents to nearly 30,000. M-PESA's success has attracted interest from imitators in emerging markets such as Tanzania, South Africa, Afghanistan, India, and Egypt.

*Table 3.4* M-PESA fees (Kenyan shillings[6])

| Transfer sum interval | | Transfer to other M-PESA users | Transfer to non-M-PESA users | Withdrawal from M-PESA agents |
|---|---|---|---|---|
| 10 | 49 | 3 | N/A | N/A |
| 50 | 100 | 5 | N/A | 10 |
| 101 | 500 | 25 | 60 | 25 |
| 501 | 1,000 | 30 | 60 | 25 |
| 1,001 | 1,500 | 30 | 60 | 25 |
| 1,501 | 2,500 | 30 | 60 | 25 |
| 2,501 | 3,500 | 30 | 80 | 45 |
| 3,501 | 5,000 | 30 | 95 | 60 |
| 5,001 | 7,500 | 50 | 130 | 75 |
| 7,501 | 10,000 | 50 | 155 | 100 |
| 10,001 | 15,000 | 50 | 200 | 145 |
| 15,001 | 20,000 | 50 | 215 | 160 |
| 20,001 | 25,000 | 75 | 250 | 170 |
| 25,001 | 30,000 | 75 | 250 | 170 |
| 30,001 | 35,000 | 75 | 250 | 170 |
| 35,001 | 40,000 | 75 | N/A | 250 |
| 40,001 | 45,000 | 75 | N/A | 250 |
| 45,001 | 50,000 | 100 | N/A | 250 |
| 50,001 | 70,000 | 100 | N/A | 300 |

| The amount interval | | ATM withdrawal fee |
|---|---|---|
| 200 | 2,500 | 30 |
| 2,501 | 5,000 | 60 |
| 5,001 | 10,000 | 100 |
| 10,001 | 20,000 | 175 |

Note: The maximum M-PESA account balance is 100,000 Shillings and transfers cannot exceed 140,000 Shillings. Daily transfers and per transfer amounts cannot exceed 70,000 Shillings, M-PESA agents do not accept cash under 50 Shillings.

### 2.3.2 Wizzit (South Africa)[7]

Wizzit was launched in November 2004 by a joint venture between mobile operator MTN and Standard Bank. It is a virtual bank with no branches. Target users are the 16 million strong low-income group in South Africa (48% of the adult population). In addition to financial services such as transfer, payment, prepaid recharge, wage payment, and account query by phone, Wizzit also offers a Maestro debit card. Users can use the card for withdrawals at ATMs and deposits at bank branches. It uses more than 2,000 WIZZ Kids[8] to advertise and serve as agents (including registration for the service) rather than placing advertising in conventional media.

Wizzit has no minimum balance requirement or fixed costs, which makes it attractive to groups not normally covered by financial services. Its greatest advantage is its low transaction costs, which are sustained through high volumes. Despite being founded partially by a telecom company, Wizzit is compatible with all mobile operators. Like similar services, it monitors user accounts and suspends transactions that cross certain thresholds for transaction amount or total account volume.

### 2.3.3 GCash (Philippines)[9]

The Philippine mobile operator Globe Telecom founded GCash in 2004. Users register with text messages, then deposit or withdraw funds through agents.[10] GCash can make transfers between bank accounts, but does not function as a bank. Banks and other financial institutions act only as agents in their model.

At present, GCash's has more than 1.2 million users and its transactions total more than 60 billion Philippine Pesos, charging only for withdrawals.[11] The Philippine central bank has taken a relatively relaxed stance in the regulation of GCash. Requirements focus on information disclosure, client fund ring-fencing, transaction limits, and anti-money laundering.

### 2.4 The risk and regulation of mobile banking

Banks faces two types of risk when they use mobile phones for banking in poor areas. The first risk is related to agents, who often have a shortage of trained employees and insufficiently developed security systems. Banks are thus subject to risks such as theft, fraud, and improper transactions. Policymakers and regulators are seriously considering how to deal with these risks emanating from agency arrangements.[12] For example, Brazil has facilitated branchless banking development by opening up the agency function to all retail stores with a POS machine, but has mitigated risk by holding the banks responsible for agents, requiring central bank approval for new agents, mandating data collection, and placing limits on clearing time for transactions. The result is to both create incentives and give the proper tools for banks to properly manage their agents. In contrast, India's central bank placed severe restrictions on which entities can serve as agents. This is to a certain extent justified by the poor track record of many retail entities, but has impeded the development of branchless banking services in India. This is in stark contrast to Kenya, in which operators like M-PESA both freely choose and are not responsible for their agents.

The second type of risks relates to misconduct or mistakes committed by operators. For example, client funds may be misappropriated for use in risky investments, which can lead to client losses. Electronic currency must be regulated. If a bank issues electronic currency, regulators monitor the flows of stored value or unpaid funds. For example, Smart Money in the Philippines records its funds on cooperating banks' books as accounts payable rather than savings to reduce regulatory costs, but customers get a lower degree of protection. In non-bank mode, however, mobile operators open virtual accounts for the customer and directly establish a contractual relationship between clients and mobile operators rather than opening a contractual relationship with the bank. In this case, the electronic currency is less regulated. Once a risk occurs, customers can put in a claim to the provider, but not the bank. Therefore, there is a need to formulate special regulations to ensure the provider has enough capital to deal with and prioritize customer claims for compensation.

## 2.5 Mobile banking in China

### 2.5.1 Developments

Some banks in China have launched mobile banking, including big state-owned banks such as Bank of China (BOC), Agricultural Bank of China (ABC), Industrial and Commercial Bank of China (ICBC), Construction Bank of China (CBC), and Bank of Communications (BCM); nationwide joint-stock banks; city commercial banks and rural commercial banks; rural cooperative banks; new-type rural financial institutions; and rural credit cooperatives. Mobile banking through regional banks is basically network banking on the phone. Mobile banking is relevant to rural finance when it includes cardless cash withdrawal, small loans to farmers, on-site remittance, and mobile finance.

BCMs first launched mobile banking with cardless cash withdrawal, then China Guangfa Bank (GDB), Shenzhen Development Bank (SDB) and ICBC launched similar services. Cardholders prearrange the withdrawal on the platform and then can withdraw funds without their card. This can protect the client from card theft, allow emergency withdrawals, and permit others to remotely complete the withdrawal for them (if they keep the money, this becomes a quasi-transfer). The ATM requirement has led to this service expanding more in cities than the countryside.

Small loans to farmers was first launched by ABC's Guangxi and Henan branches as pilot programs. They provide six basic functions including self-help borrowing, self-help payment, reimbursement trial, loan contracts, information queries, and reimbursement queries. This service is a win–win; farmers can obtain loans without leaving home, ABC expands the rural market with lower transaction costs, and the government promotes financial inclusion.

Postal Savings Bank of China (PSBC) was the first to launch site-based remittance services. This service allows farmers to remit funds by delivering the notice of withdrawal with a listed beneficiary. The farmers with no bank card in remote areas can complete the remittance by address.

Mobile banking can also merge other financial services. The mobile bank of Chongqing Rural Commercial Bank (CRCB) highly integrates basic financial services including: a mobile payment application, cross-industry mobile payments, remote payments, online shopping, prepaid phone cards, game cards, ticket and hotel booking, and many others.

### 2.5.2 Improving financial services with mobile banking

Rural financial institution branches in China cannot satisfy the increasing demand for rural financial services. At the same time, regulators have realized the importance of mobile banking to bridge the financial gap in villages and towns. In 2011, the China Banking Regulatory Commission (CBRC) issued a policy pronouncement titled "*continue providing basic financial services for the absence of finance in villages and towns*" to push financial institutions in this direction.

Cash access is the key for mobile banking to solve the general inclusion problem, but cash business generally requires an agent. The specific operation is as follows: mobile bank users can use the card provided by a bank as a mobile virtual bank account provided by mobile operators and agents install POS equipment or phones with mobile banking functions. If customers want to make a deposit with the agent, the bank will automatically deduct the amount from the agent's account as the customers' deposit funding. The customer cash offsets the deduction to the bank/mobile operator's account. If the customer wants to take out cash, the opposite occurs. Clients can thus obtain important financial services without commuting to a specific bank branch.

The conditions are ripe for promoting mobile banking in rural China. First, mobile phones are on the rise. At the end of October 2012, China's mobile phone penetration rate reached 80.6%. By the end of 2011, the accelerated development of wireless mobile communication networks will cover all counties and most of the villages and towns throughout the country. At present, 3G network transmission speeds reach 2 mbps and support encryption.

Second, mobile banking does not require a network. Without additional equipment and personnel, mobile banking saves on transaction costs. Empirically, bank teller transactions outside China cost an average of US$1.07, but mobile banks only require US$0.16. At Chinese bank counters, transaction costs an average of RMB 4 yuan, compared with mobile banking transactions at only RMB 0.6 yuan.

Third, branches of existing rural financial institutions cannot cover vast rural areas, so the absence of rural financial institutions provides the market demand for mobile banking development. In addition, rural income level, education level, and consumption habits support the promotion of mobile banking in rural China.

Fourth, the rural income level has increased. Since China's reform and opening up, China's rural residents' per capita net income has increased from US$133.6 in 1978 to RMB 5,153.2 in 2009, up by a factor of 38. This laid a solid economic foundation for the promotion of mobile banking.

Fifth, the rural education level has increased. Generally speaking, a high school education is sufficient to use mobile banking. Those in rural areas who have completed middle schools and high school degrees has risen steadily from 34.7% of the rural population in 1985 to 64.4% in 2009.[13]

Sixth, rural consumption habits are changing. It remains unclear whether Chinese rural areas will change from the current cash transaction model into a mobile payment mode. As incomes, educational attainment, and culture change, we may see very different consumption patterns in the future, patterns that will also be influenced by mobile banking.

## SECTION 2: NETWORK SECURITIES COMPANIES

The network securities business refers to investors taking advantage of resources including the Internet, LANs, private networks, wireless Internet, and other electronic means to transmit information, data, and deals relating to securities and exchange. It includes a series of activities such as real-time price acquisition, market information, investment consultation, and online trust products.[14]

Once, the stock exchange was full of gesticulating traders in red vests racing against time to place orders over the phone. The online trading system has made this history. The trading floor of securities firms is also gradually being replaced by online transactions. E-Trade launched online securities trading in the United States in 1992, and from then on the online securities trading business has boomed. Now most customers are accustomed to online trading. All one needs to do is open an account and download a simple trading software, then it is possible to trade stocks from home or even from one's cell phone, anywhere in the world.

The impact of information and communication technologies on China's securities markets has been profound. China has experienced successive stages of centralized trading, online securities trading, and mobile securities trading. The first stage was centralized trading, marked with the establishment of Shanghai stock exchange in 1990 and the Shenzhen stock exchange in 1991. The second stage was online trading, marked with an online trading system launched by Huarong Trust Investment Company in March 1997. The third stage was mobile securities trading, meaning securities trading entered the mobile era.

## 1 Business models worldwide

Based on the depth of the use of the Internet, we divide network securities companies into three models: the first is a pure Internet securities brokerage company such as E-Trade and TD Ameritrade, the second is a comprehensive securities brokerage firm like Charles Schwab and Fidelity, and the third is a traditional securities brokerage such as Merrill Lynch and A.G. Edwards.

E-Trade was formally established in 1992. It first provided investors with online securities services through AOL, and then established its own online trading site www.etrade.com in 1996. At present, E-Trade is the world's largest personal online investment services site, with customers in over 100 countries. Its most salient advantage is low transaction costs. E-Trade has strong technical capabilities and a convenient online trading channel, all without physical locations. Thus, they are able to offer trades with a commission average of only about US$10. The disadvantage of E-trade lies in its lack of experienced investment advisers.

Charles Schwab has become one of America's personal financial services market leaders. In the mid-1990s, Charles Schwab made a major breakthrough when it launched an online financial services platform. Charles Schwab offers investors a relatively inexpensive service mainly through telephone, fax, and Internet trading. Unlike E-trade, Schwab is not a pure Internet securities company because it has a few physical locations for customer service. The Schwab mode has low cost, but its research and development ability is weak.

Merrill Lynch was one of the world's leading financial management and consulting companies. Unlike Schwab, Merrill Lynch focused on high-end customers, providing customers with face-to-face, comprehensive asset investment advisory services. Merrill lynch had strong investment research and portfolio consulting, but it had a limited potential customer base due to the cost of providing personalized service. Its use of the Internet was not nearly as deep as the other two modes.

## 2 Chinese models

Internet securities companies in China mainly provide information and financial services. We divide them into three forms: brokerage website mode, independent third-party site, and brokerage and bank cooperation.

The brokerage website mode is common for the securities companies, such as GF Securities Guotai Junan, CITIC Securities, and Haitong Securities. These trading and service sites are part of the company's inner service centers. Their services are not limited to the traditional brokerage business. Customers can also buy information products and funds on the platform. The advantage of this model is that the securities company can directly provide traditional market services for online clients through the website, and brokerage service advantages can be fully displayed. The problem for small and medium-sized brokerages is that special website construction requires significant funds.

In independent third-party site mode, the Internet services company, consulting firm, and software system developers build websites to provide consultancy services for customers, and brokerages are in the background providing online securities trading services to customers. This model is an open platform. If the client needs securities trading, he/she can just open "add broker" on the software. Flash and Great Wisdo are some of the leaders in this area for the Chinese market. Some websites only provide consulting services, such as Oriental Wealth. The advantage of this mode is that technology and information advantages can be fully reflected. The disadvantage is that the content of the securities service and professional level trust by clients need a time to develop.

Bank-Securities Link exemplifies a new type of financial services business between brokerage and bank. On the basis of banks' network with securities firms, investors can directly use the current savings account provided by bank branches as a securities margin account. They can buy and sell securities through the bank's trust system or through securities firm commissioned systems. The model permits commercial banks to get involved in the securities market business. The advantage is convenience, low fees, and protection from margin appropriation risks. The drawback is that there is legal risk; for example Bank-Securities Link shut its doors for this reason in 2006.

## SECTION 3: NETWORK INSURANCE COMPANIES

Online insurance refers to insurance companies or other intermediary institutions, which use the Internet to facilitate their business. There are narrow and broad definitions. In the narrow sense, online insurance refers to insurance companies or other intermediaries that provide information about insurance products and services over the Internet. They may also directly complete the sale of insurance products and services online. More broadly, online insurance includes web-based internal management activities and transactions, information exchange activities, insurance regulation, taxation, and management institutions.[15]

## 1 Development

In the insurance industry, information and communication technology originally was used for electronic insurance products. Marketing is also increasingly electronic. With the development of IT, e-commerce platforms gradually developed, through which customers can self-service, obtain quotes, and buy products.

The first insurance company to promote its insurance products entirely through the Internet was founded in 1999 in Japan as a joint venture between AFLAC and Japan Telecom. It focuses on customers under the age of 40. INSWEB (US) is the world's largest and most respected insurance e-commerce site. Forbes once called it the best site on the Internet. The site covers insurance of just about everything, including cars, housing, medical treatment, personal life, and pets.

China's online insurance is still at a rudimentary stage. Most insurance companies just set up their own web portal with little comparative information. In June 2012, "Rest Assured Insurance" put B2B and B2C trading online. It is also a third-party insurance sales platform. In 2013, Alibaba, China's Ping An Insurance, and Tencent jointly established an online property insurance company that will disrupt the existing Chinese insurance marketing model.

## 2 Major types

The online insurance businesses can provide insurance services online, use specialized companies, or collaborate together online.[16] The first type operates sales through the company's website. This helps promote the company and its products through new channels. The insurance company can then manage customer data to provide other value-added services, such as providing free SMS and personalized e-mail subscriptions. The disadvantage of this scheme for its consumers is a lack of comparability. It only shows one company's products and has high technical requirements. The eCoverage (US) was the first company to provide customers with service from quotation to claims service on the Internet.

Another model uses a network platform to put all related insurance company products information online. Users search for and choose insurance products, then are linked to a fitting insurance company. These platforms can charge comparatively lower commission and fees. In this mode, users can quickly find what they need by comparing different insurance companies. Huize.com was the first third-party insurance electronic commerce platform in China to provide product comparisons, vertical transactions, purchases, and professional insurance consulting interaction in one place. It combined with several large insurance companies to provide real-time online insurance. INSWEB is a typical example in foreign countries; it inked agreements with more than 50 insurance companies all over the world and cooperates with more than 180 websites. There are three main profit points for this platform mode. The first is the intermediary fee paid by consumers, the second is a "finder's fee" paid by the agent, and the third is advertising and other fees.

In the Taobao network insurance mode, the insurance site does not list insurance products or information. It just provides a platform for insurance suppliers and demanders to match themselves. The core of this website is to provide help both sides make an independent choice and provide some "soft" information for the insurance market. Many insurance companies are now on Taobao, such as China's Ping An Insurance and China Life Insurance, who now do online sales of insurance, car insurance, health insurance, and other products.

A network insurance support platform does not directly provide insurance products. It provides information and technical support for insurers, and is generally founded by a non-insurance agency. These generally have a very deep industry background with strong information superiority and social credibility. Firms such as China Insurance Network provide theory and policy, member communication, real-time news, data, information, training information, and information related to insurance companies, insurance agents and brokers, and other information for insurance practitioners and consumers. Network insurance technical support provides information technology specifically for insurance companies. Typical representatives such as the Yi-Bao network only provide technical guarantees and services for insurance companies.

## SECTION 4: NETWORK FINANCIAL TRADING PLATFORMS

### 1 SecondMarket

SecondMarket was established in 2004 to provide online trading services for products such as equity of non-listed companies, fixed income securities, bankruptcy claims, warrants, and alternative assets.

#### 1.1 Basic information

Barry Silbert, the founder of SecondMarket, once worked at a Wall Street investment bank with a focus on financial restructuring, mergers and acquisitions, and corporate finance. He was involved in major events such as the bankruptcies of Enron and WorldCom. He found that in a restructuring project, creditors often get shares of the new company, but there was no effective channel to resell these shares. This gap inspired Silbert's idea to establish a centralized and transparent market for trading alternative assets.

SecondMarket initially traded restricted stock, warrants, and convertible bonds of public companies. Gradually, its business extended to include fixed income securities, bankruptcy claims, and equity of non-public companies. In early 2009, there were only 2,500 investors, but this reached 75,000 in 2011. Now, equity in more than 50 companies, including Internet startups such as Facebook and Twitter, trades on SecondMarket. In 2008, SecondMarket reached an annual trading volume of US$30 million, but grew to US$100 million in 2009. In 2011, it reached US$558 million. Thanks to its broad prospects for development, SecondMarket has attracted investments from New Enterprise Associates, the Li KaShing, and Temasek Holdings. Its market valuation is about US$200 million.

SecondMarket has now been registered as a trade broker by SEC and as a member of FINRA. It also operates an alternative trading system (ATS).

#### 1.2 Policies

1   The willingness of companies to trade their equity is a precondition for transactions. Non-public companies vary widely. Some companies value the control and operating flexibility, while others may pay more attention to liquidity and enterprise value. Therefore, SecondMarket only provides the trading services for non-public companies after obtaining their consent. It also allows the company to set restrictions, including trade restrictions and investor qualifications. Some companies only allow former employees to trade, while others only allow existing shareholders to purchase. A majority of companies are opposed to excessively frequent trading.

2   Disclosure of certain information is required to participate in SecondMarket. It requires non-public companies to disclose financial information to its registered members on the online trading platform, including the audited

annual reports of last two years and other risk factors. SecondMarket strictly controls the database to prevent leaks.

3  Individual investors must have net assets of more than US$1 million or annual income of more than US$200,000 to invest in SecondMarket's traded companies.

4  The trading mechanism involves sellers who post assets for sale on the website's board. The system automatically finds proper buyers in the database according to the members' interests or past transactions. SecondMarket will then notify both parties over the phone. After the buyer and seller reach an agreement, SecondMarket processes legal, settlement and payment issues of transactions. It charges a transaction commission of 2%–4%.

### *1.3 Statistical data*

Based on the data from completed transactions in 2011, approximately 27.2% of the shares were purchased by individual investors, 72.8% by institutional investors such as asset management companies, hedge funds, private equity funds, venture capital, and mutual funds. Here the majority are asset management institutions. The main source of equities is former employees of the companies whose shares are up for sale. These account for 79.3% of the total trading volume. Current employees are the next largest source of shares, at 11.1%. Investors and founders' shares make up most of the rest, at 10%.

## 2 SharesPost

SharesPost was founded in 2009. It focuses on the market of trading non-listed companies' equity. SharesPost also provides services such as financing through private equity, index preparation, and third-party research reports.

### *2.1 Background*

In 2009, Greg Brogger and Scott Painter founded the SharesPost website to establish an exchange market for equity of non-listed companies. Brogger worked as a securities lawyer after earning a JD and MBA from the University of Pennsylvania. The other founder started his own business in 1993. In 1998, they started a company together, zag.com, that provided an online platform for purchasing cars. It disrupted the traditional sales model of cars and quickly swept the nation. Subsequently, they found that private equity transactions were still realized through telephone, which followed the traditional brokerage model pervasive in the 1930s. They believed that its disruption would be a tremendous opportunity, so they founded SharesPost.

SharesPost has already attracted 83,000 investors. There are more than 150 stocks traded on the platform, with a total value of up to US$1 billion. The most frequently traded stocks include hot stocks such as Facebook and Yelp. Even a single quarter (Q4 2011) has seen a trading volume up to US$180 million in Sharespost's secondary market. It shows both momentum and a large potential for growth.

## 2.2 Main policies

1   Threshold for investment: Although SharesPost is an open market, in order to conform with securities regulations, SharesPost sets the criteria for qualified investors along the lines of those for private placement: individual investors must have net assets of more than US$1 million or have annual income of more than US$200,000. Institutional investors must possess net assets of at least US$100 million.

2   Private equity transfer: SharesPost is similar to a BBS or forum. Buyers and sellers on SharesPost register as members and trade equities through the website platform. The two parties agree on a time to discuss the transaction, and then process the negotiation. Finally, the deal reached between the parties is submitted to the registered broker of SharesPost for an audit. In contrast with SecondMarket, equity transfers do not need the approval or authorization of the company.

3   Private placement financing: In addition to private equity transfers, SharesPost has a private placement market. Start-ups and their agent investment banks can post offers on SharesPost's bulletin board. The buyers and sells can then contact each other directly.

4   Creation of indices: SharesPost created the first private equity index in US history—the SharesPost Index. The Index consists of thirty representative companies traded on SharePost's platform. It is reported in real time during trading hours.

5   Providing third-party research reports: To find the intrinsic value of the stocks, SharesPost offers up to 450 reports provided by nine third-party research institutions. The reports cover many well-known venture enterprises such as Twitter, Yelp, Facebook, Zynga, and so on.

6   Providing transaction information: Currently, through the Bloomberg terminal, it is possible to browse real-time quote and transaction information on SharesPost. Historical transaction data is also available.

7   Cost mode: SharesPost charges US$34 to each party in completed transactions, not distinguishing between private or institutional investors.

## SECTION 5: DISTRIBUTION NETWORKS FOR FINANCIAL PRODUCTS

Essentially, Internet sales of financial products match the suppliers and demanders of financial products through Internet channels. The demanders of financial products play a dominating role in the matching process. They search for financial products and conduct asset allocation. Financial product providers aim at maximizing the probability and amount of their financial products that are selected into demanders' "allocation bracket" (a concept of collection of trading possibility). To achieve this goal, they focus on demanders' preference, disclose the risk-return characteristics of their products, and conduct certain promotional activities. Some financial products of low-volatility and high mobility are often linked to payment. It not only meets demanders' needs of investment needs, but also their needs for payment.

Next, we introduce the main model of Internet sales of financial products, then analyze Yu'E Bao. Yu'E Bao significantly and unexpectedly changed the structure of China's fund industry when it started in 2013. Finally, we discuss the principles of economics supporting financial products as payment instruments.

## Notes

1  Yin, Long. 2012. "Internet Banking and Monetary Electronics - Network Theory of Finance," Southwestern University of Finance and Economics doctoral thesis.
2  Jiang, Jianqing. 2000. "Financial Development of High Technology and In-depth Impact Study," China Financial Publishing House.
3  Porteous, David. 2006. "The Enabling Environment for Mobile Banking in Africa," working paper.
4  Safaricom. 2013. www.safaricom.co.ke/.
5  Vodafone is a multinational mobile operator. Headquartered in Newbury, UK and Dusseldorf, Germany, is one of the world's largest mobile communications operators, its network covering 26 countries directly and providing network services together with partners in another 31 countries.
6  At year-end December 2013, one Yuan equaled about 14 Shillings.
7  Wizzit. 2013. www.wizzit.co.za/.
8  WizzKids are generally young people who sign up as agents.
9  Globe. 2013. http://gcash.globe.com.ph/.
10  Retail stores, banks, Globe Telecom locations, and myriad other locations serve as agents.
11  At year-end 2013, 1 RMB = 6.6 pesos.
12  CGAP (Consultative Group to Assist the Poor). 2006. "Use of Agents in Branchless Banking for the Poor: Rewards, Risks, and Regulation."
13  Rural Social and Economic Investigation Department of National Bureau of Statistics of China. 2010. "China's Rural Household Survey Yearbook 2010," China Statistical Publishing House.
14  Zhang, Jin, and Yao Zhiguo. 2002. "The Network Finance," Peking University Publishing House.
15  Zhang, Jinsong. 2007. "The Theory and Practice of Network Finance," Zhejiang Science and Technology Publishing House.
16  Zhang, Jinsong. 2010. "The Network Financial," Mechanical Industry Publishing House.

# 4　Mobile and third-party payments

Paul Volcker, the former chairman of the Federal Reserve, once said that: "The only useful thing banks have invented in 20 years is the ATM machine." However, we believe that the most significant innovation in the financial industry over the past 20 years arose in the field of payments.

## SECTION 1: BASIC CONCEPT AND DEVELOPMENT

### 1 Mobile payments

Mobile payments involve the transaction of monetary value with mobile communication equipment and wireless communication technology, thus clearing and settling the positions of creditors and debtors.[1] These are made possible by the spread of mobile terminals and the development of mobile Internet. With the popularization of mobile terminals, it is possible that mobile payments will be widely accepted in the transaction of products and services as well as in the liquidation of debt. It will then be able to replace currency and credit cards, thus becoming a key form of electronic currency. The basic traits of mobile payments are as follows:

1　They use mobile communication equipment, especially smartphones, as the carrier.
2　They employ wireless communication technology.
3　Electronic currency is the basis for mobile payments' existence, but they only really function when they coexist.
4　Mobile payments change the form of money without touching upon its essence.
5　The development of mobile payments relies on third-party payments.

In China, Mobile payments have been developing rapidly. According to data from iResearch, mobile payments reached Renminbi (RMB) 296.51 billion in transactions by the third quarter of 2013, an explosive growth of 185.3%. The number of smart phones in China reached 580 million in 2013, a year-over-year (YoY) increase of 60.3%, while mobile shopping made up 38.9% of the mobile Internet market. 2013 also witnessed the growth of mobile games, the market for which amounted to RMB 11.24 billion, a YoY increase of 246.9%. The development of mobile Internet markets has also driven the development of mobile payments, which itself is adding diverse formats such as SMS payments, near field communication (NFC) payments, QR code payments, mobile banking payments, and even payments with facial recognition, and so on.

## 2 Third–party payments

Third-party payments refer to helping clients quickly realize the function of currency payments and fund settlements by making connection between clients, third-party payment companies, and banks over the Internet, thus playing the role of credit guarantor and technical support as well. According to data from iResearch, the scale of market transactions of online third-party payments in China added up to RMB 1.4 trillion in the third quarter of 2013, a link-relative growth rate of 26.7%. Alipay makes up 48.8% of this market, while Tenpay takes the second place with 18.7%. At the same time, Easylink, quick money, remittance world, EPRO pay, and IPS are also developing quickly (Figure 4.1).

## 3 Third–party mobile payments

Third-party mobile payments are executed by third-party payment companies via mobile payment terminals. According to data from iResearch, the online third-party payments market in China reached RMB 1.4 trillion in the third quarter of 2013, a link-relative growth rate of 26.7%. Third-party payments in China added up to RMB 1.2 trillion, an increase of 707% YoY. Remote mobile Internet payments

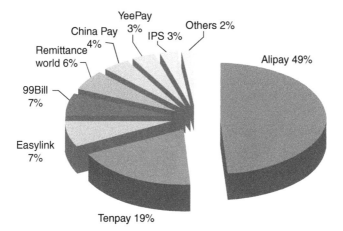

*Figure 4.1* The market structure of online third-party payments.
Data source: iResearch, by the third quarter of 2013

make up 93.1% of this total market, while near field mobile payments occupy only 0.8%. From this data, we conclude that the share of near field mobile payments is still small. There thus remains vast space for development. Payment methods such as voice payments, QR-code payments, as well as the integration of personal accounts continue to drive change in this sector.

Alipay, Lakala, and Tenpay are the market leaders in this field, with respective market shares of 58%, 21%, and 6% (Figure 4.2).

## SECTION 2: BASIC PRINCIPLES AND THE ACCOUNT SYSTEM

### 1 Mobile payments: Forms and principles

While the forms of mobile payment in developed countries are similar to those in China, that of developing countries is mobile banking, which usually does not require third-party payments. Mobile payments executed by Chinese banks require mobile banking. They may also need NFC-enabled mobile phones for near field payments. If the payments go through the three major telecom operators,[2] the process uses microchips planted in SIM cards (such as the sticker cards on the cellphone, or the RFID-UIM[3] card used for Bestpay payments). If the mobile payment products are provided by pure third-party payment companies, mobile banking is unnecessary and the payments can be completed directly. Examples of this include "Pengpengshua" by Alipay and Wechat payment by Tencent. These methodologies provide speed and convenience. However, the mobile payments from third-party payment companies are generally less secure than mobile banks and tend to be underwritten by insurance companies.

Mobile banking in African areas requires forward storing, while Chinese mobile banking uses transaction size ceilings. Mobile payments provided by mobile

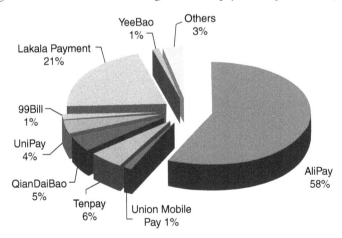

*Figure 4.2* The market shares for mobile third-party payment.
Data source: Enfodesk, by the second quarter of 2013

operators in China do, however, require forward storing. However, it is not necessary for payments done by third-party companies such as Tencent and Alipay. As forward storing makes mobile payments less convenient, those without the forward storing will prove to be more popular in the future.

The relationship between mobile banking and mobile payment is reflected in two aspects. First, mobile payments are more focused on banking. However, as mobile banking has relatively high device and security requirements, one must register in bank branches or on the online banks websites. This means less convenient payment operations with more complications, such as repeated entry of account numbers and passwords. The second point is that mobile payments are more focused on payments, which means a more streamlined process.

## 2 The principle of third-party payments

Third-party payments go around direct account settlement between clients and banks. This is beneficial for a reason: third-party payments can play the role of guarantor, numerous banks can be combined and payments completed without online banking or mobile banking services, and it saves transaction costs. Mobile third-party payments then reduce the costs even more.

Mobile payments ostensibly use mobile phones rather than computers as the payment terminals. However, it is this kind of transformation that may lead to revolutionary changes in the field of payments. As payments refer to the transaction of currency between different accounts, payment itself indicates mobility, while the most significant strength of terminals like mobile phones is also mobility. The combination of mobile payments and the third-party payments then magnifies this advantage.

Before the emergence of the third-party payments, the payment and clearing system included the connection between commercial banks and clients, as well as the connection between commercial banks and the central bank. As the commercial bank's payment and clearing counterparty, the central bank can conduct liquidation by netting. In the already existing payment and clearing patterns, as the clients are not able to establish a direct connection with the central bank, they have to establish a connection with each commercial bank individually. This reduces the efficiency of payment and clearing. After the emergence of third-party payments, clients can build connections with the third-party payment companies, then the third-party payment companies represent their clients when establishing the connection with commercial banks. The third-party companies become payment and clearing counterparties between clients and commercial banks, so they can net large amounts of trading capital through intermediate accounts established at different banks, while only small amounts of interbank payments are completed by the payment and clearing system of the central bank. The third-party payments complete the clearing of large amounts of small transactions after the third-party payment companies net them with secondary settlement. They thus undertake the functions of the central bank in payment clearing, as well as offering credit guarantees. Before the emergence of mobile payments, computers mainly undertake the connection between clients and third-party companies. However, after the birth of mobile payments, the connection will gradually migrate to mobile phone terminals.

## 3 The function and categories of accounts

There is a close connection between payments and accounts. Accounts are the sine qua non of payments, and they gain even more importance in the era of electronic currency. The chairman of Guotai Junan Securities once said, "He who wins the accounts wins power over the future of finance."[4] In the era of electronic currency, it is essential to have a personal account to ensure that the currency has the payment functions and qualifies as a financial product, which is not necessary for cash transactions. A financial product that can be used as means of payment generally has low volatility and high mobility (see more details in Chapter 3).

There are many different formats for accounts. One includes personal accounts at traditional financial institutions. Payments based on these accounts still dominate the market. Inside a certain financial institution, this kind of account is forming gradually (such as the Yiwangtong accounts of the China Merchants Bank and Junhong accounts of Guotai Junan). This kind of account has not been totally integrated between different financial institutions. However, after the emergence of Internet banking, parts of these functions, such as balance inquiries, will be integrated between banks. The securities company accounts may also implement the integration. When clients open an account at securities companies, they actually open an account at China Securities Depository and Clearing Co., Ltd. The clients can thus use securities accounts at different companies by only applying for custody transfer.

The second type includes accounts in third-party payment companies or financial services companies such as Alipay. Alipay began to open its account system to third-party applications such as Dingding Discounts and iReaders in July 2013. Clients can now log into the third-party applications directly with their Alipay accounts, thus eliminating the cumbersome registration process. Clients can also use the information in their Alipay accounts when they need to pay within these applications, which is both convenient and safe.

The third type includes social networking platform accounts, such as QQ, which can be used to buy various virtual goods with virtual currency. The QQ account system is now gradually opening to third-party applications.

In conclusion, various kinds of accounts have only implemented the integration of partial functions within certain categories. They have not completed the integration of different kinds of accounts. This greatly limits the development of mobile and third-party payments. However, with the development of information technology, personal accounts will take shape gradually and become consolidated accounts, integrating all the personal business and all the assets and liabilities. It will thus serve as the beginning of personal financial activities and even of daily life. The account integration in turn promotes the development of mobile and third-party payments, because people will be able to use the mobile payments anywhere once the integration is complete. Without the integration, despite the existence of the basis of mobile payments, people will abandon mobile payments because they either lack a necessary account or tire of the cumbersome registration process.

With the rise of Internet finance, personal financial accounts are no longer confined to the traditional financial institutions. They can now be provided by Internet companies such as Alipay and Tencent. The account providers will also proliferate. And with the gradual integration of personal accounts, even the central bank may begin to provide them (see Chapter 2), because integrated personal accounts have a nature similar to public goods.

## SECTION 3: PROPERTIES OF FINANCIAL PRODUCTS AND MONETARY CONTROL

### 1 Payments and electronic currency

The essence of both mobile payments and third-party payments is the fund flow of electronic currency. Despite the different definitions of electronic currency, it generally has the following features: currency value represented by virtual accounts, stored in electronic devices, and possesses a general purpose. It thus becomes an acceptable method of payment for issuers and entities beyond close business partners. Electronic currency is considered a form of currency, so it is not only a means of payment but also has the functions of means of exchange and store of value. Electronic currency includes that based on bank cards (issued by commercial banks, including savings and digital checks), or products that need transform between bank deposits, cash, and electronic currency. Jin Chao and Leng Yanhua call this type "electrified currency," which includes phone cards, meal cards, and digital cash.[5] The second is based on virtual accounts, such as M-PESA and Internet currency (for more on Internet currency see Chapter 5).

Electronic currency can not only be transformed with the sovereign currency issued by the central bank, but can also be separated from it, thus taking on an independent existence as an Internet currency. Enterprises seeking profit maximization and the central bank may also issue currency at the same time.

If this pattern of currency and payment methods (the mobile third-party payment) which is conventionally accepted is going to rise to become acknowledged by law, it will require the gradual enlargement of the range of application (including network scale effects) and its irreplaceability in the social economy. It can then in turn force the law to stipulate it as a kind of currency pattern and payment method.

Mobile payment, including third-party payments, which is limited by network and scale effects, still has a long way to go to be popularized. However, the combination of mobile and the third-party payments will accelerate this process. During the initial period, as the scale of mobile payment users is limited, suppliers are unwilling to provide while consumers are reluctant to use. To break through the chicken-egg problem, effective measures taken by each involved party are needed, such as vigorous advocacy of the advantages of mobile terminals and broad prospects for the mobile payment, thus promoting the use of mobile payment. In the beginning, the government can provide subsidies or promote the construction of related infrastructure, while suppliers need to take preferential measures to encourage consumers to participate in mobile payments.

The mobile payments have both network externalities and positive externalities. The utility that consumers can get from consuming certain commodities such as mobile payments relies on the consumption of other consumers. The core of the network scale effects of mobile payments is the establishment of basic users. According to rationality in economics, the premise of using mobile payments as a payment method is that the benefits of using it are larger than its costs. To establish the premise, the number of mobile payment users must reach a scale that is big enough to make this the case. Consumer acceptance is important to make the number of mobile payment users sufficient. Only if they except that large quantities of people will use the mobile payments, can the number of users reach a certain scale.

We can use the analytical framework proposed by Nicholas Economides and Charles Himmelberg to analyze mobile payments.[6] The framework is mainly used to analyze the network scale effects of the telecommunications industry. There are many similarities between mobile payments and the telecommunications industry, mostly in relation to network effects.

We suppose that the utility function of consumers is $u(y, n^e) = y(a + b(n^e))y$. (a) $y$ represents the income of consumers. The function shows that the utility consumers gain from mobile payments are linked to their income; the higher the income level, the more ability they have to participate in mobile payments. (b) $a$ represents the intrinsic value of mobile payments when there are no other users. There is no necessity for the existence of mobile payments if there is no other user, so $a$ equals zero in this condition. (c) $n$ represents the proportion of mobile payment users among total users. $0 \leq n \leq 1$. $b(n^e)$ is used to measure the benefits that consumers get from the network scale effects of mobile payments. $b(n^e)$ is an increasing function of $n^e$, and $b(0) = 0$. $n^e$ is the proportion of mobile payment users among the total users.

Given the price $p^7$ and basis users $n^e$, we have $u(y, n^e) = y(a + b(n^e)) > p$. The aggregate demand function for mobile payments can be represented as $n = f(n^e, p)$. For the given user $n^e$, the aggregate demand of mobile payments moves inversely with the price. However, if the basic users $n^e$ increase, the aggregate demand of mobile payments moves with the price. The above-mentioned aggregate demand function can also be represented as $p = p(n, n^e)$ (Figure 4.3), there is $n = n^e$ when the equilibrium is achieved, and then we call it the aggregate demand curve of perfect information, which is represented as $p = p(n, n)$. The curve $p = p(n, n_1^e)$ and $p = p(n, n_2^e)$ represent consumers' willingness to pay for mobile payments, in which $n_2^e > n_1^e$. The more users the consumers accept, the higher their willingness to pay and the more actual users of mobile payments.

The aggregate demand curve of perfect foresight is not monotone because when the number of users reaches a certain value, the marginal cost of mobile

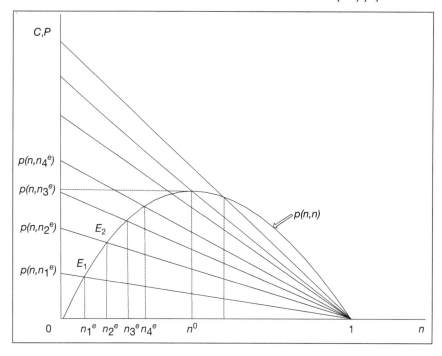

*Figure 4.3* The demand curve for mobile payments.

payments become quite low, so the actual price that consumers pay becomes lower. That is before reaching $n_0$, the price of mobile payments moves the same way with the number of users, while after $n_0$, the two move inversely. When $n$ is big enough, $\lim_{n \to 1} p(n, n) = 0$.

The key to understand the network scale effects is the consumers' expectation of the users of mobile payments. When people expect that the number of base users is large, that is there will be a bright future for mobile payments, people are willing to get involved. They are also willing to pay a higher price now because the price will be low when the number of mobile payment users is large enough. Sometimes the costs can approach zero. To make people expect that the number of mobile payment users will be high in the future, service providers and the government need to cooperate. For instance, the government should lead the development of basic infrastructure for mobile payments and set related rules and laws. This will send a positive signal that leads to an improved outlook for mobile payments. On the other hand, suppliers can provide consumers with subsidies and a more convenient experience to make the consumers truly feel the advantages of mobile payments.

In conclusion, with the importance of network scale effects for mobile payments and electronic currency, the range of application of electronic currency issued by private enterprises will become wide spread. It can be used to purchase both virtual commodities online and physical products in real life. Therefore, the importance of network scale effects for mobile payments and electronic currency means that electronic currency will either replace the sovereign currency issued by the central bank or coexist with it, which will have a significant impact on the monetary policy.

## 2 Payments and financial product properties

In the era of electronic currency, with the rapid growth of information technology, mobile and third-party payments have developed traits that resemble financial products. This trait has not only made mobile and third-party payments more attractive, but also has increased the difficulty of control over monetary conditions. This trait is defined by having the potential to make profit for clients, while being sensitive to the changes of currency. This resemblance to financial products has one defining characteristic—either the currency in the payment method is a financial product itself, or it can create value by switching between being a financial product and being a payment method.

Currency can be used as a financial product when it is not making payments. This is true for both precious metals and electronic currency. The main difference is that during payment, the transaction costs of currency and financial products were higher in the era of precious metals than in the era of electronic currency. Besides, in the era of electronic currency, the mobility of mobile payments is consistent with that of payments. This greatly reduces the transaction costs between currency and financial products.

In the era of electronic currency, as long as one has an online account, such as an Alipay account, currency can be linked to financial products with a few clicks or the swipe of a finger. When no payment is being made, the balance on personal accounts is a financial product. During a payment, the balance can be used as currency. This transformation can be made within a second, which was previously unimaginable. However, the power of technology also brings new challenges to monetary control.

## 3 Payment and monetary control

The rise of mobile and third-party payments has affected monetary control in the following ways: First, the low transaction costs of mobile and third-party payments have reduced the need for cash. Second, the financial product resemblance of mobile and third-party payments has obscured what counts as money, which could have an influence on the monetary base and multiplier. At last, with the rapid development of mobile and third-party payments, a private supply of electronic currency is available, which could change the currency supply system of the central bank and commercial banks.

With financial innovation, technological development, and the emerging third-party and mobile payments, other assets with relative high yield can be used as currency. This phenomenon is especially obvious in the era of electronic currency, as low transaction costs help to reduce the demand for interest-free electronic currency. For the first time, people can enjoy financial services anytime, anywhere, and any way. This also includes converting high yield assets into electronic currency. People will put electronic currency into bank accounts or virtual accounts to collect interest. Only when there is a purchase will withdrawals be made through a simple operation on computers or mobile phones for the exact amount to complete the purchase. The emergence of mobile and third-party payments will reduce the demand for currency as well as accelerate the velocity of circulation.

The emergence of mobile and third-party payments obscures the boundary of currency arrangements. Using mobile terminals to send instructions, one can quickly transform non-liquid currency into liquid currency. It is now hard to distinguish whether a currency is a demand deposit, a saving deposit, or cash. Furthermore, some nonbanking institutions have begun issuing electronic currency. For example, mobile carriers can issue electronic currency through virtual accounts. Many of these electronic currencies were not considered currency before, which greatly increased the difficulty of regulation.

Mobile and third-party payments are accompanied by private issuance of electronic currency. Some nonbanking institutions are able to issue electronic currency autonomously. Most of them are mobile carriers and Internet companies. Since there is not enough regulation, the reserve ratio of electronic currency is a company's own decision. Of course, companies will put some money aside as reserves because their reputations are at stake. However, this is only a soft constraint. As long as electronic currency issuance remains unregulated, companies may minimize their reserve in order to maximize profit. This could be a shock to the currency supply.

At the current stage, the private supply of electronic currency will not end the fundamental system of central bank currency issuance. However, changes in the format of currency demand, the unclear boundary of currency arrangements, and the diversification of currency issuers will certainly pose a threat to central banks.

## SECTION 4: ANALYSIS OF TENCENT'S WECHAT PAYMENT

### 1 A brief history

Since its start in 2013, Wechat Payment has rapidly spread across China. Businesses that are currently supporting Wechat Payment include QQ top-up, Tencent voucher center, Guangdong Unicom, WeLOMO, McDonald, Wechat Group Purchase, and others. Banks' personal financial services are also cooperating with Wechat, and Tenpay has already started its cooperation with several banks, experimenting with less risky fixed-rate products. Wechat Payment has also extended itself to payment for everyday expenses. One example is the "Shenzhen Power Supply" service provided by Shenzhen Power Supply Bureau, which provides services such as online payment of electricity bills, electricity price checks, and balance inquiries. Paying for everyday expenses may not be as profitable as credit cards and electronic payments, but may increase client stickiness.

In order to make payments more convenient, Wechat is gradually partnering with some companies to push voice payments. Clients can simply say the products they desire on their mobile phones, and then both purchase and payments are processed. Wechat also allows payments to be made through QR code scanning. Wechat clients do not have to exit the Wechat application and while paying, they simply need a bank card attached to a Wechat account to pay for products provided by public accounts on Tenpay. The entire process takes less than a minute.

However, the progress of financial institutions' adoption of Wechat Payment is relatively slow. By December 2013, more than 40 securities companies have opened accounts on Wechat. Most of them, however, do not involve payments. If there is a need for financial products, these companies need to go on fund company websites with their cell phones. The banking industry is the same. Furthermore, merchants who joined Wechat Payment are predominately from the Chinese mainland. Since it can only accept payment transactions from the Chinese mainland. The Wechat platform cannot yet make overseas purchases.

## 2 Operating principles

The name "Wechat Payment" implies two things: It is a mobile payment application where transactions are made through the Tenpay third-party payment platform. It is also a payment method in which payments are made through mobile banking by accessing banks' Wechat public accounts. The Wechat Payment that we generally refer to is the former. It integrates social network platforms, third-party payment companies, as well as mobile banking, thus maximizing the client experience.

The bank must have a Wechat public account to handle payments. Banks can interact with clients on Wechat, and then direct their clients to their mobile banks to complete the payment. Of course, the clients must have a mobile bank account. The core characteristic of Wechat Payment is its integration of a social networking platform, third-party payments, and mobile banking. It combines their strengths to provide a new service to clients (Figure 4.4).

## 3 Risk and risk management

The main risk facing Wechat is IT risk (see Chapter 10). This includes damage to hardware, software failures, viruses, operating errors, potential mistakes in data transmission and data processing, and various online frauds.

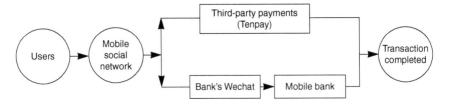

*Figure 4.4* The process of Wechat payment.

The information technology risk of Wechat Payment cannot be managed with just one method. A system of risk control must be in place, attacking the problem with both technological and non-technological means. Some examples of technological means include setting a separate password for Wechat Payment, sending confirmation text messages, requiring voice authentication, verifying client identity by using big data analysis, and so on. When a risk to client accounts is confirmed, the system must notify the client immediately, and a series of protective measure must be turned on to provide real-time protection for clients. For example, Alipay developed a real-time risk monitoring system for its accounts and transactions in 2005 to preempt and avoid losses. Non-technological means include providing insurance, which can be negotiated with insurance companies. In fact, Wechat Payment is now fully covered by Peoples Insurance Company of China (PICC).

## SECTION 5: A BRIEF ANALYSIS OF YU'E BAO

### 1 Creation and development

Yu'E Bao is a Chinese service developed by Alipay. It targets individual users to provide interest on their savings. Since its creation in June of 2013, Yu'E Bao has seen tremendous growth. According to Tian Hong Asset Management, in December of 2013, Yu'E Bao reached over 43 million users, with total savings of RMB 18.53 Billion. The assets under management ranking of Tian Hong Asset Management soared from 46th in the first quarter of 2013 to 2nd by the end of 2013.

Yu'E Bao has posed a threat to banks by challenging their deposit savings. It has attracted numerous small investors and low value added money market funds. Cumulating tiny savings was an exclusive right for the banks that is now threatened. With the development of technology, Yu'E Bao may become a universal account in the future, providing services in lending, saving, securities purchases, and asset managing products, on top of its current services.

### 2 The fundamentals of Yu'E Bao

The success of Yu'E Bao lies in its ability to create value for all involved. The securities companies increase their sales through Alipay, and Alipay earns a commission for bridging the gap between securities companies and individual buyers. Moreover, the individuals can collect interest on savings with Yu'E Bao while keeping their savings liquid. The innovation of Yu'E Bao is in purchasing and redemption.

In purchasing, because Yu'E Bao is not a qualified trustee, funds from the customers must be quickly transferred to Tian Hong Asset Management's escrow account. Otherwise, there could be a suspicion of misconduct. The funds actually go through two steps: purchase and transfer. During purchase, the balance in Alipay moves to Yu'E Bao. In transfer, the balance is automatically transferred to Tian Hong's escrow account.

The greatest innovation of Yu'E Bao with respect to redemption is real-time redemption. If redemption is simply a reversal of purchasing, then there is no misconduct. Through this process, however, redeeming T + 0 cannot be achieved. In order to achieve real-time redemption, there are two other methods. Both of them, nevertheless, are on the edge of being illegal. One of them is to have Alipay cover the cost, which Tian Hong later reimburses. The second method is for Tian Hong to keep a reserve in Alipay's payment account. When redemptions occur, the reserve can be used to transfer money to the users (Figure 4.5).

Although Yu'E Bao has bypassed banking sales, it still cannot exist without banks. Third-party payment companies needs banks to verify client information, transfer funds and liquidate positions when necessary.

## 3 Risks

On top of IT risks, Yu'E Bao also has legal and market risks. Legally, Yu'E Bao lacks risk disclosure to its users. "A Guide on Securities Investment Sales Applications" states that institutions selling securities should investigate and evaluate the investor risk tolerance at or before their first purchase. For investors who have already bought securities, they should also investigate and evaluate the investor's historical risk tolerance. On Yu'E Bao redemptions, if Alipay covers the payments, it may violate clause 23 of "Regulation on Excess Reserve for Payment Institutions" by completing payments requested by clients ahead of time. Tian Hong may also violate the "Interim Measures for the Administration of Securities Investment Funds" with its subscription and redemption activities.

There may also be market risks, since Yu'E Bao is not exactly savings. Users may face interest rate declines or even losses due to mistakes in management. The initial high return rate was possible due to a shortage of funds in the market, which is likely to continue. Yu'E Bao may also be investing in non-monetary products with high risk. If the economy slows down, Yu'E Bao could decide to take more risks in pursuit of higher returns.

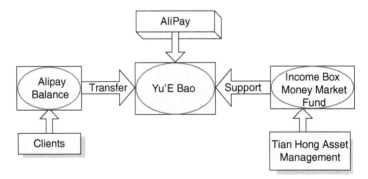

*Figure 4.5*[8] The operational structure of Yu'E Bao.

## 4 Financial products as instruments of payment

The existence of Yu'E Bao gave rise to numerous financial products involving third-party payment and funds. These products provide interest to users and can be an instrument of payment when needed. This has blurred the line between investment and payment, as well as financial products and currencies. With interest rate marketization, these products are likely to grow in the next years. If their total market cap reaches RMB 1 trillion, they could exert tremendous influence to the financial system.

To be an instrument of payment, a financial product must have low volatility and high liquidity. These two characteristics are closely correlated, but there is no causality between them. Other than the composition of financial products, these characteristics are also results of the market environment.

Statistically, low volatility requires a product to be stable in price over time, which makes the product maintain its value. This is similar to the store of value characteristic of currencies. Two approaches can be used to achieve low volatility. Either the product is a diverse portfolio of securities, or the product has low risk due to high quality issuers or counterparties, advantages in capital structure, short maturities, or good contract terms.

Liquidity refers to a financial product's ability to convert quickly to cash. On some occasions, it may also refer to the product's collateral quality—the higher the quality, the lower the haircut.[9] Market liquidity is plotted by the bid-ask spread in the secondary market. If the spread is low, the liquidity is invariably high. In most occasions, when the risk of securities is low, the secondary market is often well equipped with high liquidity.

Most money market funds invest in treasury bonds, commercial paper, and short-term financing bonds. They are generally low in volatility and highly liquid, which makes them ideal for payments. In fact, M2 statistics include money market funds and savings accounts with the ability to issue checks.

Nevertheless, money market funds are not risk free, and they are not protected by deposit insurance as some savings accounts are. They are not always low in volatility and highly liquid. In fact, money market funds experienced a major crisis in September of 2008. Therefore, we can conclude that there are indeed risks to financial products combining third-party payment and funds. As a result, implementation of appropriate regulations will be very important.

## 5 Main models

### *5.1 Self-built platforms to sell financial products*

With the rise of Internet-based finance, major commercial banks have gradually established their own e-commerce platforms. They provide both payment and other one-stop financial services. For example, the "ShanRong" service of China Construction bank is both a B2B and B2C platform. It is an in-depth incorporation of e-commerce and financial services. Self-built platforms aim to develop customers. However, because of the closed nature of the platform, less-diversified product portfolio, and non-existence of a price advantage, customers are not very active on these platforms. This is evidenced by the shutdown of ICBC's online store.

### 5.2 Utilizing third-party channels to sell financial products

There are various ways to run this model: to sell products through third-party e-commerce business platforms, such as Taobao flagship stores; routing through third-party financial products such as Yu'eBao (accomplished mainly through collaboration with mutual funds); and marketing through a supermarket of funds, loans, or insurance. An example of each type of site is Shumi Funds (funds), Ron 360 (loans), and Huize (insurance).

### 5.3 Using social networks to sell financial products

This model refers to financial institutions that utilize social platforms to connect financial institutions and users. This model takes full advantage of big data analysis, data flows, cloud computing, and relationships on social network platforms to capture "soft" information. Simultaneously, by creating a virtual online VIP room, customers can enjoy the feeling of being served over the counter. Selling financial products through social networking platforms can fundamentally change the relationship between financial institutions and customers. It achieves real-time dialogue between financial institutions and customers. The more opportunities there are for dialogue, the more information will be shared. Financial institutions can therefore more accurately determine customer needs. Typical representative include microblog banks, Wechat bank, and Baidu finance.

### 5.4 Integration of relationships and the Internet to launch a financial supply chain

In this model, what is sold is more than just a financial product; it is a package of financial services. The customers form a customer cluster in relationship with a core enterprise. Through the "transfer" of target customers, the financial supply chain can be an effective solution to information asymmetry. Because Internet supply chain financing can achieve a high degree of integration of information flows, capital flows, logistics, and online control, lending efficiency, and safety are vastly improved. The financial supply chain of Jingdong is indicative of this trend. It is an e-commerce company that provides guarantees for merchants to obtain loans from financial institutions. Through guarantees, merchants more easily obtain loans.

Finally, not all financial products are suitable for online marketing, especially products of high complexity, high customization and high risks, or products requiring investors to make many sophisticated judgments.

# Notes

1  Shuai, Qinghong. 2011. "Electronic Payments and Settlements," Dongbei University of Finance & Economics Press.
2  The services are actually provided by the subsidiaries of the telecom operators, including Wing e-commerce(China Telecom), Unicom WO easypay(China Unicom), e-commerce of CMCC(CMCC).
3  RFID-UIM card is a kind of mobile phone card with the function of radio frequency identification.
4  Wan, Jianhua. 2003. "E-era of finance," China Citic Press.
5  Jin, Chao, and Yanhua Leng. 2004, "Electronized Currency, Electronic Currency and Money Supply", Shanghai Finance.
6  Economides, Nicholas, and Charles Himmelberg. 1994? "Critical Mass and Network Evolution in Telecommunications?" Working paper.
7  The $p$ here can be understood as the transaction costs of mobile payments.
8  This diagram is built on "A Construction Bank's Interpretation of Risks: How Will Yu'E Bao Impact Banks", especially its content involving Yu'E Bao's structure.
9  Haircuts refer to reductions in the amount one can borrow based on collateral of a certain present value.

# 5 Internet currency

This chapter examines the form of money in the Internet world. The core of our idea is that many quality online communities with payment functions will issue their own "Internet currencies." Internet currency will be widely used for economic activity on the Internet, and society will revert to the state where currency issued by the central bank and that issued privately coexist. It will create new challenges to the foundations of current monetary, currency, and central banking theory.

## SECTION 1: THE CONCEPT OF INTERNET CURRENCY

Virtual currencies have already emerged as a rudimentary form of Internet currency. Classic examples include Bitcoin, Qcoin (created by the Tencent, one of the key Chinese Internet companies), Facebook Credits, Amazon Coins, Gold (World of Warcraft), and Linden Dollars. These virtual currencies can be used in social networks, online games, or virtual worlds to purchase goods (hereafter referred to as digital products) and services. This activity has already developed into an extremely complex market mechanism.

Some of these virtual currencies are not exchangeable for legal money, such as World of Warcraft's G coin, a currency that may only be used in the online game's environment. Other virtual currencies such as Amazon Coins employ legal currency to allow holders of virtual currency to buy both online and physical products and services, but they cannot be directly exchanged for legal currency. Bitcoins and Linden Dollars are in a final category that can both be exchanged for legal currency and be used for purchases. According to research conducted by the European Central Bank,[1] virtual currency transactions in the United States amounted to $2 billion in 2011, a level that surpasses the gross domestic product (GDP) of a few countries. Traditional payments companies are also jumping into the virtual currency area. For example, in 2011 Visa spent $190 million to buy PlaySpan, a company that manages electronic goods transactions for games, online media, and social networks. American Express entered this market through its $30 million purchase of the virtual currency platform Sometrics. Virtual currencies will prove even more beneficial once the development of mobile payments improves their ability to transact.

We identify the following characteristics that define virtual currencies:

1   Issued by an online community
2   Either not regulated at all or very lightly regulated, especially by central banks
3   Exists in digital form
4   Issuing online community has an internal payments system
5   Accepted and used by the members of the online community
6   Can be used to purchase the online community's virtual goods or real goods
7   Serves as a unit of exchange for online products

Number five indicates that the virtual currency can be used as a unit of exchange. A few online communities have user numbers that surpass the population of many countries. For example, Facebook's monthly active users (MAU) come from many countries and have now surpassed 1 billion. The sixth indicates the unit of exchange function, and the seventh means it can function as a price discovery mechanism. If we consider the purchasing power of Internet currency and the relative prices of goods purchased, it also has the "store of value" function. Internet currencies thus fulfill all of the standard requirements to be considered a currency (unit of exchange, store of value, and price discovery). Internet currencies also defy borders. They are both international and exceedingly powerful.

Up to now, most Internet currencies are essentially fiat money with a centralized issuer. The value depends on the trust people have in the issuer. Bitcoin is thus an exception. There is no central issuer, and its characteristics more approach that of money backed by precious metals. Later sections will go into further detail on this point.

## SECTION 2: THE ECONOMICS OF INTERNET CURRENCY

## 1 Online communities and network economics

Internet currency's benefits for online communities include the following:

1   Independent pricing for digital goods
2   Wealth effect due to online accounts
3   Facilitation of transactions between members
4   Increased "stickiness" due to more effective use rules than legal currency
5   New income sources such as seigniorage, exchange with legal currency, and use of inactive members' funds
6   Creation of economic activity on the online network
7   No counterfeit currency

The distinction between digital and physical goods is becoming increasingly unclear. Digital goods such as software, e-books, music, films, and news are all digitized information. This means that consumer utility does not vary with their form. More and more people recognize the value in these products. In the future, many products that do not require physical delivery will be produced, traded, and consumed online (see Chapter 11). This type of goods will continually increase as a percentage of total goods. For example, Tencent makes Renminbi (RMB) 22.8 billion from online games, 51% of its total income. It is not necessary to use legal currency for this type of activity.

It is also important to note that the relationship between the Internet economy and the real economy is getting ever closer. Imagine the following scenario: someone creates a software product online and sells it in exchange for Internet currency. He then uses this currency to buy food at McDonalds, which in turn uses this currency to buy digital products. The real and Internet economies combine perfectly. Legal money is excluded and unnecessary.

## 2 The new form of currency: Facilitating network payments

Chapter 4 predicted the coming integration of forms of payment such as bank cards and mobile payments. We will have the convenience of payments anytime, anywhere, and any way. This reality is already upon us if we consider virtual currency accounts as a type of deposit. One can make quick payments over the Internet. A possible future state may occur if everyone has both virtual and legal currency. Internet currencies are both easily exchangeable across online communities and into legal currency. Online currencies would be far more integrated with the real economy, and we could even witness the emergence of Internet stocks, bonds, deposits, and credit.

Up to the present, there have been three stages of currency development:

1  Barter economy, no currency exists
2  Hard goods as currency, such as gold, silver, or paper money redeemable for precious metals. Money creation was mainly determined by discovery and mining of precious metals
3  Fiat money without intrinsic value or guaranteed convertibility

Private organizations were the primary issuers at the beginning of stage three. Legal currency only emerged when law specified the central bank's currency as that used in payment, settlement, and clearing, excluding others. The central bank, commercial banks, savers, and lenders all participate in money creation. Base money includes money in circulation and the reserves commercial banks store at the central bank. Commercial bank credit and bond investments cause deposits to expand to many times over. We separate money into three levels: M1, M2, or M3 based on liquidity (from highest to lowest). Legal currency replaced private currency due to the central bank's creditworthiness and deep involvement in payment, clearing, and settlement systems.

However, we have not yet reached the end of money's evolution. Hayek and Friedman already expressed doubts about this system all the way back in the 1950s. Hayek argued that government currency issuance since the eighteenth century was not natural, and he saw it as an important contributing factor of both inflation and the business cycle. He recommended a return to multiple issuers to reinstate competition for issuance that would lead to more stability and societal benefits. Friedman wanted to do away with the central bank and replace it with an automated mechanism that would increase the money supply at a stable rate.

Although private money no longer circulates in large amounts, quasi-private money is still common. In the twentieth century, China's universities issued cafeteria cards that could be traded or used to buy food and household products. Today, rewards programs, frequent flier miles, gift cards, and other forms of quasi-private money are everywhere. Internet currencies combine fiat money and private money. There are two main reasons why legal currency is unable to replace Internet currencies: some areas of online activity cannot accept legal currency, and Internet technology permits payment outside the central bank's systems. Since payments and money follow the same evolutionary trajectory, currency's fourth stage will witness the coexistence of legal money and Internet currency.

## 3 The risks of Internet currency

One of the key risks inherent to Internet currency is that its issuers are unable to match neither the creditworthiness nor the effective payment and clearing of a central bank. For example, Bitcoin's main risk is an insufficiently reliable clearing process. It is impossible to avoid credit risk, liquidity risk, operations risk, and payment problems. Since these currencies allow for significant anonymity, they are difficult to regulate. They are thus more susceptible to illegal activities such as money laundering, which give rise to both legal and reputational risk.

Internet currency may also affect price stability. Before the emergence virtual deposits, the creation of virtual currencies did not involve the central bank or commercial banking system. They did not create a multi-tiered monetary system. However, excessive emission of Internet currency could create inflation in digital goods. When digital goods enter the consumer price index (CPI) basket, they will enter as relative prices between digital goods to create an average. Price risk is thus low.

Internet currencies can also affect physical goods prices. Once it integrates into the real economy, it may even replace legal currency in some areas. This would then affect legal money velocity through a contractionary effect. Monetary policy and the quality of the central bank's statistics would then be affected; since the central bank does not necessarily have access to key information on Internet currency. As for financial stability, fluctuation in the rate of exchange between the Internet currency and legal currency is the main source of risk. This is especially clear for Bitcoin.

## SECTION 3: BITCOIN

Bitcoin is the first ever electronic currency based on P2P technology. It is both issued and traded online. It was announced by Satoshi Nakamoto in 2008 and officially entered circulation on January 3, 2009.[2] By the end of December 2013, 12 million Bitcoins had been issued.[3] Assuming a value of $900 per Bitcoin,[4] the total value amounted to $10 billion, higher than the GDP of more than 60 countries.[5]

Cryptography and universal Internet serve together as Bitcoin's foundation. Its uniqueness comes principally due to its ability to process payments and issue currency without either the central bank or third-party payments, and its modern verification system allows for relatively high anonymity. Its initial supporters were tech fanatics, anarchists, and criminals, who viewed it as an embodiment of the spirit of democracy. It challenges the banking system and those in power by breaking the state's monopoly on issuing currency. It protects its holders from expropriation through inflation. As it increased convertibility with physical currencies, it gained the attention of the media, governments, scholars, and others. It also sparked significant controversy. Competitors such as Litecoin, Peercoin, and Primecoin have already emerged.[6] These competitors retain Bitcoin's main idea, but they differentiate themselves through special characteristics.

## 1 Working mechanism

In early 1998, Dai Wei explained the thinking behind Internet currency in a cryptography-focused e-mail newsletter. It would be "provided to and by untraceable entities" and "the government is … unnecessary."[7] Bitcoin is the development and extension of this thinking. The most important innovation is the decentralized model it uses for its payment system (Figure 5.1)

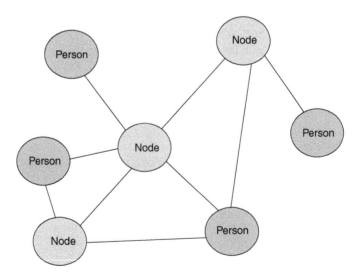

*Figure 5.1*  A decentralized payment system.

In an entirely decentralized system, one can have any number of payment terminals to confirm transactions and protect the accounts system. Payments are confirmed in two steps: it begins when a node successfully completes the initial step
through competition and finishes when this information is broadcast and finally
confirmed by the entire network.

Bitcoin's new model requires it to deal with two important questions: how
to protect the anonymity of those transacting and how to ensure that the same
money is not used in two transactions. Bitcoin has dealt very creatively with these
problems. It uses public-key encryption to protect anonymity. There is a public key
that corresponds roughly to one's address or account number at a bank, and there
is a private key held only by the Bitcoin holder. The public key acts as the address
for reception of Bitcoins, and the private key provides access to the account, its
Bitcoins, and payments. Thus the public key functions like an e-mail address, the
private its password.

Figure 5.2 shows how both keys are used for Bitcoin transactions. Assume that
in N transactions, person A wants to make a transfer to B, and in N + 1 transactions
B wants to further transfer the coins it received from A to a new person D. This
transaction requires four steps.

Person "A" first generates the information from the past N transactions, including
the connection from the last transaction, information from the current transaction
(including the amount to be transferred), and the public-key corresponding to
person "B". "A" then uses his/her private key for the electronic verification process

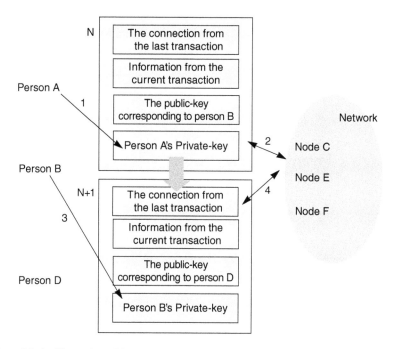

*Figure 5.2* An illustration of Bitcoin transaction.

and sends it to the network. In the second step, the network checks and confirms A's request, including whether it was sent from A, whether it possesses sufficient Bitcoins, and whether these Coins have already been used. If this is confirmed, it will be sent over the entire network and saved. In the third step, B undertakes the same steps for transaction N + 1 as A did in transaction N. In the fourth, the network then undergoes the same confirmation process as in the second step.

This is the complete process for Bitcoin transactions. It must prevent that the same coins are used multiple times. In a traditional economy, the central bank performs this function. It uses a centralized account system for the requisite checks, while Bitcoin uses decentralization and real-time technology. Each computer in the network verifies new transactions by referring to the entire "transaction chain" of those previously completed. Only transactions checked and confirmed against this chain become official. In fact, each new transaction is responsible for addition to the end of the transaction chain, and there is only one valid transaction chain. Thus, although it is on every computer (decentralized), it is in actuality a system based on one central confirmation (Figure 5.3).

Bitcoin requires complex calculation for a node to add a transaction to the chain due to failed transactions, fraud, and other risks. The calculation requires expenditure of a great deal of computing power, which serves as proof of work performed. The incentive to perform this work comes in the form of "Bitcoin mining", the way in which new Bitcoins are created and the payment platform continues to function.

Bitcoin's reliance on the Internet allows it to easily cross borders. Its unlimited nodes allow it to easily withstand attacks on any individual or group of nodes. Users are completely anonymous and can possess any number of accounts. Bitcoin is also cheap for users, as the transfer fees and exchange charges are extremely low.

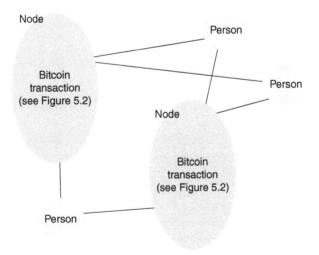

*Figure 5.3* The full Bitcoin transaction chain.

One rare characteristic is the irreversibility of transfers. There is no way to cancel or reverse a transfer that has already been confirmed except through instituting a new transfer in the opposite direction. It is both open and transparent, and all transaction data are available on the Internet. Finally, it is divisible up to eight decimal places, or 0.00000001 Bitcoin.

Bitcoin is, however, not perfect. Some believe the massive expenditure of computing power to create new transactions is a waste. Microsoft's Moshe Babaioff and collaborators published research point out a potential "red balloon effect" in Bitcoin mining in which the decentralized network do not contribute to the transmission of transaction information.[8] For example, some Bitcoin miners could change their distribution codes so that other nodes are unable to receive new transaction information.

## 2 Issuance mechanism

The payment terminals that successfully confirm transactions receive newly minted Bitcoins. The system therefore does not need a central bank. At the beginning, each completed transaction link creates 50 Bitcoins, but this number will decline by 50% every four years until the total Bitcoins in circulation maxes out (expected in 2040 at 210 million total Bitcoins, see Figure 5.4). This create scarcity, which in turn could very well lead to a deflationary tendency that manifests itself in declining goods prices in terms of Bitcoins. This increase in Bitcoin value could cause hoarding that reduces liquidity and further increases deflationary pressure. This deflationary tendency becomes a barrier to financial products based on Bitcoin prices due to the continually increasing real debt repayment burden. All currencies, even Bitcoin, need price stability. Although Bitcoin has dealt with the inflationary tendency of other currencies through a fixed issuance schedule, its deflationary tendency will encumber its future growth. However, it remains possible to change the code. For example, the issuance could be changed to base itself on a certain level of inflation. We recommend a report by the Paolo Alto Research Center[9] to readers particularly interested in this subject.

Another problem is the diminishing returns on Bitcoin mining. In the early days of Bitcoin, individual "miners" with personal computers could receive Bitcoins. Today, the computing power required to harvest the same number of Bitcoins is extremely high, so many computers have to work together and split the winnings, giving rise to a "mining pool" (see Figure 5.5).

The "mining pool" distribution implies a somewhat monopolistic payment mechanism. If there is a limited number of effective payment nodes, then Bitcoin supporters' belief in its democratic purity declines along with the distinction between Bitcoin and money issued from a central bank. The biggest question is how to keep the mechanism afloat once Bitcoin miners cannot receive any more Bitcoins for their efforts. Bitcoin's founder has suggested a transaction fee to maintain the system, and the Bitcoin Association has created a plan to implement it. Transactors would pay the confirming nodes to confirm their transactions in

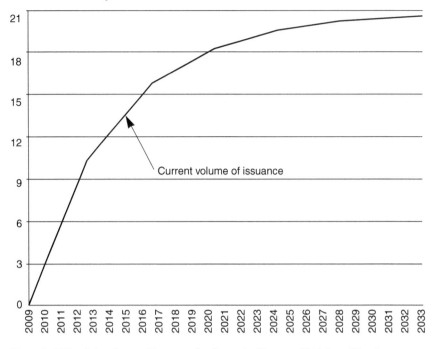

*Figure 5.4* Bitcoin's volume of issuance (by the end of January 2014, in millions)

this model. However, these are all in the planning stages. The current system does not involve nodes that collect confirmation fees.

## 3 Bitcoin's effect

Bitcoin has already run up an impressive transaction volume and is convertible into many currencies at rates that fluctuate freely with demand. Mt. Gox is the world's largest Bitcoin exchange. It is responsible for over 80% of Bitcoin exchanges and publishes daily exchange rates between Bitcoin and major currencies. Other Internet sites such as Bitcoin.local allow accountholders to directly exchange with each other.

Bitcoin's price is famously unstable. Both user numbers and prices increased dramatically from June to July 2011. The price started below $1, then quickly rocketed up to $30. Prices have fluctuated up ever since. Figure 5.6 indicates the staggering price volatility in 2013, reaching $1,200 and then receding. Although Bitcoin has had a relatively small footprint, some service, software, and clothing companies accept Bitcoins. Some questionable uses have also emerged out of its anonymity. WikiLeaks began to accept donations in Bitcoins when it was cut off from traditional payments. Some drug dealers on the "Silk Road" Online Marketplace accept payment only in Bitcoins. Nicholas Christin of Carnegie Mellon University estimated that this website generated monthly transactions of

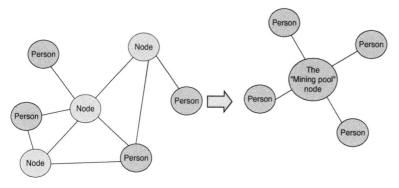

*Figure 5.5* The "mining pool" distribution mode.

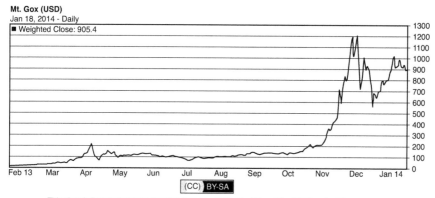

*Figure 5.6* Bitcoin's price volatility in 2013.

$1.2 million in 2012.[10] In May 2013, the FBI closed the site and took possession of its Bitcoins.

In a systematic analysis of Bitcoin, Ron and Shamir discovered that Bitcoins are mostly untraded and highly concentrated.[11] Most existing Bitcoins have not moved from their initial accounts, an indication that they have been either lost[12] or hoarded. 90% of accounts have made less than ten transactions and possess very few Bitcoins, an indication that Bitcoin can hardly be considered a lively marketplace. The breakdown in Table 5.1 shows that 97% of accounts possess 10 Bitcoins or less.

Table 5.1 confirms Bitcoin's scarcity and tendency to both deflation and appreciation expectations. Bitcoin holders tend to remain just that, holders who do not use them. This cannot be good for Bitcoin's popularization.

## 4 Innovation and insufficiency

Bitcoin sparked a deeper discussion about the nature of money. We believe it is a fitting reference point for questions about innovation and the future of money,

*Table 5.1* Balance on Bitcoin accounts[13]

| Greater or equal to | Lesser than | Number of users | Accounts |
|---|---|---|---|
| 0 | 0.01 | 2,097,245 | 3,399,539 |
| 0.01 | 0.1 | 192,931 | 152,890 |
| 0.1 | 10 | 95,396 | 101,186 |
| 10 | 100 | 67,579 | 68,907 |
| 100 | 1,000 | 6,746 | 6,778 |
| 1,000 | 10,000 | 841 | 848 |
| 10,000 | 50,000 | 71 | 65 |
| 50,000 | 100,000 | 5 | 3 |
| 100,000 | 200,000 | 1 | 1 |
| 200,000 | 400,000 | 1 | 1 |
| 400,000 | | 0 | 0 |

including a possible world currency. Bitcoin's main innovation is its independence from the banking system, which allows even international payments to be both direct and cheap. It could play a leading role in a future with many forms of money. It has even inspired J.P. Morgan to apply to create its own digital currency.

The fixed issuance schedule has inspired new thinking on an issue that has plagued monetary policy since the collapse of the gold standard and transition to fiat money: inflation's wealth destruction. Mainstream ideas focus on central bank independence and monetary policy transparency. Bitcoin's idea is something new. It does not require a central bank and separates the payment and money issuance functions in favor of a rules-based issuance.

However, a lack of stable purchasing power is holding Bitcoin bank from being a completely developed currency. There is neither an intrinsic value (gold standard) nor an issuing body (fiat money) to ensure this. This instability, combined with holders' high concentration and hoarding behavior, mean Bitcoin badly needs a redesign.

## 5 Risk and regulation

In a fiat money system, base money includes bank reserve requirements and money in circulation. Money and credit are inextricably linked through credit expansion, which both creates money and causes deposits to proliferate. Bitcoin decouples credit and money, it is not a fiat currency. A look at money creation under the gold standard, with Bitcoin mining as a replacement for gold mining, gives us a better idea of why Bitcoin behaves as it does. The total amount of both gold and Bitcoins is fixed, and the costs to extract them increase as the easiest accessible stocks are exhausted.

Fiat money is priced based on faith in the issuer and total issuance. That of metal-backed currency is supported by its intrinsic value (use in jewelry and other products) and stabilized by the tendency for gold to exit circulation when prices decline and enter when prices rise. Bitcoin's price combines elements of both. It could decline if faith in its mechanism declines due to worries of hacker attacks, loopholes, Bitcoin seizures, or counterfeit coins. The cost of computing power that miners expend could also influence the price. Just like gold, it is influenced by the price of fiat currencies in which the prices are expressed.[14]

The February 2014 hacker attack on the Mt. Gox Bitcoin exchange demonstrates the risks associated with Bitcoin. The Bitcoin losses were so staggering that the exchange applied for bankruptcy, and the price of Bitcoins fell 50% in a single day. The emergence of similar, competing currencies such as Litecoin, Peercoin, and Primecoin all pose risks to Bitcoin's value.

Bitcoin currently resides in a legal gray area. Should Bitcoins be classified and protected as wealth? Does it violate current laws? How should policymakers and regulators deal with Bitcoin? How can we adjust current laws to deal with Internet currencies? Many users doubt that Bitcoin is ready for an expanded role due to this uncertainty. Its anonymity facilitates money laundering along with drug and weapon sales. This must be changed. Insufficient regulation has inhibited tax collection on Bitcoins and focused attention on a Bitcoin transaction tax. For example, the United Kingdom is considering classification of Bitcoin as a money replacement, which will allow it to impose a 20% value added tax.[15] Norway, Germany, and Singapore have already provided for Bitcoin taxes.

How does Bitcoin fit into the existing US legal framework? In a comprehensive review published in 2011, Ruben Grinberg, now a lawyer at Davis Polk, argued that the Stamp Payments and federal counterfeiting statutes would need substantive revision to apply to the issuance of Bitcoin.[16] They also do not quite fit the many definitions of securities under securities laws. He did, however, point out significant risk for the Bitcoin community in relation to money laundering laws, as Bitcoin does not fulfill the registration requirements for money services and it is, "generally known that Bitcoin is used to promote illegal activities." Nikolei Kaplanov argued strongly against the regulation of Bitcoin in a paper published by the Temple University Law Review.[17] He compared Bitcoin with existing community currencies and questioned the legal basis for the federal government, including the Federal Reserve, to regulate the use of Bitcoins for transactions between willing parties. These admonitions appear not to have convinced the federal government.

Bitcoin's greatest risk is uncertainty regarding its regulation. Regulators around the world are paying ever-increasing attention to Bitcoin's development. In August 2013, a federal judge officially ruled that Bitcoin is subject to regulation according to American Securities Laws. European officials are issuing warnings about the threat it and other virtual currencies pose to the central bank's ability to safeguard fiscal and monetary stability. Russia, India, and Hong Kong have all issued warnings and taken various steps such as investigation and temporary closure of Bitcoin trading platforms (India) and bans on domestic transactions parallel with the Ruble (Russia). However, these pale in comparison with the strict response from China. In December 2013, the People's Bank of China (PBoC) issued a directive banning Bitcoin's use as a liquid currency.[18] The ban extended to financial institutions, payments companies, and retail businesses, which were forbidden from processing or accepting payments in Bitcoins.

America's attitude toward Bitcoin is still developing. Former Federal Reserve Chairman Ben Bernanke expressed hope for Bitcoin's ability to overcome legal and supervisory questions to create a more effective international payments system over the long term. On the state level, California's House of Representatives passed a bill permitting use of any alternative currency with monetary value in payments and retail transactions in the state.[19] It would put Bitcoin on the road to full legality in California, but the bill still needs to pass through the state senate and receive the governor's approval to become law.

Based on this analysis, we have two recommendations. The first is that China delays its clarification of Bitcoin's legal role until the technical and market foundations are fully developed. The second is to research ways to effectively regulate it so as to protect consumers and prevent money laundering, speculation, and price manipulation. The circulation of Internet currency indicates that it could one day become an able competitor with central bank-issued legal money, especially if an online currency emerges whose issuance is rules-based rather than predetermined like Bitcoin. It could sensitively adjust issuance to take economic risk into account rather than price and quantity, thus avoiding the deflationary pitfalls of Bitcoin and the myriad issues with central bank-issued currency. There is a great deal of work to do, but we see a bright future with many forms of currency on the horizon.

## Notes

1  European Central Bank. 2012. "Virtual Currency Schemes."
2  Nakamoto, Satoshi. 2008, "Bitcoin: A Peer-to-Peer Electronic Cash System."
3  Blockchain.info. 2013. http://blockchain.info/charts/total-bitcoins.
4  Mt. Gox. 2012. www.mtgox.com/.
5  Gross Domestic Product. 2013. World Bank.
6  Sprankel, Simon. 2013. "Technical Basis of Digital Currencies," Technische Universitaet Darmstadt.
7  Source: http://weidai.com/bmoney.txt
8  Babaioff, Moshe, Shahar Dobzinski, Sigal Oren, and Aviv Zohar. 2012. "On Bitcoin and Red Balloons." "Red Balloons" refers to a 2009 DARPA experiment in which participants were to locate ten red balloons placed randomly across the United States. The winner received $40,000. The core of the Red Balloon Phenomena is cooperation and competition.
9  Barber, Simon, Xavier Boyen, Elaisn Shi, and Ersin Uzun. 2012. "Bitter to Better—How to Make Bitcoin a Better Currency."
10  Christin, Nicolas. 2012. "Travelling the Silk Road: A Measurement Analysis of the Silk Road Anonymous Marketplace."

11 Ron, Dorit and Adi Shamir. 2013. "Quantitative Analysis of the Full Bitcoin Transaction Graph."

12 Bitcoins can be linked to a specific piece of computer hardware. If that hardware breaks or is lost, it may be impossible to access its linked Bitcoins.

13 Up to May 3rd 2012.

14 If the US Dollar depreciates (appreciates), Bitcoin and Gold as expressed in dollars appreciate (depreciate).

15 Chaturvedi, Neeblah. "U.K. Weighs How to Tax Dealings in Bitcoin." 21 January 2014. Wall Street Journal. http://online.wsj.com/news/articles/SB10001424052702304302704579334790053233278

16 Grinberg, Reuben. 2011. "Bitcoin: An Innovative Alternative Digital Currency."

17 Kaplanov, Nikolei. 2012. "Nerdy Money: Bitcoin, the Private Digital Currency, and the Case Against its Regulation." Temple Law Review.

18 "Notification on containing the risks of Bitcoin." 5 December 2013, People's Bank of China www.pbc.gov.cn/publish/goutongjiaoliu/524/2013/20131205153156832222251/20131205153156832222251_.html.

19 California House of Representatives, AB129.

# 6  Big data

*Big data* is a new concept that also goes by *Big Scale Data* or *Massive Data*. So far, there exists no universal definition for the concept. However, it is well understood that the so-called Big data has four features, that is 4Vs: large *Volume*, low in *Value* density, *Variety* in sources and features, and rapid *Velocity*.

The concept has emerged from society's digitization process (see Chapter 1), especially with the development of online social networks and sensory devices. Updated cloud computing and search engines provide efficient ways to analyze big data. Yet the core lies in how to quickly identify valuable information from the wide range and massive data sources. Big data is playing an increasingly significant role in social analysis, scientific discovery, and business decision making. Finance is only one example of such an application.

Today Big data has become a hot topic. Some believe that it is an important or even strategic component of a nation's resources, just like oil and gas. We will not discuss each idea in detail. Rather, we believe that most of the discussion is theoretical. Since it does not explain the mechanism of big data analysis technically, we aim to fill this gap.

Based on the findings of data science and data mining literatures, we start by introducing the main types of big data, and then discuss the goals for big data analysis. In the end, we will compare it to econometrics. Chapter 7 will focus on the big-data-based credit investigation and Internet lending. Chapter 12 will discuss the application of big data in securities investment and actuarial science.

## SECTION 1: BIG DATA: CONCEPTS AND MAIN TYPES

The basic unit of big data is a data set. First we will introduce two relevant concepts for data sets: data objects and properties, and discuss the three different types of data set: recorded data, graphic-based data, and ordered data.

## 1 Basic concept

A data set is a collection of data objects. Accordingly, the data objects are its components. In statistics, data objects are equal to statistical units or sample points and are sometimes called records, points, vectors, models, events, cases, samples, observations, or objects. The data objects are described via a set of properties.

The number of the data objects' properties is called the "dimension." A common problem in the analysis of high dimensional data is the so-called curse of dimensionality. The difference between the number of data objects and their dimensions is the degrees of freedom. As the degrees of freedom decrease, some statistical methods will become inapplicable and the results will be less reliable. One way to deal with this is dimensionality reduction, that is combining original dimensions into a new one to reduce the number of dimensions. Usually, linear algebra methods such as principal component analysis and singular value decomposition are used to project high-dimensional data sets into lower ones.

In some data sets, object values in most properties are zero, and in most cases, the nonzero terms account for less than 1%. This is known as sparseness. There are certain ways to deal with the sparseness. Properties are equal to the variables in statistics, which stand for the data objects' features or characters and vary from object to object or from event to event. Properties are also called characters, fields, features, or dimensions. The rules that connect numbers or symbols with the objects' properties are the measurement scale. For example, GPA is one property of students, and identifying a certain student's score is actual measuring.

Properties can be divided into four categories based on their applicable calculation types (i.e. comparison, order, addition and subtraction, multiplication and division). The first category is a nominal property, of which the values are set as different labels that provide sufficient information to identify each data objective. For example, different IDs, genders, and so on. belong to this category. The second category is the ordinal property, of which the values give information to order different data objects. House numbers belongs to this category. The third is the interval property. The interval property has measurement units with meaningful differences in properties. One example of this category is temperature. The fourth category is the ratio property, of which the difference and ratio are both meaningful. For instance, length and weight belong to this category. Of the four categories, nominal and ordinal properties are qualitative properties while interval and ratio ones are quantitative properties.

The possible number of values of each property can be divided into two categories. The first is a discrete property with limited or infinite numbers of values. The second is the continuous property with values from the whole set of real numbers. Usually, nominal and ordinal properties are discrete and interval and ratio properties are continuous.

## 2 Recorded data

Recorded data is a collection of records (i.e. data objects) and each of them contains fixed data fields (i.e. properties). For most basic forms of recorded data, the records have no clear relevance to the fields. The recorded data is usually stored in flattened files or relational databases. It is structural data and can be presented as a data matrix. There are two conditions for this.

Condition I: If all data objects have the same data property set, these data objects can be regarded as points (or vectors) in multi-dimensional space. Each dimension represents a different property. Cross-sectional data used in econometrics can therefore be regarded as a data matrix, whose analysis method is represented by matrix signals and computing.

Condition II: After it is transferred, some recorded data can be represented by a data matrix, such as file data. If we ignore the order of words that appear in a file, we can use word vectors to represent the file, of which each word is a component of a vector (property). The value for each component corresponds to the times of a word appears in the file. Data matrices based on this logic are called document-term matrices. Transaction and market basket data are other examples of this type. In a supermarket, the products bought by one customer at one time can be regarded as "one transaction," within which each commodity is one term. Each customer buys different products, and each product type is of a different amount. Still, the complete market basket can be represented by commodity vectors, each of which is a component of the vector (property), and each vector's value corresponds to the market basket's commodity type, commodity amount, and expense. It is important to note that the data matrix under the second condition tends to have "sparseness."

## 3 Data based on graphs

**Data with relationships among data objects.** The relationship among data objects tends to carry important information. For example, website pages include text and links that refer to other web pages. These links carry information about the importance of this web page. Google's Page Rank computing method is based on link analysis, which we explore in detail below (see Link analysis in Section 2). We can use graphs to represent this kind of data. Generally, data objects will produce mappings on the graph's nodes, and the relationship among data objects can be represented by the direction and weight of links between different nodes.

**Data with graph objects.** If data objects have structure (i.e. objects include sub-objects), they are usually represented by graphs. For example, the structure of a compound can be represented by graphs, among which the atom is the nodes and the chemical link is the link between different nodes.

## 4 Data in order

**Sequential data** is an expansion in recorded data in which each record includes time-related information. For example, a supermarket cashier records the market basket information for each customer. The recorded information is sequential data. Also, all the time series data (such as macroeconomic series and financial price series data) belong to sequential data.

**Sequence data** is the sequence of each entity. It is quite similar to time series, except that sequence data do not have a timestamp. Typical sequence data includes genome, word, or letter sequences.

**Spatial data** can also be regarded as an expansion in recorded data, only that each record includes the space of the area feature related to this data. Typical spatial data includes meteorological data collected from different geographic positions and different points in time, such as temperature, humidity and atmospheric pressure.

## SECTION 2: PRIMARY TASKS FOR BIG DATA ANALYSIS

Big data analysis is primarily used for prediction or description. For prediction, it uses a set of independent variables to estimate or predict the value of the dependent variable. Description summarizes potential correlations, trends, clustering, and abnormal trajectories in the data. Descriptive tasks are usually exploratory and often need post-processing to verify and interpret results. These two types of tasks can be divided further into classification, regression, association analysis, cluster analysis, recommender systems, anomaly detection, and link analysis.

## 1 Classification

Classification aims to place data objects into a pre-defined target class. Typically, these target classes are mutually exclusive. For example, credit rating agencies use issuer data to place debt into categories based on creditworthiness from AAA (the best rating) to D (default).

The input data is a collection of records. Each record is represented by the tuple, (x, y), in which x is a collection of attributes and y is a special attribute that indicates the class label record (also called categorical attributes or target attribute). The core of classification is to determine a target function by learning and map each attribute set x to a pre-defined class number y. Sometimes, instead of determining the set of attributes mapped to a certain category number y, x may be mapped to all the target classes as long as it is subject only to a certain probability distribution.

The general classification task has two steps. The first step requires a training test consisting of records in which the label is known. It can develop into classification models, including the Logit model, Probit model, decision tree classification, rule-based classification, artificial neural networks, vector machines, and Bayesian supported classification method (part of this model will be described in detail in Chapter 7). Next, the classification model is applied to a test set consisting of records in which the label is unknown. We then evaluate the classification model's performance by seeing which records were correctly classified.

Confusion matrices are often used in these problems. Table 6.1 is a typical confusion matrix for a binary classification problem. There are positive and negative types (a positive class usually represents a rare category while negative classes represents the majority); in each table entry, $f_{ij}$ indicates its actual class is $i$ but is predicted to be class $j$. The table contains four specific conditions:

*Table 6.1* Confusion matrix

|  |  | Predicted Class | |
| --- | --- | --- | --- |
|  |  | Positive | Negative |
| Actual Class | Positive | $f_{++}$(TP) | $f_{+-}$(FN) |
|  | Negative | $f_{-+}$(FP) | $f_{--}$(TN) |

- True positive (TP) or $f_{++}$: number of positive samples of correctly predicted to be positive;
- False negative (FN) or $f_{+-}$: number of positive samples erroneously predicted to be negative;
- False positive (FP) or $f_{-+}$: number of negative samples erroneously predicted to be positive;
- True negative (TN) or $f_{--}$: number of negative samples correctly predicted to be negative.

According to the confusion matrix entries, the total number of correctly predicted samples by classification model equals to $f_{++} + f_{--}$ and that of erroneously predicted ones equals to $f_{+-} + f_{-+}$. Accuracy and error rates are two common indexes of the classification model's performance. The accuracy rate is equal to the proportion of correct predictions, $\dfrac{f_{++} + f_{--}}{f_{++} + f_{+-} + f_{-+} + f_{--}}$, and the error rate is the proportion of wrong predictions, $\dfrac{f_{+-} + f_{-+}}{f_{++} + f_{+-} + f_{-+} + f_{--}}$.

Another common tool to measure the performance of classification models is the receiver operating characteristic (ROC) curve based on the true and false positive rates (FPRs). The true positive rate (TPR) is defined as the proportion of correctly identified positive samples, $TPR = \dfrac{TP}{TP + FN}$, and FPR is the proportion of negative samples predicted to be positive by the model, $FPR = \dfrac{FP}{TN + FP}$.

ROC curves can be applied to classification models that produce output values continuously (such as Logit models, Probit models, artificial neural networks, and Bayesian classifications). These output values can be used to sort orders into categories from the most likely to be positive to the least likely, specifically in the following five steps:

Step 1 (assuming a continuous value output for the positive class) sorts samples by their output value. The higher the output value, the more likely the sample is to be positive.

Step 2 selects the sample with minimum output value and defines others as positive. This makes centralized test samples positive. If all positive samples have been correctly classified, then all negative ones must be wrongly classified, so $TPR = FPR = 1$.

Step 3 selects the next sample from the sorting list and defines it and those with higher output values as positive. Samples with lower output values are negative. Recalculate $TPR$ and $FPR$.

Step 4 repeats the third step; the test selects the sample with the highest output value.

Step 5 connects all $(FPR, TPR)$ in turn and get the ROC curve (Figure 6.1).

Two classification models' ROC curves are rather special. One is perfect classification $TPR = 1, FPR = 0$. Its ROC curve is the horizontal line at the top of Figure 6.1. The other is random classification, that is divide samples randomly into positive category according to a fixed probability and get a diagonal ROC curve. Other models' ROC curves are between that of perfect classification and random classification. Models with curves closer to the upper left corner curves perform better. Thus, area under curve (AUC) also functions as a performance metric.

## 2 Regression

Regression is similar to classification. The key difference is that in regression, the target attribute $y$ is continuous. In classification, however, the target attribute $y$ is discrete. In other words, classification predicts whether something will happen, while regression is to predict how much.

Regression is the most commonly used tool in econometric analysis, especially the linear regression model:

$$y = \alpha + \beta_1 x_1 + \beta_2 x_2 + \ldots + \beta_p x_p + \varepsilon \tag{6.1}$$

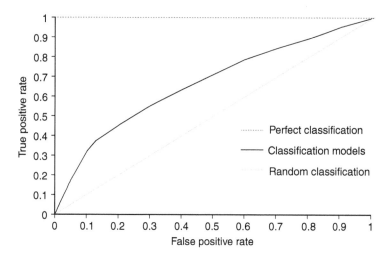

*Figure 6.1* ROC curve.

Here, $y$ is the dependent variable. $x_1$ to $x_p$ are independent variables. $\beta_1$ to $\beta_p$ are parameters to be estimated. $\varepsilon$ represents random disturbance.

Mean square error (MSE) is a prime measurement of a regression model's performance. Suppose there are $n$ samples and the $i$ sample's dependent variable value is $y_i$ which is predicted to be $\hat{y}_i$ by the regression model. Then the MSE is:

$$MSE = \frac{1}{n}\sum_{i=1}^{n}(y_i - \hat{y}_i)^2 \tag{6.2}$$

In the linear regression model, the least squares method (LSM) gets parameter estimates by solving the MSE minimization problem.

## 3 Association analysis

Association analysis focuses on market basket data. The goal is to find hidden meaningful relations in big data sets. One popular (and humorous) example is diapers and beer. Retailers found that many customers buy diapers and beer at the same time, so they placed diapers and beer together in stores to promote cross-selling. Association analysis tries to find a link rather than an explanation. Here, we face two essential issues: first, the calculation cost may be too high; second, some correlations may occur by accident. The core of the association analysis algorithm is to deal with these problems, expressed as follows:

$I = \{i_1, i_2, \ldots, i_d\}$ stands for all the items in the market basket data, and $T = \{t_1, t_2, \ldots, t_N\}$ represents all matters. Every item contained by matter $t_i$ is subset of $I$. For item set $X$, its support is:

$$\sigma(X) = \#\{t_i | X \subseteq t_i, t_i \in T\} \tag{6.3}$$

In it, $\#$ represents the number of elements in the collection.

Association rules are expressed as an implication expression like $X \to Y$ in which $X$ and $Y$ are disjointed item sets $X \cap Y = \varnothing$. Support and confidence show the strength of association rules.

Support depicts the frequency of $X$ and $Y$ occurring together (i.e. $X \cup Y$) in $T$:

$$s(X \to Y) = \frac{\sigma(X \cup Y)}{\#T} \tag{6.4}$$

Occasional rules have low support. From business perspectives, low support rules are mostly meaningless. Therefore, support is used to delete those pointless rules.

Confidence depicts the frequency of $Y$ in matters that contain $X$ and reflects reasoning by the rule:

$$c(X \to Y) = \frac{\sigma(X \cup Y)}{\sigma(X)} \tag{6.5}$$

The association rule's mining problem is for a given set of matters $T$ to identify all rules whose supports are greater than or equal to minsup and confidences are greater than or equal to minconf, where minsup and minconf are the thresholds of support and confidence. Here, we usually complete two steps:

First, generate frequent item sets to find all item sets that meet the minimum support threshold;

Second, produce rules with high confidence from the previous step, which are then called strong rules.

Typically, the amount of calculation to generate frequent item sets is much larger than that of desired rules. Generating item sets frequently uses either the Apriori or FP growth algorithm.

## 4 Cluster analysis

Cluster analysis divides data objects into groups based on descriptive objects and their relationship information in the data. Objects are related within a group and uncorrelated among different groups. The greater the homogeneity within the group, the greater the gap between the two groups, which then improves the clustering effect.

Cluster analysis and classification are similar. Clustering classes (clusters) can also be considered as a data object classification, but this classification information can only be derived from the data. In classification, however, the class labels are known when the development of the object model is done. We then assign numbers to new and unmarked objects. Thus, classification is also called supervised classification, and clustering analysis is called unsupervised classification.

Common clustering algorithms include K-means, agglomerative hierarchical clustering, and DBSCAN. They can be hierarchical/agglomerative or use point assignment. The first type of algorithm regards each data object as a cluster at the beginning and combines clusters according to their closeness, which can be defined in many different ways. When the further combination leads to pre-defined undesired results, the above combination process is ended. For example, combination can stop when it reaches a pre-given number of clusters. The second category involves point assignment process, which means considering each data object in a certain order and assigning it to the most appropriate cluster. The process typically has a short initial phase to estimate clusters. Some algorithms allow merging or splitting for temporary clusters. They may also identify outliers when the data object may not be assigned to any cluster.

## 5 Recommender system

The recommender system predicts user preferences. For example, an online newspaper provides news reports based on the prediction of user interest, and online retailers recommend products to customers that they might want to buy on the basis of their shopping and/or goods search history.

There are two types of elements in recommender systems: users and items. User preference for some items can be expressed as utility. Suppose there are $N$ items and $R(u,i)$ represents user $u'$s utility from item $i$. Since it is impossible to observe $R(u,i)$, the recommender system must work this out and get prediction $\hat{R}(u,i)$. After obtaining $N$ predicted utility values $\hat{R}(u,i_1), \hat{R}(u,i_2),\ldots,\hat{R}(u,i_N)$, the recommender system will first recommend $K$ (usually much smaller than $N$) items on the principle of utility maximization.

One type of recommender system is content-based. Such recommender systems use customers' past preference to recommend similar ones. Similarity between items is determined by calculating the similarity between attributes. Amazon uses this to recommend books similar to the one currently viewed.

Another is collaborative filtering, which recommends items according to other customers' choice who have similar taste. The similarity between users depends on their browsing and scoring records. For example, Dangdang's "those bought this item also bought" feature is a type of collaborative filtering. Collaborative filtering is the most popular and also the most widely applied of all types.

Recommendations can also base themselves on demographic characteristics. Such recommender systems recommend appropriate items based on users' demographic characteristics (such as age, language, and country).

Knowledge-based systems make out yet another category. Such systems use domain-specific knowledge to judge whether an item meets users' needs, preferences, and practicability. The core is a similarity function used to measure users' needs (i.e. description of the problem) and match degree of recommendations (i.e. answers).

Community-based systems rely on the user's friends. The basis for such recommender systems is that people tend to accept the recommendation of friends. The popularity of social networks has also promoted its development.

Hybrid recommender systems mix the above systems together. For example, content-based recommender systems can make up for the new-item problems of collaborative filtering.

## 6 Anomaly detection

Anomaly detection identifies characteristics that are significantly different from other observed values. The abnormal observation value is called an anomaly or outlier. Anomaly detection tries to find real outliers and avoid false labeling. In statistics parlance, a good anomaly detector must have a high detection rate and low false alarm rate. Anomaly detection applications include fraud detection (such as credit card fraud detection), network attacks, unusual disease patterns, and ecosystem disturbance.

There are three main sources of outliers. First, data may come from different classes. The statistician Douglas Hawkins defines outliers as observations with differences so large that it seems impossible they come from the same mechanism. For example, people who use credit cards fraudulently and legally are two different types. The second source is natural variation. Many data sets can be modeled with a statistical distribution (e.g. normal distribution) in which the probability of an observation appearing decreases as it departs from the mean. The third source is data measurement and collection errors. Such anomalies reduce the quality of the data analysis and should be thrown out.

There are a variety of ways to detect abnormalities. Many anomaly detection techniques first create a model without points that are not perfectly fit. For example, the data distribution model can be created by the parameter estimation of probability distributions. If an object does not fit well with the model (that is, not subject to the distribution), it is an outlier. If the model is a set of clusters, then the outlier is not the object of any significant clusters. When using the regression model, anomalies are relatively far from the predicted value of the object.

Proximity-based techniques, on the other hand, measure the distance between objects. Outliers are those objects furthest away from most of the other objects. When the data can be displayed in a two-dimensional or three-dimensional scatter chart, outliers can be detected visually by finding points separate from the majority.

We also have techniques based on density. The relative density of an object can be estimated directly, especially when there is already a proximity measure between objects. Low-density areas relatively far from the nearest neighbor objects may be seen as outliers. A more sophisticated approach is to consider that the data set may have different density areas. Only if the local density of a point is significantly lower than most of its neighbors can they be classified as outliers.

## 7 Link analysis

Google's PageRank is representative of the link analysis algorithm. Before Google, there were many search engines, most of which used a web crawler to obtain data from the Internet, and then list the lexical items of each page with an inverted index. When a user submits a search query, all pages containing these words are extracted from its inverted index and listed in a way that that reflects inside items. Therefore, words appearing on the page header items have a higher correlation than lexical items that appear in text, and the more occurrences of lexical items, the more relevant the web page. In this case, "term spam appeared" in large numbers and some unrelated Web pages modified themselves (such as a large number of duplicate keywords) to deceive search engines. To solve lexical item falsification, the PageRank algorithm has developed two innovations.

First, it simulates the behavior of Internet surfers. These imaginary surfers start from random web pages and pick a next destination link randomly selected from current page. This multi-step process can be iterated. Ultimately, these surfers will converge on a page. Pages with more visitors become more important than those of few visits. PageRank measures this "importance" of web pages. Google lists pages according to PageRank when answering queries.

Second, in determining the content of the page, both lexical items that appear on the page and word entry point links to the page should be considered. The implicit assumption is that web owners tend to link to good or useful web pages instead of bad or useless ones. Even if spammers can easily add false lexical items on pages under their control, they can hardly do the same thing on pages referring to theirs. Link spam has been developed to work against link analysis, which builds a webpage collection that is called a "junk farm" to increase the PageRank of certain pages. Correspondingly, some anti-spam methods appeared such as TrustRank and "garbage quality."

In this way, the PageRank algorithm actually uses the Internet as a directed graph where pages are graph nodes: two can be connected with a direct edge if there is a link between them. The PageRank algorithm simulates the behavior of Internet surfers and gives transition probability meaning to edges. For example, suppose a surfer is currently on page A, while page A has three links pointing to page B, C, and D. It is believed that the surfers' probability to visit B, C, or D is equally 1/3, but staying on A has zero probability. Thus, a Markov process can characterize surfers' behavior on the Internet.

Assume webpages denoted by $\{1, 2, \ldots, N\}$ are in the state space of a Markov process. $X_t$ represents surfers' location at the moment of $t$ and is a random variable ranging from $\{1, 2, \ldots, N\}$. The sequence of random variables $\{X_t, t = 0, 1, 2, \ldots\}$ is a random process. In the PageRank algorithm, this random process satisfies Markov properties (visual description is given now, past and future are not relevant):

$$\forall t, n \quad f\left(X_{t+1} \middle| X_t, X_{t-1}, \ldots, X_{t-n}\right) = f\left(X_{t+1} \middle| X_t\right) \tag{6.6}$$

In Equation (6.6), $f\left(X_{t+1} \middle| \cdot\right)$ indicates $X_{t+1}$'s conditional distribution.

Thus, $\{X_t, t = 0, 1, 2, \ldots\}$ is a Markov process and its dynamic change can be characterized by a transition matrix. Use $N \times N$ matrix $P$ to represent the transitional probability matrix, then $p_{ij}$ in line $i$ and column $j$ means:

$$p_{ij} = \Pr\left(X_{t+1} = j \middle| X_t = i\right) \tag{6.7}$$

Using a $N \times 1$ matrix $V^t$ to describe surfers' locational distribution on the Internet at moment of $t$, the $i$ component $v_i^t$ means:

$$v_i^t = \Pr\left(X_t = i\right) \tag{6.8}$$

So, at the time $t + 1$, surfers' locational distribution $V^{t+1}$ satisfies:

$$V^{t+1} = P \cdot V^t \tag{6.9}$$

If the Internet is a strongly connected corresponding digraph, that is starting from any node we can reach all other nodes and there is no end point (i.e. the node does not exist in the chain), then regardless of the surfers' initial locational distribution on the Internet, after long enough, it will be close to a stationary distribution $\pi^1$. The rigorous formulation is:

$$\forall V^0, \lim_{t \to \infty} V^t = \pi \tag{6.10}$$

The steady-state distribution $\pi$ satisfies $\pi = P \cdot \pi$ (i.e. starting from the steady state, the next moment is still a steady-state), so $\pi$ is actually an eigenvector of Matrix $P$ with corresponding eigenvalue 1.

$\pi^i$ is the $i$ component of $\pi$ in the steady state that shows surfers' probability to stay on page $i$ and PageRank value of page $i$.

In reality, the corresponding figure of the Internet generally does not have strong connectivity features. For example, there may be no termination point for the chain or there may be a set of pages that have a chain, but the chain does not point to other web pages outside of this group. The PageRank algorithm solves these problems by modifying the transition probability matrix, such as "taxed" law, which will not been discussed here.

## SECTION 3: COMPARISON OF BIG DATA ANALYSIS AND ECONOMETRICS

## 1 Introduction to econometrics[2]

Econometrics is the dominating quantitative empirical analysis used in the economic and financial fields. Econometrics adds empirical content to economic theory, which allows theories to be tested and used for solving real problems, especially for forecasting and policy evaluation of government and enterprises. Econometrics studies random economic relations by dealing with data from real observations, usually without artificial control, with mathematic methods to build models and reveal quantitative relations for an objective economic system.

Econometric analysis is generally based on four steps: variables and data selection, model specification, model fitting and testing, and applications. It should be noted that model specification and testing are closely connected in real studies.

### 1.1 Variables and data selection

First, model variables are based on research purpose, theory, and empirical studies. There are two kinds of variable: dependent and independent. These variables must be observable and quantifiable.

Secondly, we select samples to assign data to each variable that has been chosen. There are three main types of data: cross-sectional data that refers to observations of many different individuals (subjects, objects) at a given time (each observation belonging to a different individual), time series data that refers to a sequence of observations which are ordered in time or space (each observation belonging to the same individual), and panel data that refers to multi-dimensional data frequently involving measurements over time. Panel data contains observations of multiple phenomena obtained over multiple time periods for the same firms or individuals.

The data sample has a direct impact on an econometric model's quality. General samples must meet the following requirements: the sample should be representative and randomly selected from the same population, the data should be comparable to the same variable and have a consistent statistical standards, data should be as accurate as possible to reduce errors caused by measurement and merging, and data should be as complete as possible.

### 1.2 Model specification

When one has selected the variables and sample, one can set the mathematical form of the econometric model. In principle, the model should be in line with economic theory and reality. The models should also contain the important influential factors. Econometric models can be abstracted into the following general form:

$$Y = g(X,\theta) + \varepsilon \qquad (6.11)$$

In Equation (6.11), $Y$ is the dependent variable, $X$ is independent variable, $\varepsilon$ is a random disturbance term, and $\theta$ is the parameter to be estimated.

First, $g(\cdot)$'s function (often a linear or log-linear model) and explanatory variables are the core problems that can generally be determined after repeated attempts, inspection, and adjustment.

Second, the random disturbance $\varepsilon$ is a random variable. $\varepsilon$ is the sum of all factors that influence the dependent variable but are not included in the model. It comes mainly from omission of an explanatory variable, mathematical omission, observation error, accidental factors, and merging errors. $\varepsilon$ is unobservable and generally assumed to be white noise (expected value is zero; variance is constant; covariance is zero; and sometimes assumed to be normally distributed).

Third, the role of the parameter $\theta$ is to describe the stable characteristics of the economic system, generally having economic implications and used to analyze the direction and strength of the relationship between explanatory and explained variables. Parameter $\theta$ is objective but always unknown. The general range of $\theta$'s values is provided by economic theory. Its estimated value is derived from sample data based on econometric methods.

### 1.3 Model fitting and testing

Model fitting generally requires Stata, Eviews, SAS, SPSS, R, or other professional software. Output includes the parameter estimates and various test statistics. There are a variety of testing models. One uses the effect of model fitting tests, including goodness of fit tests for the entire model or individual parameters, the residuals (estimates of random disturbance) of the test, and whether the main test item meets the same random noise variance, irrelevance, and normal distribution assumptions. It also refers to improper specification, such as the presence of unrelated variables, the omission of important variables, and mathematical form error. The second category tests economic rationality, including symbols, numerical size of the parameter estimates, and whether the relationships meet the predictions of economic theory.

## 1.4 Applications

First, one must predict. For example, one may use time series models to predict future macroeconomic variables. Model predictions need certain conditions. History, reality, and future must have a consistent economic structure for the same econometric model to have stable parameters. Explanatory variables for the next period are known. The model must also have predictive ability and reach desired accuracy. If economic development processes are not steady, lack standardized behavior, or the model is out of date, then prediction will fail.

Second, we have the economic structure of the analysis, including fit with predictions of economic theory and quantitative relations between economic variables, such as marginal analysis, elasticity analysis, and comparative static analysis.

The final step is policy evaluation. Econometric results can help us both evaluate existing policies and select the appropriate solution for future policy.

# 2 Differences between big data analysis and econometrics

## 2.1 Different data types

Econometrics deals with structured data, including cross-sectional data, time series data and panel data, which are generally presented in tabular form in Excel. They have clear economic implications and consistent statistical standards for each rank. These data can also be transformed into data matrices. Many of the basic concepts of econometrics, analytical tools, and algorithms can be expressed as matrices or matrix operations.

Big data analysis can handle unstructured data, including documents, video, and images, which are generally difficult to present in tabular form. These unstructured data need quantification before analysis, and quantification is generally accompanied by loss of information. For example, in big data analysis, presentation of documents must be transformed into word vectors in order to do further processing. Word vectors only reflect words' location and frequency in the document, but cannot abstract semantic information in words' arrangement.

The curse of dimensionality exists both in econometrics and big data analysis. However, in big data analysis, because of big data amount and lower signal noise, the curse of dimensionality is more prominent, so the use of dimension reduction techniques is more common.

## 2.2 Different focuses

Econometric analysis focuses on hypothesis testing. Its core concept is very close to Popper's falsificationism. In general econometric analysis, it is a must to first define a number of hypotheses deduced from economic theory. Secondly, econometric analysis must build null hypotheses that may be falsified. For example, correlation tests usually take "no association between the two" as the null hypothesis, while independence tests take "a link between the two" as the null hypothesis. The null hypothesis often constrains parameters to be estimated, such as whether an argument is 0 or two arguments are equal. If the null hypothesis is valid, the sample data or its constructed test statistics should follow a known probability distribution. If the actual value of sample data or the test statistic only occurs with small probability (i.e. the confidence level, for example 1%, 5%), then the sample data are considered to correspond to the null hypothesis. One negates the null hypothesis under a certain confidence level. Otherwise, the null hypothesis cannot be rejected (but never say "accept the null hypothesis"). Through hypothesis testing, econometrics falsifies or supports (not confirms) economic theories.

In addition, parameter estimation is one of the important contents in econometric analysis. However, hypothesis testing for parameters is more important than parameters' specific values. Econometrics can forecast, but mainly in policy research areas. In leading academic research, econometrics is mainly used to test economic theory.

In contrast, big data analysis is more pragmatic. Prediction occupies a large proportion of the big data analysis. We use classification and regression to reveal relations between variables and further predict unknown variables. Association analysis, cluster analysis, recommender systems, and anomaly detection detect potentially relevant data, trends, clustering, trajectory, and abnormal patterns. These patterns are expected to be useful on other occasions or in the future and have practical value. Therefore, the assessment of predicted effect is an important part of data analysis embodied in the confusion matrix, ROC curves, and other tools.

## 3 Inherent contact between big data analysis and econometrics

### 3.1 Based on probability theory and mathematical statistics

Although big data analysis uses a number of specific terms, concepts and methods from computer science, it has no essential difference from econometrics in terms of random questions. Both are based on probability theory and statistics. Recognizing this helps us to clarify certain misconceptions about big data.

Viktor Mayer-Schonberger and Kenneth Cukier believe that big data analysis is for all the data, not random samples.[3] This is debatable. While the data collection and analysis methods are sophisticated enough for data collection and analysis, it is not always necessary to do so. According to the central limit theorem, there is a square root relation between the quality of statistical analysis and quantity of the sample. For example, when the number of samples increase 100-fold, quality of analysis will increase 10-fold. Yet the statistical analysis workload has a linear relationship with the number of samples. For example, as the number of samples increases 100-fold, increase in storage and computing capacity is generally 100-fold. Thus, the cost of additional work to improve the quality will exceed the corresponding benefits generated as the sample size grows. Therefore, to obtain a representative sample through sample surveys of scientific design, data analysis is still of great value.

Secondly, they believe that big data analysis seeks correlation rather than causation. This statement is a cliché in statistics. Statistical correlation between cause and effect relationships can only be used for falsification instead of proving causation. Theoretical analysis of big data is also based on theory of probability and statistics.

Third, big data analysis is not a panacea. Estimation based on big data can be abstractly described as: $X$ is known information; $Y$ is unknown information; looking for a function $h(X)$ of $X$ to forecast $Y$. Prediction error is $Y - h(X)$. $E[Y - h(X)]^2$(similar to the MSE) used to measure the predicted effect. It can be proved[4] for any $h(X)$,

$$E[Y - h(X)]^2 = E[h(X) - E(Y|X)]^2 + E[Y - E(Y|X)]^2 \qquad (6.12)$$

and

$$E[Y - h(X)]^2 \geq E[Y - E(Y|X)]^2 \qquad (6.13)$$

The equal sign is valid when $h(X) = E(Y|X)$. So $E(Y|X)$ is also known as the best predictor.

Here we arrive at two conclusions. First, in big data analysis, optimal algorithms' core task is to make $h(X)$ as close as possible to the theoretical prediction $E(Y|X)$. Second, even in the best prediction, prediction error represented by $E[Y - E(Y|X)]^2$ still cannot be eliminated and is endogenous to information structure. For instance, even if information technology is well developed, some information cannot be digitized (and thus cannot be used in big data analysis). This "mixed" message determines the efficient frontier of big data analysis.

### 3.2 Unification of our understanding

Both big data analysis and econometrics can use points, collection/space, distance, and other concepts to unify understanding if data objects are regarded as points and data set as a collection or pace.

#### 3.2.1 Big data analysis

In classification, attributes can be recorded as points and divided into classes in different collections. In correlation analysis, the item sets can be viewed as points; their support and confidence are like a kind of distance. In cluster analysis, an object is a point, cluster is a collection, and proximity can be seen as distance. In a content-based recommendation system, options and users in collaborative filtering can be seen as points, while the same user's utility differences between the different options can be seen as a kind of distance. In anomaly detection, object is the point that is characterized by abnormal deviation from the normal point of collection, and proximity is a distance.

Big data analysis has developed many dissimilarity or proximity metrics to proxy for distance. For example, Euclidean distance, Manhattan distance, Hamming distance, Minkowski distance, correlation coefficient, Jaccard distance, cosine similarity, Mahalanobis distance, Bergman divergence, and edit distance are used in this way. Big data analysis can flexibly use various distances, such as nearest neighbor classifier in classification, K-means method in clustering analysis, and outlier detection based on the proximity in anomaly detection.

## 3.2.2 Econometrics

### 3.2.1.1 LINEAR REGRESSION

Consider the following linear regression model

$$y = \beta_1 x_1 + \beta_2 x_2 + \ldots + \beta_p x_p + \varepsilon$$

Suppose there are $n$ samples. In the $i$ sample, the dependent variable is $y_i$, and the independent variable is $(x_{i1}, x_{i2}, \ldots, x_{ip})$. Introducing the following notation

$$Y = \begin{pmatrix} y_1 \\ y_2 \\ \vdots \\ y_n \end{pmatrix}, \quad X_i = \begin{pmatrix} x_{i1} \\ x_{i2} \\ \vdots \\ x_{ip} \end{pmatrix}, \quad X = \begin{pmatrix} X_1' \\ X_2' \\ \vdots \\ X_n' \end{pmatrix}, \quad \beta = \begin{pmatrix} \beta_1 \\ \beta_2 \\ \vdots \\ \beta_n \end{pmatrix}$$

According to the least square method, the coefficient is estimated

$$\hat{\beta} = \left( X'X \right)^{-1} X'Y \tag{6.14}$$

Consider a new sample. The independent variable $X_0 = \begin{pmatrix} x_{01} \\ x_{02} \\ \vdots \\ x_{0p} \end{pmatrix}$ is known, so the dependent variable is predicted to be

$$\hat{y}_0 = X_0' \hat{\beta} = X_0' \left( X'X \right)^{-1} X'Y$$
$$= \sum_{i=1}^{n} \left[ X_0' \left( X'X \right)^{-1} X_i \right] y_i \tag{6.15}$$

The positive definite matrix $\left( X'X \right)^{-1}$ can be decomposed as $\left( X'X \right)^{-1} = \Gamma' \Lambda \Gamma$, in which $\Lambda$ is a diagonal matrix. Thus, $\hat{y}_0$ can be expressed as

$$\hat{y}_0 = \sum_{i=1}^{n} \left\langle \Lambda^{1/2} \Gamma X_0, \Lambda^{1/2} \Gamma X_i \right\rangle y_i \tag{6.16}$$

$\langle \cdot \rangle$ represents the vector product implying the cosine similarity concept:

$$\cos(x, y) = \frac{\langle x, y \rangle}{\|x\| \cdot \|y\|} \tag{6.17}$$

$\|\cdot\|$ represents the vector mode (length). When the angle between two vectors is 0, the cosine similarity is equal to 1. When two vectors are orthogonal, the cosine similarity is equal to 0. When the angle between two vectors is 180 degrees (i.e. the opposite direction), the cosine similarity equals to $-1$. Cosine similarity coefficient corresponds to essentially random variables.

Therefore, $\hat{y}_0$ can be further expressed as

$$\hat{y}_0 = \sum_{i=1}^{n} \|\Lambda^{1/2}\Gamma X_0\| \cdot \|\Lambda^{1/2}\Gamma X_i\| \cdot \cos(\Lambda^{1/2}\Gamma X_0, \Lambda^{1/2}\Gamma X_i) \cdot y_i \tag{6.18}$$

Equation (6.18) shows that the predicted value $\hat{y}_0$ is weighted by the known sample's dependent variable. Wherein the $i$ sample's weights is $\|\Lambda^{1/2}\Gamma X_0\| \cdot \|\Lambda^{1/2}\Gamma X_i\| \cdot \cos(\Lambda^{1/2}\Gamma X_0, \Lambda^{1/2}\Gamma X_i)$. Given $\|\Lambda^{1/2}\Gamma X_0\|$ and $\|\Lambda^{1/2}\Gamma X_i\|$, the higher cosine similarity of vectors $\Lambda^{1/2}\Gamma X_0$ and $\Lambda^{1/2}\Gamma X_i$ (i.e. more in the same direction), the bigger $i$ sample weight.

### 3.2.1.2 MAXIMUM LIKELIHOOD METHOD

The core logic of maximum likelihood is that the most reasonable estimate of the parameters should allow the largest probability to pick samples in a group that is randomly selected from the model population.

Assuming the overall distribution is $f(Y|\theta)$, $f(\cdot)$ represents the data generation mechanism. $\theta$ is an unknown parameter vector to be estimated. Assuming $X_1, X_2, \ldots, X_n$ is a set of observations from the overall sample distribution, and is independently and identically distributed. The definition of the likelihood function is the joint density function of the sample:

$$L(\theta|X) = \prod_{i=1}^{n} f(X_i|\theta) \tag{6.19}$$

The maximum likelihood method obtains estimation parameters by solving the maximum value problem:

$$\hat{\theta}_{MLE} = \arg\max_{\theta} L(\theta|X) = \arg\max_{\theta} \sum_{i=1}^{n} \ln f(X_i|\theta) \tag{6.20}$$

$LL(\theta|X) = \sum_{i=1}^{n} \ln f(X_i|\theta)$ is known as the log–likelihood function.

The maximum likelihood method has tight logical link with anomaly detection in big data analysis. An anomaly detection method based on density supposes an object outlier score is the inverse of density. The common definition of density is the number of objects around in a specified distance. Next, we use the density and anomaly score to interpret the maximum likelihood method.

Assume the value of the parameter vector $\theta$ is estimated within $\Theta$. For every $\theta \in \Theta$, we generate independent and identically distributed random variables $Y_1, Y_2, \ldots, Y_m$ following $f(Y|\theta)$. In the random variable space, the distribution $f(Y|\theta)$ is represented by point set $\{Y_1, Y_2, \ldots, Y_m\}$. Thus, there is a series of point sets corresponding to different values of $\theta$.

Consider the distribution $f(Y|\theta)$ with a representative point set $\{Y_1, Y_2, \ldots, Y_m\}$ and an observation sample $X_i$. With reference to the anomaly detection approach, $X_i$'s relative density to $\{Y_1, Y_2, \ldots, Y_m\}$ is:

$$\text{density}(X_i, d) = \frac{\#\left\{Z | Z \in \{Y_1, Y_2, \ldots, Y_m\} \text{ and} \|Z - X_i\| \le d\right\}}{m \cdot \int_{\|Z - X_i\| \le d} dZ} \tag{6.21}$$

$\#$ represents the number of elements in the set. $\|Z - X_i\| \le d$ means that the distance between $Z$ and $X_i$ is no more than $d$. $\int_{\|Z - X_i\| \le d} dz$ represents the volume of a sphere with center $X_i$ and radius $d$.

When $\{Y_1, Y_2, \ldots, Y_m\}$ is sufficiently dense (i.e. $m$ is sufficiently large), there comes:

$$\lim_{m \to \infty} \text{denisty}(X_i, d) = \frac{\int_{\|Z - X_i\| \le d} f(Z|\theta) dZ}{\int_{\|Z - X_i\| \le d} dZ}$$

Further, when $d$ is sufficiently small, we have:

$$\lim_{m \to \infty, d \to 0} \text{denisty}(X_i, d) = f(X_i|\theta) \tag{6.22}$$

In abnormality detection, $X_i$'s abnormal point score is $\frac{1}{\text{denisty}(X_i, d)}$. Because in the observed sample $X_1, X_2, \ldots, X_n$ are independent of each other, as a whole, their relative outlier scores to $\{Y_1, Y_2, \ldots, Y_m\}$ are $\prod_{i=1}^{n} \frac{1}{\text{denisty}(X_i, d)}$. According to the above analysis, when $m$ is sufficiently large and $d$ is sufficiently small, the abnormal-point scores of observed sample are close to the inverse of the likelihood function:

$$\lim_{m \to \infty, d \to 0} \prod_{i=1}^{n} \frac{1}{\text{denisty}(X_i, d)} = \prod_{i=1}^{n} \frac{1}{f(X_i|\theta)} = \frac{1}{L(\theta|X)} \tag{6.23}$$

Therefore, to maximize the likelihood function is equivalent to minimizing the outlier score. Maximum likelihood and anomaly detection solve the same problem from different points of view.

Finally, we would like to stress two points. First, unifying understanding of big data analysis and econometrics by using point, collection/space, distance, and other mathematic concepts reflects the deep connections among the probability theory, statistics, and functional analysis (or topology). Second, if data relation issues can be flexibly expressed as points, collection/space, and distance, it may create many new analytical methods. This shows that big data analysis still has much room for innovation beyond the seven major tasks in this chapter.

## Notes

1   Qian, Minping, and Gong, Guanglu. 1998. "The Application of Stochastic Processes," Peking University Press.
2   This chapter mainly refers to: Jin, Yunhui and Sainan Jin. 2007. "Advanced Econometrics," Peking University Press.
3   Mayer-Schonberger, Viktor, and Kenneth Cukier. 2013. "Big Data: A Revolution That Will Transform How We Live, Work And Think," Eamon Dolan/Houghton Mifflin Harcourt.
4   Durrett, Richard. 1996. "Probability: Theory and Examples," 2nd ed., Duxbury Press.

# 7 Big data-based credit and Internet lending

The core of loan provision is the management of credit risk. This begins with an evaluation of the creditworthiness of borrowers, and then determines the interest rate and term of the loan. Thus, creditworthiness is also the basis of Internet loan provisions. In this chapter, we first introduce the process of credit provision based on big data by contrasting the credit center of People's Bank of China (PBoC), a typical traditional means of credit, and that of Alibaba, one based on big data. We then introduce lending based on big data by contrasting Kabbage (USA) and Ali Small Loan (China).

## SECTION 1: BIG DATA-BASED CREDIT

## 1 Basic concepts[1]

Credit is mainly about evaluating clients' willingness and ability to repay loans based on their financial status, behavior, occupation, and credit record. The result of this evaluation is manifest in credit ratings and credit scores.

Credit rating involves the use of models and analytical methods to comprehensively evaluate different economic entities' credibility and ability to repay principal and interest. This process is undertaken by professional credit rating agencies. It is also an overall evaluation of repayment risk. Credit rating consists of the evaluation of willingness and ability to pay, with ability as an objective parameter and willingness as a subjective one. The credit rating procedure combines quantitative and qualitative methods. It emphasizes qualitative methods and uses quantitative estimates for reference. The results of credit rating is presented in simple grades, such as AAA, AA, A, BBB, BB, B, CCC, CC, C, and D. Every grade can be subdivided into three subcategories, positive such as AA+, the neutral AA, and negative such as AA−. In addition, each grade suggests a certain probability of default (PD). For example, the historical default rate of BBB bonds is approximately 3%, while that of AAA bonds is 0.003%.

A credit score is a score for individuals or small companies. Credit agencies extrapolate them from mathematical models based on credit reports to evaluate and estimate their creditworthiness. The higher the credit score, the better the creditworthiness.

Credit then becomes a problem of categorization (see Chapter 6). It categorizes individuals and companies according to their default probabilities. Mathematically, if we use X to represent the characteristics, features, and historical information of individuals and companies as independent variables and use $Y$ to represent the credit rating, default probability and credit score as dependent variables, we actually use g(X), a function of X, to predict $Y$ based on an empirical analysis. The banking industry put a great deal of effort into setting and adjusting their predictive functions[2] for the Internal Rating-Based Approach in Basel II & III.

In contrast with traditional credit, big data–based credit mainly absorbs new sources of data, but does not differ from traditional credit in approaches and modeling techniques. The principal difference thus lies in new independent variables available for model input. In the next two sections, we briefly introduce the PBoC credit rating center (CRC) and the credit rating system at Alibaba. Here we focus on the differences in their data sources. After that, we introduce the main credit rating approaches.

## 2 Brief introduction of the credit rating center of People's Bank of China

The CRC of PBoC collects, matches, and processes data related to credit. It also produces credit reports and credit service to lenders. The flow of information is divided into data collection, product processing, and external service (Figure 7.1).

### 2.1 Data collection

The CRC collects credit trade information and material non-credit trade information that has direct and specific influence on credit institutions, especially credit information in the financial industry. It includes the following:

1   Lending information is provided by credit institutions certified by the China Banking Regulatory Commission (CBRC). This is the main source of information, as the CRC's right to collect data from these agencies is guaranteed

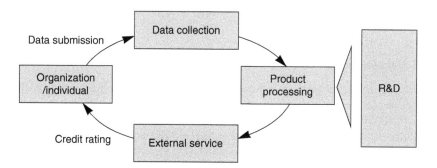

*Figure 7.1* Business model of the credit rating center.

by laws and regulations. These institutions are technically advanced, and the quality of their data is generally reliable.

2   Uncertified credit institutions provide lending information. This is a supplementary source of data, and the CRC's right to collect data from these agencies is also guaranteed. However, these organizations are small in scale and may lack the requisite information systems to provide reliable data.

3   Data is also collected from public sector entities that handle credit transactions, such as telephone bill records. These data are collected by permission of or through negotiation with the public sector. The quality of data is much influenced by the information quality of these public entities.

4   Information is also produced through law enforcement. These data have an essential impact on the credit report of the credit body. As the government enlarges the scope of information disclosure, this information can be collected from public channels.

5   Information from courts on the registration, litigation, judgment, and execution of lawsuits. Barring extreme situations, judicial information will be disclosed and can be collected through public channels.

### 2.2 Data processing

Data processing requires sorting, filtration, and processing of client-related information. The framework of data processing at the CBC has six levels (Figure 7.2):

1   Data provision: extracts data in various ways from queues, documents and databases

2   Data exchange: verifies data in format and logic and loads it into the basic library

3   Basic data: stores verified data as post source layer and provides data for further data processing

4   Data processing: differentiates and integrates credit institution information

5   Product processing: processes basic and value-added products

6   Data movement: includes dispatch, transfer, formatting, and other functions.

### 2.3 Main product

After examining, filtering, matching, storing, and managing the data, the CRC processes data into products according to the product design and research results. The CRC is designed to be a basic database in financial credit information, in addition to its service for credit institutions and the government. According to diversified scale and demands of clients, the CRC for now supplies five categories of product: data products, tools, solution products, outsourced service products, and credit institution service products (Figure 7.3).

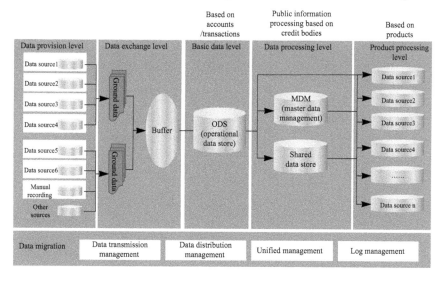

*Figure 7.2* Data processing framework of the credit rating center.

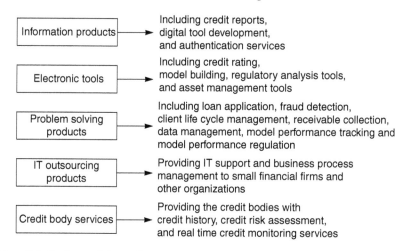

*Figure 7.3* Products of the credit rating center.

## 3 Brief introduction of the Alibaba credit system[3]

The Alibaba credit system (ACS) emphasizes borrowers' behavioral data automatically recorded in the Alibaba internal system (Table 7.1).

Data analysis is the core of business decision making in Ali Finance, with the goal to provide objective and reliable analysis, recommendations, and optimal solutions to improve business procedures by inputting basic data on risk, sales, and policy into analysis models. It serves business decision-making on micro loans, wealth management, insurance and retail, and procedures of marketing, loan approval, credit, payments, supervision, and debt repayment.

*Table 7.1* Sources of Alibaba credit system

| System | | Alibaba credit system | PBoC credit system |
|---|---|---|---|
| Number of businesses | Corporate credit | Over 6 million (TaoBao alone) | Over 10 million |
| | Individual credit | 145 million (Taobao alone) | 600 million |
| Credit information | Corporate credit | All information relating to business operation, including identification, volume, activity level, inventory, rating, cash flow, and utility bills, etc. | Identification, credit information, social security payments and housing acquisition fund, quality control information, salary arrears, and telecom payments, etc. |
| | Individual Credit | Buyer's information and corporate credit system, buyer's identification, online expenditures, utility expenses, and social activeness, etc. | Personal credit information, identification, social security, payments, and housing acquisition fund, etc. |
| Source of data | | Automatic recording | Commercial banks and government |

The core of data analysis is the PD model, mainly applied in loan provision, automatic approval of loans, and post-approval risk monitoring.

## 4 Main credit evaluation approaches

Credit evaluation methods can be divided into qualitative and quantitative categories. A representative qualitative method is the 5C assessment. It is based on experts' assessment of borrowers' character, capacity, capital, condition, and collateral. As statistical methods and technology improve, quantitative methods play an increasingly important role in credit assessment.

Based on the current practical applications of quantitative methods, we focus on the Merton model, credit default swap (CDS) model, Logit model, and Bayesian Criterion. Among these methods, the Logit model and Bayesion Criterion are applicable to credit assessment for both companies and individuals. They evaluate creditworthiness according to borrower characteristics and historical credit information. The Merton model and the CDS model can only be applied to companies with outstanding stock and CDS respectively. They extrapolate creditworthiness from market information such as stock prices or CDS spreads, assuming that markets can fully reflect credit information. The Merton model is classified as a structural model because it analyzes credit risk through causality. The other three models are based on correlation, and are thus called reduced-form models. The difference between these two kinds of models will be discussed further in Chapter 11.

### 4.1 Merton model

The Merton model was first developed by the renowned economist and Noble laureate Robert Merton. The Merton model takes the stock of a company as a call option with the asset of the company as underlying asset and the total liabilities of the company as the strike price (Figure 7.4). First, it calculates the market value of the company and volatility of stock based on historical stock prices, and then calculates the probability that the company becomes insolvent. The Moody's KMV model is a commercialized form of the Merton model, and the progressive single factor risk model applies the same logic.

The mathematics of the Merton model are illustrated here. We assume the following: the total debt of a company is $D$ and matures at time $T$; (to simplify, we ignore interest payments), the market value (not the book value) of the company assets is $V_0$ at the present and will be $V_T$ at time $T$, the volatility of the stock price is a constant $\sigma_V$ (these three variables cannot be attained directly but can be calculated from market data), the market value of equity is $E_0$ at present, and will be $E_T$ at time $T$, and the volatility of the equity value is a constant $\sigma_E$ (these three variables also must be calculated).

Due to limited liability, we have the equation $E_T = \max(V_T - D, 0)$. Thus, $E_0$ can be deemed the present value of a European call option with $V_T$ as the underlying asset and $D$ as the strike price. According to the Black–Scholes formula,

$$E_0 = V_0 \cdot \Phi(d_1) - D \cdot e^{-rT} \cdot \Phi(d_2) \tag{7.1}$$

with

$$d_1 = \frac{\ln(V_0 / D) + (r + \sigma_V^2 / 2)T}{\sigma_V \sqrt{T}}$$

$$d_2 = d_1 - \sigma_V \sqrt{T}$$

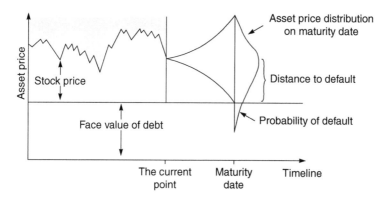

*Figure 7.4*[4] Merton model.

$\Phi(\cdot)$ as the cumulative distribution function of a standardized normal distribution.

According to the Ito formula

$$\sigma_E \cdot E_0 = \Phi(d_1) \cdot \sigma_V \cdot V_0 \tag{7.2}$$

After calculating $E_0$ and $\sigma_E$ from market data, we solve the simultaneous Equations (7.1) and (7.2), and then we can solve $V_0$ and $\sigma_V$. Thus, we have the PD

$$PD = \Pr(V_T < D) = \Phi(-d_2) \tag{7.3}$$

In practice, the capital structure of a company is much more complicated than the model we have discussed, so we should set triggering conditions for default and adjust the Merton model accordingly.

### 4.2 CDS model

A CDS is essentially insurance on the credit risk of one or more institutions, called the "underlying." Any CDS transaction requires a buyer and seller of the protection. The buyer periodically pays a fixed amount, called the CDS spread, to the seller. In return, if the underlying institution defaults or restructures its debt before the CDS expires (also called a "credit event"), the seller has the obligation to compensate the buyer for its loss. The CDS market is very active, and involves significant disclosure.

Intuitively, to make CDS transactions fair, the CDS spread should equal the expected loss of the underlying institutions' default. Approximately[5]

CDS spread $\approx$ PD $\times$ (1 − reclaim rate of debt after default)

Given the recovery rate, (the recovery rate of a senior debt is usually assumed to be 40%), the PD can be inferred from the CDS spread. The higher the CDS spread is, the higher the PD.

Chapter 2, Section 2.1 discusses a simplified version of CDS, suggesting that the CDS spread pools the credit information that CDS market participants have. This is the economic basis of the CDS model.

### 4.3 Logit model[6]

The Logit model is simple in form and easy to regress. These advantages have made it one of the most commonly adopted models in the banking industry for individual and company credit evaluation. The Logit model is a nonlinear probability model and is derived from the latent variable model.

We use the binary variable $Y$ with the value of 0 or 1 to represent the credit status of clients. $Y = 1$, means borrower default, while $Y = 0$ means no default. Also, we use the scalar $X$ to represent the features, characteristics, and historical information of clients, including their demographic characteristics, financial status, and behavioral information.

Assume that $Y$ and $X$ are connected by the latent variable $Y^*$. Though we cannot observe the specific value of $Y^*$, we assume that

$$Y^* = X'\beta + \varepsilon \tag{7.5}$$

With $X'\beta$ as a linear indicator function and constant $\beta$ as indicator coefficient. The cumulative distribution function of random disturbance $\varepsilon$ is noted as $F(\cdot)$. The value of $Y$ is determined by $y^*$:

$$Y = \begin{cases} 1 \text{ When } Y^* > 0 \\ 0 \text{ When } Y^* \leq 0 \end{cases} \tag{7.6}$$

Thus, the probability distribution of $Y$ is

$$\Pr(Y = 1 | X) = \Pr(\varepsilon > -X'\beta) = 1 - F(-X'\beta), Y = 1 \tag{7.7}$$

or, the probability distribution of $Y$ when $Y = 0$ can be similarly derived.

If the cumulative distribution function of $\varepsilon$ is the logistic function $F(\varepsilon) = \dfrac{e^{\varepsilon}}{1 + e^{\varepsilon}}$,

Then Equation (7.7) can be transformed into

$$\Pr(Y = 1 | X) = \frac{e^{X'\beta}}{1 + e^{X'\beta}} \tag{7.8}$$

Equation (7.8) is the core of the Logit model. By determining what independent variables to include in X and examining the methodology according to empirical data, such as the borrower characteristics, category, empirical information, and default status, we can estimate the indicator coefficient $\beta$, Equation (7.8) that can then be used to estimate PD.

The Logit model is very flexible in the selection of independent variables. For example, more than 100 indicators in 7 categories can be adapted to non-retail clients, such as: financial leverage indicators including asset–liability ratio, adjusted asset–liability ratio, all-capitalization rate; solvency and liquidity indicators including liquidity ratio, quick ratio, cash ratio, interest coverage ratio, operating net cash flow/ total debt ratio, operating profit/total loan ratio; profitability indicators including operating profit/sales revenue ratio, EBIT/sales revenue ratio, and profit margin volatility in the last three years; return indicators including ROA, ROE, adjusted ROA and adjusted ROE; operating efficiency indicators, including asset turnover, fixed asset turnover, inventory turnover, accounts receivable turnover and liquid asset turnover; scale indicators including total assets, equity, sales revenue, operating profit, and the average of these indicators over the last three years; and growth indicators including total asset growth rates, sales revenue growth rate, equity growth rate, profit growth rate, and time since establishment. For online business, Internet-based indicators such as online sales, numbers of hits, client comments, shipment rates, logistics records, and promotion and activity on social networks.

### 4.4 Bayesian Criterion[7]

We use $\Omega$ to represent the sample space. Assume that there are $k$ overall distributions, with probability density functions $f_1(x), f_2(x),\dots, f_k(x)$. The priory probability is sequentially $q_1, q_2,\dots, q_k$, while $\sum_{i=1}^{k} q_i = 1$.

Assume that $D_1, D_2,\dots, D_k$ divide the sample space into $k$ non-overlapping comprehensive regions. Thus $\bigcup_{i=1}^{k} D_i = \Omega$ and $D_i \cap D_j = \varnothing$ for any $i \neq j$, $\varnothing$ referring to the empty set. We define the criterion as if a sample $x \in D_i$, we take that $x$ is from overall distribution $G_i$. We use $D = \{D_1, D_2,\dots, D_k\}$ to represent the criterion.

Under criterion $D$, the probability that a sample from the overall distribution $G_i$ is mistaken as from $G_j$ is:

$$\Pr(j|i, D) = \int_{D_j} f_i(x)\, dx \tag{7.9}$$

We use $L(i, j)$ to represent the loss caused by mistaking one sample from $G_i$ for being in $G_j$. Thus, the total average loss under criterion $D$ is:

$$g(D) = \sum_{i=1}^{k} \sum_{j=1}^{k} q_i \cdot \Pr(j|i, D) \cdot L(i, j) \tag{7.10}$$

The Bayesian Criterion is an improvement on Equation (7.10) to find a criterion $D = \{D_1, D_2,\dots, D_k\}$ to minimize the total overall loss $g(D)$.

When $k = 2$ (in this case, overall distribution $G_1$ represents clients with good credit, while $G_2$ represents clients with bad credit), it can be proved that the Bayesian Criterion is:

$$
\begin{aligned}
D_1 &= \{x : q_1 \cdot f_1(x) \cdot L(1,2) \geq q_2 \cdot f_2(x) \cdot L(2,1)\} \\
D_2 &= \{x : q_1 \cdot f_1(x) \cdot L(1,2) < q_2 \cdot f_2(x) \cdot L(2,1)\}
\end{aligned}
\tag{7.11}
$$

If we further assume that the two overall distributions are the normal distributions $N(\mu_1, \Sigma)$ and $N(\mu_2, \Sigma)$, with $\mu_1, \mu_2, \Sigma$ known and $\Sigma$ referring to the covariance matrix of the two overall distributions, it can be proven that the Bayesian Criterion Equation (7.11) is equivalent to:

$$
\begin{aligned}
D_1 &= \{x : w(x) \geq d\} \\
D_2 &= \{x : w(x) < d\}
\end{aligned}
\qquad (7.12),\ \text{with}\ w(x) = (x - \overline{\mu})' \Sigma^{-1}(\mu_1 - \mu_2),
$$

$$\overline{\mu} = \frac{\mu_1 + \mu_2}{2}\ \text{and}\ d = \ln\frac{q_2 \cdot L(2,1)}{q_1 \cdot L(1,2)}.$$

If that Criterion function $w(x)$ is linear, there exists a weight vector A and threshold B, deducting Equation (7.12) into:

$$D_1 = \{x : A' \cdot x \geq B\}$$
$$D_2 = \{x : A' \cdot x < B\} \tag{7.13}$$

We define the credit score of clients as

$$score = A' \cdot x \tag{7.14}$$

By Equations (7.13) and (7.14), our strategy is to decline clients whose credit score is below threshold B and to accept those above it.

## SECTION 2: BIG DATA-BASED INTERNET LENDING

## 1 Analysis on Kabbage[8]

Kabbage was founded in 2008 with the goal of supplying operating capital for online businesses that do not qualify for loan requirements by commercial banks. Numerous small- and medium-sized online businesses come together on e-commerce platforms such as eBay, Yahoo, and Amazon. Their demands for capital are characterized by a short duration and small amounts. However, because these businesses' FICO credit scores are often below 720 and their owners are reluctant to put up their personal assets as collateral, it is very difficult for them to obtain bank loans. Kabbage focuses on these businesses and provide them loans by analyzing Internet-based statistics. Kabbage has now exceeded 100,000 customers, and the annual total loan amount is now around 200 million. The average Kabbage customer receives ten loans per year.

We introduce the business model of Kabbage in three aspects: data sources, loans issuance, and post-lending management (Figure 7.5).

### 1.1 Data sources

Kabbage relies on data provided by third parties rather than gathering data itself. The sharing and reading of these data connects authorized accounts, which require them to be standardizable, transferrable time series. Kabbage's main sources of data are listed in Table 7.2.

Kabbage was the first financial service institution to introduce social network analysis into credit assessment. Online businesses can gain access to a larger line of credit from Kabbage by keeping close to potential clients on social networks. Kabbage has developed its own credit scoring system, Kabbage Score, by analyzing online businesses' operation and interaction with clients. Kabbage Scores are actively adjusted to include the latest information, and can better describe the operation of online businesses than traditional FICO credit scores.

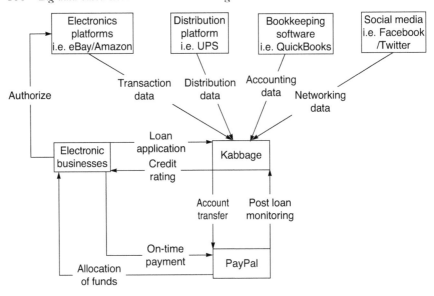

*Figure 7.5* Business model of Kabbage.

*Table 7.2* Data sources of Kabbage.

| Data type | Source | Note |
|---|---|---|
| Information flow | eBay/Amazon | Amount of views, prices, ratings, inventory, and turnovers |
| Cash flow | PayPal | Cash flow of online payment accounts |
| Distribution flow | UPS | Data on distribution |
| Social network | Facebook/Twitter | Client maintenance and socialized sales |
| Offline businesses | QuickBooks | Small bookkeeping software |

The online business has the incentive to provide more useful information in order to obtain credit, and increased information also means better terms for loans from Kabbage. The Kabbage Score and other related reports can help online business-owners supervise the operation of their businesses and may also be provided to third parties. Business owners could find their operational problems and devise solutions accordingly, thus improving both their businesses and their Kabbage Score. They would then receive a larger line of credit, which all leads into a virtuous cycle. The interests of Kabbage and the online businesses it serves are ultimately very well aligned.

*1.2 Loan issuance*

Kabbage's slogan is, "Fund your business in 7 minutes." After an online business submits its registration, the Kabbage background system automatically checks whether the business has online sales data over a sufficiently long period of time. Online businesses can only submit their application for loans after they have passed the vetting process, which is automatically carried out by Kabbage's system. It decides whether to issue lines of credit, in addition to the amounts, interest rates, and maturities based on the credit assessment. The Kabbage algorithm guarantees that the vetting results can be provided and money transferred to an appointed account in a third-party online payment system within seven minutes. The loans issuance can provide customized solutions tailored to every applicant's need, such as automatically adjusting the line of credit, maturity and interest rate according to different purposes of loans and operational situations.

Kabbage has several patents including "an approach to provide liquidity loans in online auctions and online exchanges." Online businesses can apply for loans from Kabbage by using inventories as collateral, and then repay the loans when the goods are sold and payments are received. In this process, Kabbage receives interest or fees from loans, and the online businesses receives cash flows in advance to maintain working capital.

The lines of credit that Kabbage provide range from $500 to $40,000. Interest rates are determined by maturities (up to six months) and the creditworthiness of the businesses, from 2% to 7% in thirty days and 10% to 18% in six months.

*1.3 Post-lending management*

Kabbage loan repayment is simple. On a determined repayment day, Kabbage deducts a fixed amount (including fees) from the business' payment account. Prepayment is optional and does not incur extra costs.

The core of Kabbage's post-lending management is to use multiple sources of data to cross-check. Cash flow data from the company's accounts are especially important. Kabbage has accordingly realized that the real-time supervision of sales and cash flow among online businesses can provide an early warning if cash flows become tight. If Kabbage has confirmed that a business has difficulty paying, it can directly withdraw a portion of the loan from the business' accounts and cut off future lines of credit.

Kabbage has also established a disciplinary mechanism. On payment day, if the amount in the payment account is insufficient to cover the installment, Kabbage generally charges US$35 as late fee and retains the right to refer the case to debt-collecting agencies or take legal action. However, this is a relatively rare event at Kabbage. Although bad debts average 5%–8% in US banks, Kabbage has managed a rate of only 1%.

## 2 Ali (Alibaba) small loan analysis

Ali Small Loan was jointly founded by Alibaba with Fosun Group, Wanxiang Group and Intime Group, in June, 2010. It is the first small loan company to focus on

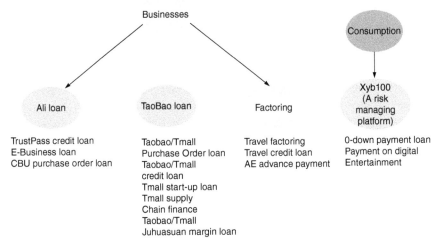

*Figure 7.6* Main categories of loans by Ali Small Loan.

small and micro companies in e-business in China. Ali Small Loan issues loans based on the mountains of data it accumulates on trade platforms such as Alibaba, Taobao, and T-mall (see Figure 7.6 for main categories of loans). It does not require collateral or guarantees, and it generally issues loans under RMB 1 million. The whole lending process is completed online and issued through Alipay, so no off-line vetting is required. The time it takes to issue a loan with this system is only three minutes. Clients with excellent credit can apply for extra loans through a manual review process to receive amounts up to RMB 10 million.

By 2013, Ali Small Loan had provided loans for more than 490,000 clients and issued loans totaling more than RMB 12 billion. Since its foundation, it has issued more than RMB 100 billion loans. On average, each client receives lines of credit of around RMB 130,000 and loans for around RMB 40,000. The bad debt rate is under 1%. As the source of capital, Ali Small Loan has around RMB 2 billion of assets and has transferred RMB 8 billion assets in 2013.

We will introduce Ali Small Loan through four aspects: loan application, loan approval, post-lending management, and IT systems (Figure 7.7).

### 2.1 Loan application

Clients first log onto the homepage of Ali Small Loan and submit application forms online. The application information includes the line of credit, the name of the company, the name of the legal representative, the mobile phone number of the legal representative, the post box of the legal representative, the marital status of the legal representative.

After receipt of the application, an investigation team accesses trade records, credit records, comparison of peers, inventory records, financial data, non-financial

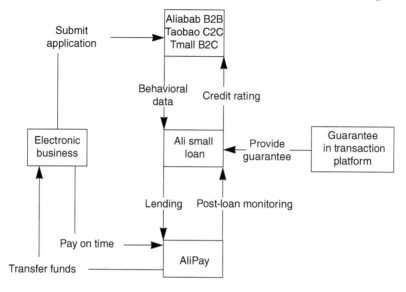

*Figure 7.7* Business model of Ali Small Loan.

comments, credit reports, and bank statements of the applicant on the B2B platform Alibaba, the C2C platform Taobao, the B2C platform T-mall, and visits to the applicant's facilities. During these visits, Ali Small Loan authorizes third-party investigators to visit companies that apply for loans and check on the operation of the companies, then the client manager of Ali Small Loan communicates with the client to confirm the materials that investigators have submitted for application.

It is worth mentioning that Ali Small Loan uses a hydrological transaction forecast model (in Figure 7.8) to actively promote its business to clients. The basic principle of the model is to use hydrological variables to forecast future transaction amounts on Taobao, excluding the seasonal business fluctuation, and to judge the amount of both client capital and ability to repay loans. It focuses on marketing when the clients are at the peak of demand for capital. All the marketing and feedback is recorded in the system and is further optimized in the response model.

### 2.2 Approval and issuance of loans

Ali Small Pay uses the PD Model to score the credit of online businesses. The model has three steps: first it gathers the client's demographic information, credit information, historical performance, transaction data, and operation status; second, according to the gathered information, it filters out the variables that significantly influence the credit status to establish the Model; third, it categorizes potential clients according to their PD scores and distinguishes clients with good or bad credit. In this model, credit records, transaction records and complaint records of

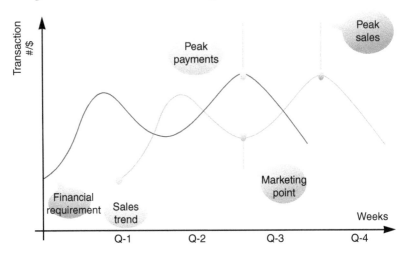

*Figure 7.8* The hydrological transaction forecast model of Ali Small Loan.

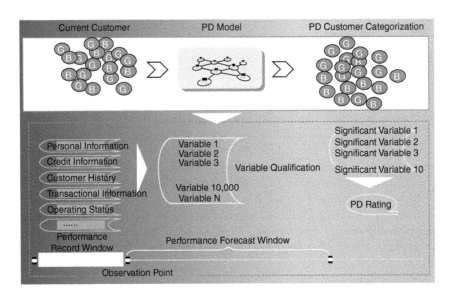

*Figure 7.9* The PD model of Ali Small Loan.

the online businesses in the Ali ecological system is fully utilized and considered as the grounds for loan approval, settling the information asymmetry and complicated procedure in loans for individuals and small and middle enterprises in traditional commercial banking (Figure 7.9).

Ali Small Loan determines the lines of credit, interest rates and maturities of loans according to the credit scores of the online businesses, financing, and guarantees in transaction platforms. If the loan is approved, the client must sign a contract with Ali Small Loan to connect the legal representative's personal account to the business's Alipay account. Ali Small Loan then verifies the applicant's real name and the Alipay account to confirm the loan in the Alipay account.

Ali Small Loan perfectly merges the transaction and financing platforms. Lenders have saved costs by providing required information as an independent third party and discovering the opportunity to provide financing as one party in the transaction in real time and at the frontier, improving the allocation of financial assets and productivity.[9]

### 2.3 Post-lending management

Ali Small Loan monitors the usage of loans and the productivity of businesses by monitoring the scoring and the debt-collection model. It does so according to transaction data and financial reports of the clients to collect loan payments. Ali Small Loan uses the installment method for repayment. Clients periodically transfer the installment from their bank accounts to Alipay accounts or leave enough money in Alipay accounts to be deducted as the installment. If the client chooses to prepay the loan, Ali Small Loan charges a fee equal to 3% of the principal. If the loan is overdue, the interest rate in the overdue period is 1.5 times the normal rate.

### 2.4 IT system

Ali Small Loan has designed a management system that covers the whole life cycle of a loan, including: management before lending, management during and after lending, anti-fraud, market analysis, and credit system.

For now, the following two types of models have been completed:

- Risk models including PD, operational risk models, monitoring and scoring models, debt-collection scoring, and loss given default model
- Marketing models including client response, churn, client loyalty, life cycle, cross-marketing, event-marketing, and client value.

These following three types of model are still being developed:

- Anti-fraud models which are essential for online financial transactions, including false trading model, false identity model, and account hacking model.
- Models for client behavior including drip-type growth analysis model, customized differentiation pricing model, and hydrological transaction forecast model.
- Ali credit model including address standardization, individual identification, natural and legal persons identification, credit scoring, credit evaluation of sellers, credit evaluation of buyers, and performance ability model.

Ali Small Loan's decision-making system processes tens of millions of clients, transactions and messages and over 10 terabytes data and outputs lines of credits for RMB tens of billions.

Considering the 79.8 million registered users of Alibaba, with 10.3 million online businesses and over one million paying members, if Ali Small Loan could obtain a banking license, allowing it to absorb public savings and opening up its ability to source capital, it would be very competitive.

## Notes

1   Niu, Luchen. 2012. "Research on Loaning Reputation: Theory and Practice in a Credit Center."
2   As is pointed out in Chapter 6, the best estimate in theory is $E(Y|X)$. Setting and adjusting predictive function is to make the function g(X) as close to $E(Y|X)$ as possible. The Internal Rating-Based approach has four parameters to predict risk: (a) Probability to Default (PD), the possibility that the borrower defaults in a certain period of time in the future; (b) Loss Given Default (LGD), the percentage of economic loss in the total risk exposure once a borrower defaults; (c) Exposure at Default (EAD), the estimate of exposure on the bank once a borrower defaults; (d) Maturity (M). IRB measures two dimensions of risk, the default risk of a borrower in Client Rating and the specific risk in trade in Facility Rating. Client Rating, the rating on the default risk of the borrower, suggests the credit status of the borrower itself, and adopts PD as the core variable. Facility Rating, the rating of risk in a specific trade, suggests the specific risk in a trade, such as collateral, priority, and the kind of trade, and adopts LGD as the core variable.
3   In this section, unless specified, all the materials on Ali Small Loan are from the speech, "How We Operate Internet Finance." by Lou Jianxun, manager of the Department of Micro Loans in Ali Small and Mini Financial Services Group, in the Second Annual Conference of the Zhejiang Finance Society in November 30, 2013.
4   Duffie, Darrell, and Kenneth Singleton. 2003. "Credit Risk: Pricing, Measurement, and Management," Princeton University Press.
5   The precise estimation of PD requires solving the CDS pricing problem. It is both very complicated and technical. Interested readers may consult Hull, John, 2006. "Options, Futures, and Other Derivatives," 5th ed., Pearson Education Asia Limited. The net premiums determined in life insurance that we discuss in Chapter 12 are in theory very similar to CDS pricing. The Default Density Model we will discuss is the core of CDS pricing.
6   Our introduction on the Logit model mainly refers to Yunhui, Jin, and Sainan Jin. 2007. "Advanced Econometrics," Peking University Press.
7   Our introduction of Bayesian Criterion refers to Shidong, Liang. 2011. "The Theory and Application of Measurement of Risk in Commercial Banking: The Core Techniques in 'Basel Capital Accord'," China Financial Publishing House.
8   Our analysis on Kabbage mainly refers to Liao, li. 2013. "Lectures on Internet Finance," PBC School of Finance, Tsinghua University.
9   This reveals the relationship between Internet exchange economy and Internet finance that we discuss in Chapter 11.

# 8    P2P network loans

The P2P network loan is a new model of person-to-person lending which has been developed in recent years. The reality that formal finance has not efficiently solved the financing problems of small and medium-sized enterprises as well as replacing private finance became the background for the development of P2P network loans. However, information technology, especially the Internet, has significantly reduced asymmetrical information and transaction costs. This gives new impetus to person to person lending which can be seen as the earliest financial model and make up for the inefficiency of formal financial institutions. P2P network loans can benefit both investors (lenders) and borrowers. In this way, borrowers can enjoy more convenient financing channels and lower borrowing costs, while investors can obtain better returns than bank deposits pay.

Zopa, the world's first P2P network loan platform, was established in the United Kingdom in March 2005. At present, in the P2P network loan industry, Lending Club and Prosper are in the spotlight. Their operation is standardized, regulatory measures are comprehensive, and information disclosure is sufficient. Between them, the development of Lending Club is the most advanced. As a result, we will focus on the analysis of Lending Club and take it as an example to discuss the economics of P2P network loans.

## SECTION 1: ANALYSIS OF LENDING CLUB

Lending Club began operations in 2007 with its head office in Los Angeles, no subsidiaries, and all business conducted by telephone or via the Internet. By the end of October 2013, Lending Club had facilitated US$2.77 billion in credit transactions and generated US$250 million interest income and now it is the world's largest P2P network loan platform. It is also still developing rapidly (Figure 8.1).

## 1 Operational framework of Lending Club

In order to conform to the laws and regulations of United States (especially securities regulations), the operational framework of Lending Club is very specific. There are four kinds of core players: Lending Club, investors, lenders, and WebBank (Figure 8.2). WebBank is a commercial bank registered in Utah and is protected by the Federal Deposit Insurance Corporation (FDIC).

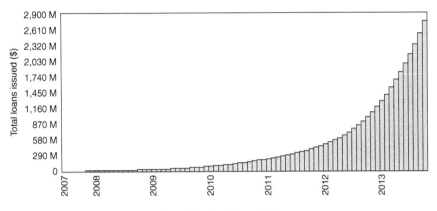

*Figure 8.1* Credit transactions facilitated by Lending Club.

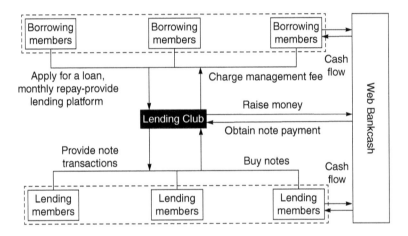

*Figure 8.2¹* Operational framework of Lending Club.

Although P2P means "peer to peer," with respect to the operational framework of Lending Club, legally speaking there are no direct obligatory relationships between investors and borrowers. In fact, they register with an account name, which is anonymous and unknown to other users. They are also not allowed to know the other party's real name and address. Investors purchase notes issued by Lending Club according to the securities laws of United States. Loans to borrowers are initially provided by WebBank and then transferred to Lending Club. Each series of notes correspond to a sum of loans, and one is similar to mirror image of the other. Excluding the service fee charged to investors by Lending Club, the monthly principal and interest collected from the borrower is paid by Lending Club to the holder of notes. If a borrower defaults, a corresponding holder of notes will not receive any payment from Lending Club (Lending Club provide no guarantees for investors). This does not constitute a breach of contract because Lending Club does not take on credit risks related to credit transactions. As for WebBank, as lending to borrowers and transfers to Lending Club occur almost simultaneously, credit risks related to credit transactions are not taken by WebBank. It is similar to the role of a custodian bank. Credit risks are borne by investors.

As a result, the key mechanism of Lending Club's operational framework is notes and loans with a mirror image relationship. Every pair of loans and notes has the same principal, interest, period, and cash flow characteristics. These types of notes are called payment dependent notes, which are similar to pass-through securities. Through arrangement of loans and notes, although there are complicated relationships among Lending Club, WebBank, and lending and borrowing parties; Lending Club and WebBank are similar in that they do not take on credit risk. Therefore, the operation of Lending Club involves the origination and transfer of loans as well as issuance and transaction of notes. It thus straddles the two fields of banking and securities.

In the process of selling notes to the investors and using WebBank to issue loans, Lending Club collects a service fee. For every payment investors receive, Lending Club charges a 1% service fee. The borrower pays a one-off origination fee to obtain funds. See Table 8.3 for a description of details.

## 2 Borrowers

Anyone who proposes to borrow money must register and then submit a loan application. There are some limits for borrower qualifications, which include: US citizenship or permanent residency, age above 18, have an e-mail address, possess a US Social Security Number and financial institution account number, have an individual credit profile, and have a FICO credit score over 660. Their debt-to-income ratio must also be below 35% (excluding mortgage loans), and the length of credit history must be over three years. One also must have borrowed money through Lending Club less than six times over the past six months.

One who proposes to apply for a loan should provide information which can reflect his/her credit status. Lending Club will review the application but not necessarily examine the authenticity of the information that borrowers provide. Loan applications are subjected to Lending Club's strict examination. Until the end of the year 2012, only 11% of the applicants received a loan. The borrowers on Lending Club generally belong to US's upper-middle class. For instance, until the end of October 2013, the average FICO credit score was 703 and the average length of credit history was 15 years. The average annual income was US$71,000, which is in the top 10% of the American income distribution.

The borrower must state three core terms of a loan: amount, period, and purpose. Permitted loan amounts are between US$1,000 and US$35,000 while the loan maturity is according to the borrower's preference. For loans which are between US$1,000 and US$15,975, the loan period is three years unless otherwise specified. The borrower lists the purpose of the loan without Lending Club's supervision. Up to the end of October 2013, the average loan amount on Lending Club was US$13,500 mainly for refinancing and paying off credit card debt (Figure 8.3). It thus basically belongs in the consumer credit category.

Risk pricing is one of the core technologies of Lending Club, consisting of two parts: credit rating and loan interest pricing. Credit ratings are divided into seven grades

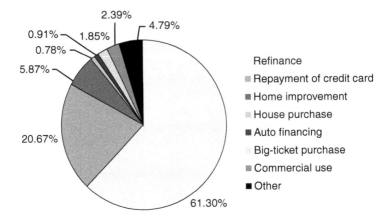

*Figure 8.3* Purpose of loans of Lending Club.

from high to low, and each grade has five segments (the total is thus thirty-five credit rating levels). The ratings are generated in two steps. Step 1 goes according to the borrower's FICO credit score and other credit characteristics. Lending Club has a model rank, and every model rank corresponds to a standard credit rating. Step 2 revises the original rating according to loan amount and gives a final credit rating. The larger the loan amount and the longer the loan period, the larger the downgrade from the standard credit rating (Table 8.1).

*Table 8.1* Credit rating method of Lending Club

| *Model rank* | | *Rank* | | | | |
|---|---|---|---|---|---|---|
| | | *1* | *2* | *3* | *4* | *5* |
| Credit rating | A | 1 | 2 | 3 | 4 | 5 |
| | B | 6 | 7 | 8 | 9 | 10 |
| | C | 11 | 12 | 13 | 14 | 15 |
| | D | 16 | 17 | 18 | 19 | 20 |
| | E | 21 | 22 | 23 | 24 | 25 |

(The relationship between standard credit rating and model rank)

| *Grade adjustment* | | *Standard credit rating* | | |
|---|---|---|---|---|
| | | *A* | *B* | *C–E* |
| Loan amount | <$5,000 | −1 | −1 | −1 |
| | $5,000–<$10,000 | 0 | 0 | 0 |

| Grade adjustment | | Standard credit rating | | |
|---|---|---|---|---|
| | | A | B | C–E |
| | $10,000–<$15,000 | 0 | 0 | 0 |
| | $15,000–<$20,000 | 0 | 0 | −1 |
| | $20,000–<$25,000 | 0 | −1 | −2 |
| | $25,000–<$30,000 | −1 | −2 | −3 |
| | $30,000–<$35,000 | −2 | −3 | −4 |
| | $35,000 | −4 | −5 | −6 |

(Loan amount and credit rating adjustment)

| Loan period | Credit rating | Downgrade |
|---|---|---|
| 3 years | A–G | 0 |
| 5 years | A–G | −8 to −4 |

(Loan period and credit rating adjustment)

On Lending Club, loan interest is market-oriented and fixed. Overall, the interest rate is connected with credit rating and is equal to the sum of risk and volatility. The purpose of the risk and volatility adjustment is to cover the expected loan losses. The lower the credit rating, the higher the loan interest is (Table 8.2).

Service fees that Lending Club charges the borrower are around 1.1%–5.0% of the loan amount, directly deducted from the principal of a loan. The service fee

Table 8.2 Loan pricing mechanism of Lending Club

| Interest | | Grade | | | | |
|---|---|---|---|---|---|---|
| | | 1 | 2 | 3 | 4 | 5 |
| Credit rating | A | 6.03% | 6.62% | 7.62% | 7.90% | 8.90% |
| | B | 9.67% | 10.99% | 11.99% | 12.99% | 13.67% |
| | C | 14.30% | 15.10% | 15.61% | 16.20% | 17.10% |
| | D | 17.76% | 18.55% | 19.20% | 19.52% | 20.20% |
| | E | 21.00% | 21.70% | 22.40% | 23.10% | 23.40% |
| | F | 23.70% | 24.08% | 24.50% | 24.99% | 25.57% |
| | G | 25.80% | 25.83% | 25.89% | 25.99% | 26.06% |

rate is related to credit rating and loan period, and the lower the credit rating or the longer the loan period, the higher the service fee (Table 8.3).

Lending Club has the exclusive power to receive monthly repayment from borrowers through normal electronic fund transfers. Lending Club also has recourse to any defaulted loans and is empowered to decide whether or when to transfer the loans to a third-party collection agency.

## 3 Investors

For investors, Lending Club has set qualifications such as minimum income and wealth (measured by net assets), and investment on Lending Club can be no more than 10% of his/her total wealth, but a credit check is not necessary. Moreover, Lending Club has established an investment consulting company called LC Advisors. LC Advisors resembles a fund manager, raising external capital to invest in notes issued by Lending Club.

Investors can choose notes that they wish to purchase on Lending Club's website. Due to the great amount of notes, it provides search and filter tools in addition to a portfolio building tool. The minimum investment in each note is US$25. For example, Lending Club will recommend a notes portfolio after the investor specifies risk and return parameters (Figure 8.4).

For investors, it is a very effective method of risk diversification. For instance, statistics indicate that if an investor purchases 100 notes, the possibility of incurring loss is 1%. If an investor purchases 400 notes, the possibility of incurring loss is 0.2%. If an investor purchases 1,000 notes, incurring loss is nearly impossible (Figure 8.5). Later we will explain this phenomenon.

*Table 8.3* Loan service fee rate

| Service fee rate | | Loan period | |
|---|---|---|---|
| Credit rating and grade | | 3-year period | 5-year period |
| A | 1 | 1.11% | 3.00% |
| | 2–3 | 2.00% | 3.00% |
| | 4–5 | 3.00% | 3.00% |
| B | 1–5 | 4.00% | 5.00% |
| C | 1–5 | 5.00% | 5.00% |
| D | 1–5 | 5.00% | 5.00% |
| E | 1–5 | 5.00% | 5.00% |
| F | 1–5 | 5.00% | 5.00% |
| G | 1–5 | 5.00% | 5.00% |

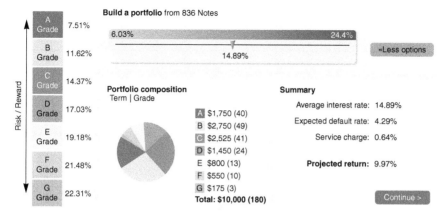

*Figure 8.4* Portfolio building tool of Lending Club.

To be clear, when investors subscribe to notes, the notes are actually not issued and loans are not made. When the subscription is full, notes are issued to investors and Lending Club receives the subscription payment (historically, 99% of notes are fully subscribed). Meanwhile, WebBank makes corresponding loans and transfers those loans to Lending Club. The notes that Lending Club issued will not be listed and traded on any exchange, but Lending Club has established a notes transaction platform called FOLIOfn to provide notes transfer services with investors, equivalent to setting up a secondary market for notes to provide liquidity.

## 4 Supervision of Lending Club in the U.S.

Supervision of Lending Club in the United States reflects a concept of functional supervision (in contrast with that of institutional supervision), which means that it is supervised by the business in which it engages and the risk it generates (Figure 8.6).

The US Securities and Exchange Commission (SEC) is the main regulator of Lending Club, because it issues notes to investors that are regarded as securities issuance. The priority of the SEC's supervision is to ensure that Lending Club follows its disclosure guidelines rather than to check or to monitor the operation of Lending Club or audit the notes themselves.

Lending Club has adopted shelf registration, which means registration of prospectuses at the SEC. The prospectus should disclose the operational mechanism and corporate governance structure of Lending Club, along with basic clauses of notes and detailed disclosure of possible risk to investors. At the time of issuance, Lending Club will make a representation to SEC about the notes (called sales reports), including anonymous information like terms of corresponding loans, purpose of loans, borrower's job, income, and so on. The information Lending Club discloses can be found on the SEC's EDGAR system and the Lending Club website.

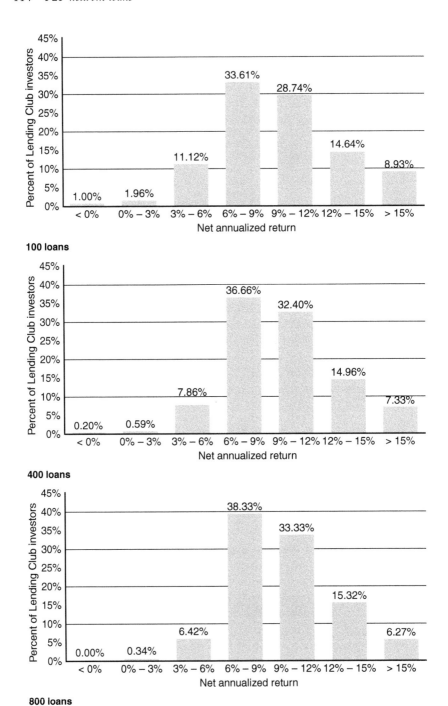

*Figure 8.5* Risk diversification effect of loan investment.

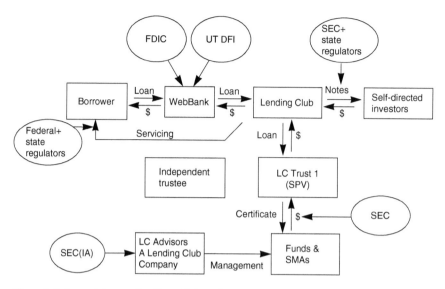

*Figure 8.6* Supervision on Lending Club in the United States.[2]

## SECTION 2: ECONOMICS OF P2P NETWORK LOANS

There are many perspectives we may use to analyze P2P network loans. The first is the legal perspective, which analyzes legal contracts and legal risks of P2P network loans. There is much debate as to whether it involves illegal fund-raising and illegal pooling of deposits. The second perspective analyzes the capital flows of P2P network loans. The third perspective is risk, which analyzes major risk types, risk-taking behavior, and risk transfer. We will follow the third perspective because we consider it the best way to examine the economic impact of P2P network loans.

## 1 Comparison with private finance

If P2P network loans do not provide guarantees for the investors, they can be seen as direct lending from peer to peer. This lending form is old but is ubiquitous in modern society as "private finance." A bidding society is the form of private finance most similar to P2P network loans.

A bidding union is one type of ROSCA, a mutually assisting credit union. Generally, an initiator (the head) invites several relatives and friends (the feet) to participate in and make an agreement to hold a meeting where they pay a membership fee to a certain member in turns for mutual help. The head of the society collects the first membership fee payment, and then they determine the collection sequence. Every member generally has an opportunity to collect the member fee, but the head of the society normally collects the first round. The head must gather and organize the bidding, collect and give out the member fees, pay other members, and deal with member fees when someone cannot pay for his/her member fee on time. Bidding societies can be either discount bid or premium bid societies. Discount means the collector receives an agreed amount of member fees and the member fee paid by other feet of society in every round should deduct the interest portion that the collector is willing to pay. In premium bid, after the member who collects member fee receives the current member fee, he/she pays other members an agreed amount of interest.[3]

The head grants a loan and repays it in amortization. The last round foot of society essentially make an installment saving. Middle feet of society participate in an installment saving and then obtain a loan with amortized repayment. To better analyze the debt and liability relationship of bidding society, we describe a four-person bidding society. Relevant conclusions are true even in more complicated situations.

Assume the member fee is $m$ dollars, the bidding price of second and third round collectors are $b2$ and $b3$, then the cash flow is

$$
\begin{pmatrix}
3m & -m & -m & -m \\
-m & 3m & -m & -m \\
-m & -m - b_2 & 3m + b_2 & -m \\
-m & -m - b_2 & -m - b_3 & 3m + b_2 + b_3
\end{pmatrix}
\tag{8.1}
$$

Each row indicates the cash flow of every participant in sequence. The first row is the cash flow of the head of society and the last row is the last collector's cash flow, and so on. Every column indicates the cash flow of participants in $t = 1, 2, 3, 4, \ldots n$ round in sequence. A plus sign signifies capital inflow while minus sign is a capital outflow. We can decompose the cash flow of this bidding society:

$$
\begin{pmatrix}
3m & -m & -m & -m \\
-m & 3m & -m & -m \\
-m & -m - b_2 & 3m + b_2 & -m \\
-m & -m - b_2 & -m - b_3 & 3m + b_2 + b_3
\end{pmatrix}
\tag{8.2}
$$

$$
= \begin{pmatrix}
m & -m & 0 & 0 \\
-m & m & 0 & 0 \\
0 & 0 & 0 & 0 \\
0 & 0 & 0 & 0
\end{pmatrix}
+ \begin{pmatrix}
m & 0 & -m & 0 \\
0 & 0 & 0 & 0 \\
-m & 0 & m & 0 \\
0 & 0 & 0 & 0
\end{pmatrix}
+ \begin{pmatrix}
m & 0 & 0 & -m \\
0 & 0 & 0 & 0 \\
0 & 0 & 0 & 0 \\
-m & 0 & 0 & m
\end{pmatrix}
$$

$$
+ \begin{pmatrix}
0 & 0 & 0 & 0 \\
0 & m & -m & 0 \\
0 & -m - b_2 & m + b_2 & 0 \\
0 & 0 & 0 & 0
\end{pmatrix}
+ \begin{pmatrix}
0 & 0 & 0 & 0 \\
0 & m & 0 & -m \\
0 & 0 & 0 & 0 \\
0 & -m - b_2 & 0 & m + b_2
\end{pmatrix}
+ \begin{pmatrix}
0 & 0 & 0 & 0 \\
0 & 0 & 0 & 0 \\
0 & 0 & m & -m \\
0 & 0 & -m - b_3 & m + b_3
\end{pmatrix}
$$

Equation (8.2) decomposes the bidding society to a series of debt and credit

between two sides. Such as: $\begin{pmatrix} 0 & 0 & 0 & 0 \\ 0 & m & -m & 0 \\ 0 & -m-b_2 & m+b_2 & 0 \\ 0 & 0 & 0 & 0 \end{pmatrix}$ means that in $t = 2$ round,

the current collector borrows $m$ Dollars and repays $m + b2$ Dollars in round $t = 3$. $b2$ is the interest amount. Other debt between two sides can be explained in the same way.

Hence we can see that bidding societies are equivalent to a series of peer to peer credit agreements in which every member is obliged to lend money to other members who precedes him/her and also has the right to borrow money from the other members who are after him/her. Among them, the head of society is a borrower. The last collector is a lender. Debt and credit relationships between member A and member B (assume A collects the member fee before B) occur when A becomes the collector and ends when B becomes the collector. Every member is a lending party before he/she becomes a collector, then turns to a borrowing party afterwards. In sum, the preceding member for collection is a borrowing party while next member for collection is a lending party.

From the above analysis, we can see that there are three common points between bidding societies and P2P network loan. First, they are essentially peer to peer lending. Second, the lending relies on credit completely without any collateral or guarantee. Third, the interest rate is market-oriented. In P2P network loans, the interest rate is determined by risk pricing mechanism. In bidding societies, interest rates fluctuate in line with market conditions, which can include the credit risk premium of the participants.

Bidding societies have an elaborate contract form and risk control mechanism, especially using social capital which is formed in a long-term cooperative game, including non-statuary ethics, custom constraints, mutual trust of acquaintances, and social sanctions as a performance bond in order to reduce information asymmetry and transaction costs. However, In comparison with P2P network loans, bidding societies have two shortcomings.

First, bidding societies are personalized transactions essentially based on social networks. Bidding society participants are largely relatives and friends, which restricts the potential scope. P2P network loans use a third party to enable impersonal transactions. Moreover, although in a bidding society the interest rate can include credit risk premium, it is basically determined by experience. Thus possibly irrational factors may influence these risk premia. P2P network loans have a more scientific risk pricing mechanism.

Second, private finance has internal instability. As private finance has to be inside a certain social network, it acts as a series of separate local markets. These local markets have different participants and risk control mechanisms without identical interest rates. Low connectivity means risk raised in a local market does not have an overall impact. However, someone may make use of differences of interest rates among private finance markets for arbitrage by borrowing in a low interest rate area and lending in high interest rate area. When arbitrage is common enough, every local market for private finance is connected, generating risk transmission channels. In this case, the activities of private finance tend to be dynamic. Private credit expands, risk control mechanisms become ineffective, and risk accumulates. Private credit will then rack up bad debts and harm social networks' trust relationship. Incremental private credit will then sharply decrease, and a credit squeeze will result. This credit squeeze will directly affect the local real economy, whose weakness will weigh on the private finance market. The squeeze can only be terminated after bad debts have been written off, balance sheets have been repaired, and private social trust relations are rebuilt. In recent years, this case actually happened in Wenzhou and Ordos in China. P2P network loans are different. They involve an impersonal transaction that does not considerably rely on social networks, so investors are sufficiently diversified. On the other hand, P2P network loans may be subject to a credit cycle.

## 2 Comparison with bank deposit

P2P network loans are similar to direct financing. They actually resemble a bond market as well if we consider notes as bonds. Investors buy the bonds and bear the borrowers' credit risk. As there is no maturity transformation, P2P network loans bear no liquidity risk. P2P network loan platforms themselves bear neither credit nor liquidity risk. Their profits come from services offered to investors and borrowers, such as facilitation of credit transactions, risk pricing, loan collection, and notes services. It is essentially an intermediary business.

Bank deposits represent another type of financing. Banks take on the maturity mismatch problem between suppliers and demanders of capital. Demanders generally need long-term capital for investment. However, suppliers generally are only willing to provide short-term capital to insure against liquidity shocks. Due to the Law of Large Numbers, a bank only needs to store a fraction of this capital in the form of high liquidity assets. Depositors' ordinary cash requirements still can be met. Banks can use other capital to grant long-term loans. Second, banks provide an agency function because they represent depositors, supervise borrowers' use of money, and control the borrowers' credit risk. By contrast, P2P network loan platforms do not confirm or supervise the real purpose of loans. Banks also bear credit and liquidity risk. They earn profit through compensation for bearing risk, which is mainly represented as the margin between lending and borrowing rates. Banks are also subject to capital adequacy ratios, liquidity risk regulations, and deposit-reserve ratios because of bearing the above risks.[4]

## 3 Core technology

### 3.1 Risk pricing

The core technologies of P2P network loans for borrowers are mainly internal credit rating and lending rate determination. Internal credit rating is essentially the classification problem discussed in Chapter 6 (the main models are in Chapter 7), which means dividing borrowers into different grades by the probability of default. If lower credit ratings mean the credit profile is worse, the credit rating system is effective. One of the measurement tools is Receiver operating characteristic (ROC) curves. The larger the area below the ROC curve, the more effective the credit rating. For instance, the ROC curve of Lending Club indicates that it is more effective than FICO08 (see Figure 8.7).

Theoretically, interest rate pricing of P2P network loans resembles bond pricing. The lending rate equals the risk-free interest rate plus a risk premium. The lower the credit rating, the higher the risk premium must be in order to reach a balance (Table 8.4).

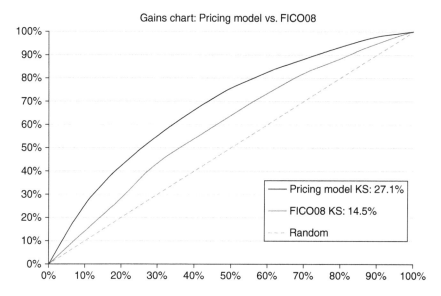

*Figure 8.7* ROC curve of Lending Club.

*Table 8.4* Characteristics of risk and return in Lending Club by rating

| Credit rating | Bad loan ratio | Average lending rate | Net annual rate of return |
|---|---|---|---|
| A | 1.38% | 7.56% | 5.48% |
| B | 2.03% | 11.74% | 8.80% |
| C | 2.41% | 15.16% | 10.61% |
| D | 4.33% | 17.98% | 11.80% |
| E | 4.86% | 20.44% | 13.23% |
| F | 5.77% | 22.76% | 13.41% |
| G | 8.81% | 23.51% | 11.40% |
| All ratings | 2.91% | 17.02% | n.a. |

### 3.2 Portfolio tools

There are many notes for investors to choose on P2P network loan platforms. For asset allocation convenience, platforms provide investors with portfolio building tools in order to recommend a notes portfolio according to investors' risk and return preferences. As notes and loans have mirror image relationship, the theoretical basis is Portfolio theory (related to the Markowitz Mean Variance Model discussed is Chapter 11). We explain it in a simple model as the following:

Assume there is $n$ sum of loans to invest. Assume in the loan portfolio, loan $i$ has weight $w_i$, which satisfies $\sum_{i=1}^{n} w_i = 1$. For P2P network loans, the core of an investor's asset allocation problem is to solve $w_i, i = 1, 2,\ldots, n$ which can make the loan portfolio satisfies the investor's preference for risk and return. Assume the interest rate of loan $i$ is $r_i$, unconditional default probability is $P_i$, and loss given default is $\lambda_i$. We use random variable $X_i$ to indicate loan $i$'s default rate, $E(X_i) = P_i$, therefore the return rate of loan $i$ is $L_i = (1\text{-}X_i)r_i - X_i\lambda_i$. The same assumptions are true for other loans.

Then the rate of return for the loan portfolio is $L = \sum_{i=1}^{n} w_i L_i = \sum_{i=1}^{n} w_i\left[(1\text{-}X_i)r_i - X_i\lambda_i\right]$. The return characteristics of the loan portfolio can be described by expected value:

$$E(L) = \sum_{i=1}^{n} w_i\left[(1\text{-}P_i)r_i - P_i\lambda_i\right] \tag{8.3}$$

The risk characteristics of the loan portfolio can be depicted by Credit Value at Risk (CVaR). Assume confidence level as $\theta$, let $\mathrm{CVaR}(L,\theta)$ indicate the credit risk value under a certain confidence level, and the definition is:

$$\Pr\left(L > -\mathrm{CVaR}(L,\theta)\right) = \theta \tag{8.4}$$

Credit risk value actually also describes the distribution of the portfolio's rate of return. For example, assuming the cumulative distribution function of $L$ is $G(l) = \Pr(L \leq l)$, we have an implicit function relationship: $G(-\mathrm{CVaR}(L,\theta)) = 1 - \theta$.

In the Asymptotic Single Risk Factor (ASRF)[5] model, the value at risk of the loan portfolio equals the sum of every sum of loan value at risk

$$\mathrm{CVaR}(L,\theta) = \sum_{i=1}^{n} w_i\mathrm{CVaR}\left((1 - X_i)r_i - X_i\lambda_i,\theta\right) \tag{8.5}$$

According to Vasicek's research[6] and Basel committee documents,[7]

$$\text{CVaR}\left((1 - X_i)r_i - X_i\lambda_i, \theta\right) = \lambda_i \Phi\left(\frac{\Phi^{-1}(P_i)}{\sqrt{1 - \rho_i}} + \sqrt{\frac{\rho_i}{1 - \rho_i}}\Phi^{-1}(\theta)\right) \quad (8.6)$$

Of which, $\rho_i = 0.12\left(2 - \frac{1 - e^{-50P_i}}{1 - e^{-50}}\right)$, $\Phi(\cdot)$ indicates a cumulative distribution

function with standard normal distribution. Equations (8.4) through (8.6) describe the risk characteristics of the loan portfolio. By similar means we can explain the risk diversification effect of P2P network loan investors. For brevity, assume in the above model that investments are even in every sum of loans and the risk charac-

teristics of loans are the same. That is, $w_i \equiv \frac{1}{n}, r_i \equiv r, P_i \equiv P, \lambda_i \equiv \lambda, i = 1, 2, \ldots, n.$

Then the rate of return for a loan portfolio is $L = \frac{1}{n}\sum_{i=1}^{n} L_i.$ We introduce an indicator

that indicates if the loan i defaults: $L_i^* = \begin{cases} 1 & \text{Default} \\ 0 & \text{No Default} \end{cases}$ and define $L^* = \frac{1}{n}\sum_{i=1}^{n} L_i^*$

to indicate the ratio of default in the loan portfolio. As $L_i = r - (r + \lambda)L_i^*$, the rate of return for the portfolio is $L = r - (r + \lambda)L^*$.

According to the ASRF model, when the risk is fully diversified or big enough, the cumulative probability distribution is:

$$F(x) = \Pr(L^* \leq x) = \Phi\left(\frac{\sqrt{1 - \rho}\Phi^{-1}(x) - \Phi^{-1}(P)}{\sqrt{\rho}}\right) \quad (8.7)$$

Of which $\rho$ is $0.12\left(2 - \frac{1 - e^{-50P}}{1 - e^{-50}}\right)$, the probability of facing a loss for the portfolio is:

$$\Pr(L < 0) = \Pr\left(L^* > \frac{r}{r + \lambda}\right) = 1 - F\left(\frac{r}{r + \lambda}\right) \quad (8.8)$$

For comparison, assume the loan portfolio is constituted by a certain loan. We might assume it is loan $i$. The rate of return for the loan portfolio is $L_i$, and the probability of facing a loss for the portfolio is $\Pr(L_i < 0) = P$.

If parameters as $r, \lambda, P$ have ordinary values, it is not difficult to prove that, compared with centralized loans portfolio, a diversified loan portfolio is more like to avoid losses (that is the phenomenon that Equation [8.5] describes).

Last, we want to point out three possible development trends for P2P network loans. The first one is the extension of "p." P2P network loans are now mainly among natural persons, but it could be extended to person to organization,

organization-to-organization, and so on. Theoretically, it has an unlimited possibility frontier. Second, along with the development of big data credit evaluation, pricing efficiency of P2P network loans will increase. Third, P2P network loan platforms can offer a credit insurance function. After investors pay a certain insurance premium (the rate is determined by big data analysis, as in Chapter 12), part or all of the borrowers' credit risk can be transferred out. This will not only provide investors with new risk control tools but also extend the transaction probability frontier of P2P network loans.

## Notes

1   Refer to "Internet Finance Handouts,"Wudaokou school of finance, Tsinghua University.
2   Abbreviations in this graph mean: (1) UT DFI, Utah Department of Financial Institutions; (2) FDIC, Federal Deposit Insurance Corporation; (3) SEC, Securities and Exchange Commission.
3   Description of bidding society in this period in cited from: Xiang Zhang, Chuanwei Zou: "Generating Mechanism of Bidding Society," "Financial Research," 2007–2011.
4   Xie, Ping, and Chuanwei Zou. 2013. "Fundamental Theoretical Research on Bank's Macroprudential Regulation."
5   Gordy, M. 2003. "A Risk-Factor Model Foundation for Ratings-Based Bank Capital Rules." Journal of Financial Intermediation, no. 12, 199–232.
6   Vasicek, O. 2002. "Loan Portfolio Value." Risk, no. 15, 160–162.
7   Mainly two documents: BCBS, 2004, "International Convergence of Capital Measurement and Capital Standards: A Revised Framework" and BCBS, 2005, "An Explanatory Note on the Basel II IRB Risk Weights Function."

# 9 Crowdfunding

Crowdfunding is equity financing raised on the Internet. Producers can obtain funding from potential consumers before incurring large costs, giving them the opportunity to carry out self-made production. Also, if the crowdfunding receives a cold welcome, producers should think twice before starting production. This saves investment cost compared with serious reflection after failure. Crowdfunding is not only a source of funds, but also a platform to evaluate product design and market prospects. In addition, it helps producers get rid of constraints frequently imposed by large funders. For consumers, they can contact the producer prior to final production to obtain the latest products. They can choose the share of their involvement according to their income level and judgment of the product's value. Compared with a fixed investment share, multi-level choices of investment scale improve consumer utility.

AngelCrunch in China and Kickstarter in the US are two typical crowdfunding platforms. This chapter starts with an analysis of Kickstarter and then introduces the operating mechanism and development of crowdfunding based on a 2013 paper[1] by Agrawal, Catalini, and Goldfarb. In the end, it will carry out an economic analysis along the lines of Hardy's 2013 paper[2] on crowdfunding.

## SECTION 1: ABOUT KICKSTARTER

### 1 The establishment of Kickstarter

Kickstarter launched on April 28, 2009. It was founded by Perry Chen, Yancey Strickler, and Charles Adler in New York. It is an online platform to publically raise funding for creative projects,[3] such as movies, music, theater, comic books, video games, and food-related items.[4] However, instead of offering cash rewards to funders, these projects can only return a unique experience or material objects, such as a written note of thanks, custom T-shirts, dinner with the writer, or the initial experience of a new product.[5]

### 2 The operating model of Kickstarter

The fundraisers of projects on Kickstarter need to explain deadlines and minimum funding targets. If the target is not achieved by the deadline, then Kickstarter will apply its refund guarantee.[6] Funds are transferred through Amazon from funder to project manager. Kickstarter is open to funders around the world as well as project managers from the United States and United Kingdom.

## 3 The pricing structure of Kickstarter

In crowdfunding cases, Kickstarter typically charges 5% of raised funds as commission. Amazon generally charges an additional 3%–5% of the cost. The platform holds neither ownership of projects nor of work produced on it. Project launches on Kickstarter are permanently archived and open to the public. After the crowdfunding round is completed, both the project and uploaded media materials cannot be edited or deleted from Kickstarter. However, there is no guarantee that all the funds will be used exclusively for realization of the project, nor to meet the expectations of supporters. Funders also have no way to confirm the status of the project other than to consult the fundraiser directly. Kickstarter proposal funders decide for themselves whether to support a project or not. It also warns project managers of possible damage compensation for funders if commitments are not met.

## 4 Projects on the Kickstarter platform

Projects released on the Kickstarter platform are divided into thirteen categories and thirty-six subcategories. The thirteen categories are: art, comics, dance, design, fashion, film, food, music, games, photography, publishing, technology, and comedy. Television and music is the biggest category, accounting for more than 50% of Kickstarter projects and attracting most of the funding.

## 5 Kickstarter guidelines[7]

In order to keep its focus on innovative project financing, Kickstarter asks all fundraisers to obey following three criteria:

- The fundraiser must have innovative projects
- The project must fit in one or more of the thirteen major categories of Kickstarter
- Fundraisers shall not engage in prohibited conduct defined by Kickstarter.

Kickstarter has additional requirements for hardware and product design projects including: prohibiting the use of photo-realistic renderings and simulations to demonstrate product, limiting the amount of individual projects or "set of ideas" project donations, requiring physical prototypes, and a requirement to lay out plans. These guidelines are intended to support Kickstarter's policy of supporting funding to complete projects rather than seek product orders. Kickstarter has also stressed the notion that the creation of a project depends on a collaboration of fundraisers and funders. All types of projects should describe the risks and challenges faced in the creative process. To educate the public and encourage their contribution to society is also one of Kickstarter's goals.

## SECTION 2: OPERATIONAL PRINCIPLE AND DEVELOPMENT

### 1 Relation between crowdfunding and crowdsourcing

Crowdfunding derives from crowdsourcing. The purpose of crowdsourcing is to effectively make use of knowledge, wisdom, and skills from potential participants in a new product and build a large pool of funds. The rapid development of the Internet provides a novel network foundation for crowdsourcing. Many specialized crowdsourcing platforms have been used as crowdfunding for enterprise incubation. There are two kinds of crowdfunding users. One is producers or project managers. They introduce new items to the platform and execute the project in accordance with funding plan once they have raised enough money. The other is crowdfunders. Although most crowdfunding platforms serve as "pay-what-you-want," they generally provide other immaterial rewards for crowdfunders such as an e-mail of thanks, Music CD, film studio visits, playing a small role in the movie, or souvenirs of cultural value. The product is the main return of crowdfunding. But for the participants who contribute a large amount, there are other incentive programs, such as a higher rate of return on equity.

Among many crowdfunding platforms, Kickstarter has two reasons to be a leader. First, it has a wide range of projects and attracted many participants and followers. Second, of the early crowdfunding models, Kickstarter's robust mechanism has been imitated or copied by latecomers.

### 2 Operational principles and project classification

Corporate funding is generally divided into accepting donations, accepting sponsorship, front-end (or pre-scheduled) sales, loans, equity sales, and so on. The complexities of these areas vary substantially, as one can see in Figure 9.1. Financing by donation is the least complex. Sponsors may add to the funding complexity by attaching other requirements. Crowdfunding usually takes a front-end sales approach. Front-end sales must have samples of innovative products, corresponding share configuration rules, and plans for prospective returns. Thus it is more complicated than donation and sponsorship. When enterprises are stable and reach a certain size, they often use more elaborate financing tools like borrowing, including bank loans and bond issuance. The highest degree of complexity is the public offering of stock.

However, crowdfunding also requires certain conditions such as sufficient crowd funders and management of a large number of micro-payment transactions. Many companies' startup projects lack either experience or interest in conducting the crowdfunding process. More often than not, they delegate the task to so called "intermediary," crowdfunding platforms. These service intermediaries often started as Internet or software companies. They had wide ranges of activities and activity

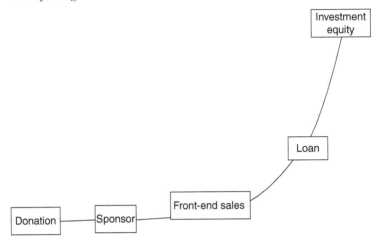

*Figure 9.1* Complexity variation of corporate finance tools.

intensity, served as an information release platform at the beginning, and acted as a neutral intermediary between the project fundraisers and public funders. With the development of participants' demands and crowdfunding mechanisms, they added functions to confirm the financing and monitor project execution capabilities, and so on. Some crowdfunding platforms also provide financing suggestions, build broader social networks for project managers, and help members find common funders.

The rise and rapid development of these platforms can be ascribed to their accordance with financing logic as well as key functions dealing with information and cost. First, as the capital demander, the innovative projects manager (producer) can communicate with the crowdfunding platform, take its advice, and promote according to its rules on detailed project information, development plans, configuration options, reward, and other information. Second, after innovative projects are released on the platform, fund providers (crowdfunders) can search for qualified projects according to their preferences, negotiate directly with project managers; or entrust banks to invest in certain or related projects, which is similar to trust loans. Of course, the majority of this process is conducted by payers of small amounts. Then, after the transfer of funds, project managers start production and give rewards to funders. Its operational relationship is described in Figure 9.2. Notably, crowdfunding platforms have certain nationality requirements for project managers that do not exist for funders.

Projects on crowdfunding platforms can be classified into non-profit, for-profit, and neutral categories. Non-profit projects generally have significant social purposes, such as public health, public infrastructure, foreign aid, general charity, and public research projects. For-profit projects generally have clear business profit targets, for example, to set up a company or provide funding for commercial projects within an existing company, internal research and development projects, commercial movies, and music albums. Neutral projects temporarily lack clear long-term business prospects. Examples include Skype, Facebook, and YouTube, which mainly provided new services or social networks on the Internet at first, and only later developed into commercial services.

Project organizations can also be divided into independent, embedded, and startups. An independent project generally does not have any organizational background and is initiated by an individual. An embedded project is originally initiated by private or public organizations, such as companies, non-governmental organizations, consortiums, or multinational corporations. It then works as part of the organization. Startup projects may start independently, but transform into a corporation, association, club, or other forms after it achieves success. A few examples in each category are laid out in Table 9.1.

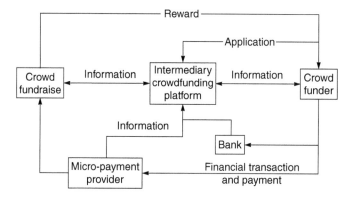

*Figure 9.2* The basic process of crowdfunding.

*Table 9.1* Classification matrix of crowdfunding projects

| Organization | Business background | | |
|---|---|---|---|
| | Non-profit | Neutral | For-profit |
| Independent | I am Verity, SmallcanBeBig, Solarimpulse, Friendly Fire | Lynch Three Project, Love Like hers, Iron Sky, The Age of Stupid, The Cosmonaut, Artemis Eternal | Million Dollar Homepage Exthanded, lunatik.com |
| Embedded | Blender, Reduce the Cost of Energy in Africa | Racing Shares, Project Franchise, Justin Wilson plc | Hotel Chocolat, Media No Mad, Trampoline Systems, Cintep |
| Startup | Buy this Satellite, 4th Revolution, Energy Autonomy | The Independent Collective MyFootballClub | Outvesting |

## 3 Development overview

Crowdfunding is booming in developed countries. Constrained by limited material, we indirectly invoke relevant data,[8] to select ten crowdfunding platforms in the United States, Britain, France, the Netherlands, Belgium, and Finland to sketch the developments (see Table 9.2). Our ten crowdfunding samples include Kickstarter (US), IndieGoGo (US), RocketHub (US), SliceThePie (UK), Sonicangel (UK), Ulule (France), MyMajor (France), PledgeMusic (US and UK), SellaBand (Netherlands and Belgium), and Grow VC (Finland and UK). From this examination, we outline a few salient characteristics of crowdfunding.

First, crowdfunding platforms can usually be classified as emerging enterprises. The longest amount of time from the launch date to the time of the literature references[9] given (as of January, 2011) is fifty-three months. The shortest is only six months. Second, crowdfunding projects depend on platform visibility and sound rules. Kickstarter issued a total number of 12,000 projects in this time period, an average of 571 per month. In total, the ten platforms we examined released 51,477 items and averaged 258 projects per month.

Second, only a small fraction of released projects will be chosen. Among Kickstarter's 12,000 items, more than 5,000 projects were funded. This selection rate (the number of projects funded by the selected/number of items released) is slightly greater than 42%. The ten platforms together selected a total of 11,414 items, with a selection rate of around 25%.

Third, the number of successful crowdfunding projects is even lower. Under the crowdfunding provision point mechanism (explained in detail below), the project cannot carry on once it failed to get enough funding during a defined period and needs to return previously raised funds to investors. Pre-selected items may not be able to reach a predetermined threshold. 3,500–4,000 projects succeeded during the period, with a success rate (number of successfully funded projects/number of items chosen by funders) of 70%–80%. The success rate over the ten platforms was 64%.

Fourth, a large number of funders participate in crowdfunding. Kickstarter funders total 400,000, an average of 19,000 per month of operation; seven crowdfunding platforms indicated that the average number of contributors is 84,200, which means each platform has an average of 3,900 funders per month of operation.

Fifth, the minimum financial contribution is low. Kickstarter raised €24.6 million for an average per project over €4,920, and the total amount over ten platforms is €45 million for an average of €3,942 per project. Each funder contributed an average of €62.9.

Table 9.2 Ten selected crowdfunding platforms' performance data[10] (2010.12–2011.2d)

| Platform (country) | Field | Start date (moment till 2011.1) | Projects amount (monthly) | Selected projects (selecting rate) | Successful amount (successful rate) | Number of funders (monthly) | Funding amount € (each project) (€) | Paid amount (€) | Average funding (€) | Platform fee |
|---|---|---|---|---|---|---|---|---|---|---|
| Kickstarter (US) | For-profit | 2009.4 (21) | 12,000 (571) | >5,000 (>42%) | 3,500–4,000 (70%–80%) | >400,000 (>19,000) | >€24.6 m (>4,920) | ? | 50 | 5% |
| IndieGoGo (US) | Any | 2008.1 (37) | >15,000 (405) | >4,000 (>27%) | Thousands | | | Million dollars | 56 | 4% |
| SellaBand (NL/DE) | Music | 2006.8 (53) | ? | 54 | 38 CDs (70%) | >70,000 (>1,320) | >€ 2.7 m (>50,000) | 2.7 m | 41 | 15% |
| RocketHub (US) | Any | 2010.2 (12) | 350 (29) | 75 (21%) | ? | ? | ? | 300,000 | ? | 8% |
| Ulule (F) | Any | 2010.10 (4) | 169 (42) | 53 (31%) | 42 (80%) | 4,818 (1,204) | €100,000 (1,887) | 70,000 | 32 | 0% |
| SliceThePie (UK) | Music | 2007.6 (43) | ? | 31 | 26 (84%) | ? | ? | 750,000 | ? | ? |
| PledgeMusic (UK/US) | Music | 2009.7 (19) | >2,700 (>115) | 2,079 (77%) | 132 (6%) | 74,000 (3,895) | ? | ? | 65 | 15% |
| Sonicangel (B) | Music | 2010.4 (11) | 1,500 (142) | 13 (0.8%) | 12 (92%) | 3,500 (318) | ? | ? | 46 | 0% (dividend) |

(continued)

*Table 9.2* Ten selected crowdfunding platforms' performance data[10] (continued)

| Platform (country) | Field | Start date (moment till 2011.1) | Projects amount (monthly) | Selected projects (selecting rate) | Successful amount (successful rate) | Number of funders (monthly) | Funding amount € (each project) (€) | Paid amount (€) | Average funding (€) | Platform fee |
|---|---|---|---|---|---|---|---|---|---|---|
| MyMajor (F) | Music | 2007.10 (38) | 18,000 (473) | 36 (0.2%) | 15 (42%) | 3,0000 (789) | €5 m (13,8889) | 360,000 | 150 | 0% (dividend) |
| GrowVC (FIN UK internat.) | Startup | 2010.8 (6) | 1,758 (293) | 73 (4.1%) | ? | 7,229 (1,205) | €11.6 m (148,904) | ? | ? | 25% of ROI |
| Total or average | | | 51,477 (258) | 11,414 (25%) | 64% | 84,200 (51.7) | >€45m (3,942) | | 62.9 | |

## SECTION 3: THE ECONOMICS OF CROWDFUNDING[11]

### 1 Common characteristics

Funds have no geographic restrictions. The advent of the Internet enables transactions between funders and fundraisers less constrained by spatial distance. For example, SellaBand is a music crowdfunding platform allowing musicians and fans to interact. Musicians can showcase their work quickly and efficiently, attract support and sponsorship of enthusiasts, and raise funds to release the album. Then through websites' exposure and support from hardcore fans, musicians can attract more supporters, expand their influence and stimulate sales of their albums. On SellaBand, over 86% of the funders are over 60 miles away from the musicians they are supporting. For a normal crowdfunding platform, the average distance is about 3,000 miles.[12]

Funds are also highly skewed. According to statistics for the general crowdfunding platforms between 2006 and 2009, 61% of the producers have not raised any money while 0.7% raised more than 73% of the total funds. One percent of the projects raised 36% of the funds on Kickstarter while 10% of the projects raised 63% of the funds.

In the early stages of crowdfunding, capital from friends and family play a key role. Friends' and family's early investments produce a signal for later funders through the promotion of capital accumulation. Crowdfunding may replace traditional sources of funding, such as home equity loans.

### 2 Incentives

Project managers, funders, and platforms are the three major players in the crowdfunding process. Here we discuss their incentives.

#### 2.1 Project manager (producer)

Two main advantages attract project managers to use crowdfunding: lower funding costs and the ability to obtain more information.

##### 2.1.1 Lower cost

Early project funding comes from personal savings, home equity loans, personal credit cards, friends and family investments, angel investors, and venture capitalists. In some cases, project managers can obtain funds at a lower cost through crowdfunding due to following reasons:

1  Better matching: Project managers can match investors with the highest willingness to fund. Funders of these projects are no longer limited to specific areas (e.g., in close geographic proximity).
2  Bundling: During the crowdfunding process, funders can get products in advance and confirm innovative value under certain conditions. However, to

some extent, crowdfunding also helps project managers bundle share sales to obtain funding and reduce the cost of capital by pre-selling the product.

3   Information: To some extent, crowdfunding can produce more information than traditional capital sourcing, which may increase funders' willingness to pay and reduce cost of capital. For example, Pebble Technology's founder Eric Migicovsky published the Pebble Smart Watch project on a crowdfunding platform after receipt of donations and funds from sponsors and friends. He disclosed relevant information to prove that some funders recognized the product's innovative value, thus attracting more funders to purchase the product and increasing the scale of funding. This improved the overall value of the product and reduced financing costs.

### 2.1.2 Information about potential demand

Project managers evaluate the innovation and practicability of products according to funders' reaction and choice, and further amend preliminary ideas and plans. Project managers can analyze the expectations for market demand, provide products to meet this demand, and enhance the probability of success for later products.[13] In addition, signals about market demand for products can assist project managers in understanding potential users' and funders' improved product recommendations that will help project managers quickly develop better products. For example, Pebble Smart Watch took users' advice and developed software applications compatible with iPhone and Android phones, expanding its functions to checking iMessage SMS, displaying caller information, Internet browsing, real-time alert messages, SMS, microblogging, and social networking information, all of which exampled new potential users.

### 2.2 Funders

One of the key benefits to funders is the ability to seek investment opportunities. Early corporate funders are traditionally located near businesses, but crowdfunding offers investment global opportunities.[14] Another benefit is early access to new products. Crowdfunding projects turn product fans into early shareholders, and their participation can enhance the value of the company. Crowdfunding also functions as a built-in social network. For investors, crowdfunding is essentially a social activity through which they can achieve improved, low cost communication with project managers. Investors can also support a product, service, or idea. Charity plays an important role on crowdfunding platforms. Some funders neither receive tangible material rewards nor participate in related online communities. Their goal is simply to find new products and new businesses with high potential.

### 2.3 Crowdfunding platforms

Crowdfunding platforms' main purpose is profit. They generally charge 4%–5% of the funding as transaction fee. Therefore, their goal is to maximize the number and size of successful projects. This requires soundly designed market operating rules to attract high-quality projects, reduce fraud and match creativity and capital efficiently. Successful crowdfunding projects have advertising effects. They can draw media attention and coverage, which further expands existing funders, enhances projects' probability of success and benefits the platforms.

## 3 Crowdfunding risks

### 3.1 Project manager

Information disclosure is the number one problem for crowd fundraisers. In most cases, a project manager must reveal some private information to early funders before selling his/her goods. However, the recipients are limited, which poses far fewer risks than posting similar information on the Internet for all, including potential competitors and imitators, to see. It could also be detrimental to bargaining power with potential suppliers.

Another problem stems from the fact that crowdfunders tend not to be professional investors. Angel investors and venture capitalists tend to bring additional value to the company through expertise and networks that can help a company further develop its capacity. Crowdfunders on the other hand provide limited investment, bring little experience or value and are not likely to make much post-investment effort.

Additionally, the cost of managing funders may rise significantly as funders multiply. Unlike angel investors or other venture capital, crowdfunding typically requires small amounts of money from a large audience in order to obtain the expected capital scale for project operational needs. This dispersion of ownership can add costs to dividend payment, voting, and eventual reorganization of a company or its equity.

### 3.2 Crowd funders

Producers may raise only a part of the funding they need and lack the ability to raise enough money for planned delivery commitments. This is a problem common to funding rounds, whether with crowdfunding or venture capital/PE, but is especially difficult due to the small amounts supplied by users. If funders are overly optimistic, they may not only invest in bad projects but also face blatant fraud. For example, project managers may use false information to make very real-looking, but fake, fundraising page. Despite all the attempts crowdfunding platforms make to filter and control, career criminals are still able to game the system. In addition, the small investment share reduces investor incentives to conduct due diligence that could mitigate this risk.

In any case, there is a high risk of project failure for early-stage projects. Even if funders can integrate risk into investment decisions, information asymmetry (i.e. creators have more information than capital providers) makes a proper evaluation difficult. Good projects may become bad due to rapid market changes.

# 4 Market design

Market design affects market performance. Currently, there are four main designs crowdfunding platforms use to reduce investment risk caused by information asymmetry: reputation signaling, rules and regulation, group due diligence, and provision point mechanisms. The first three reduce information asymmetry between producers and funders, while the fourth helps to reduce the free-rider problem.

## *4.1 Reputation signaling*

The early stage of traditional public financing largely depends on face-to-face due diligence and personal relations. On crowdfunding platforms, producers send a signal through disclosure of as much information as possible on their projects and reward programs. Market design helps market funders evaluate producers and creates market reputations. Reputation and trust are particularly important on crowdfunding platforms. Cabral sees reputation as a mechanism to reduce the risk of fraud for online transactions, "Although there are a variety of mechanisms to deal with fraud, reputation is one of the best choices for enterprises."[15] Internet market designers established many trust-building tools through reputation mechanisms. Broadly speaking, these tools can be divided into three types: quality signals, feedback systems, and trustworthy intermediaries.

### *4.1.1 Quality signals*

Waldfogel and Chen explained the importance of quality signals in online trading markets. They believe the importance of brands decreases with the ability of consumers to obtain information.[16] Lewis further tested the role of access to information and found that personal information disclosure can increase secondhand car prices on eBay.[17] Even if the product information cannot be convincingly conveyed, there are other methods to display quality. For example, Roberts showed that the guarantor can provide a reliable quality signal.[18] Elfenbein, Fisman, and McManus concluded that charitable donations send a signal of higher quality signal for Internet transactions.[19] In the early financing stages when information asymmetry is high, patents can also be used as a quality signal. Similarly, funders often regard producers' past successful experience as a quality signal, for instance, entrepreneurs or founding team members with doctoral degrees.[20] Finally, education level is positively correlated with crowdfunding success.

### *4.1.2 Feedback system*

Many crowdfunding platforms provide a system for buyers and sellers to build reputations through feedback. The most basic version simply reports sales information. Tucker and Zhang demonstrated that sales information had a significant impact on financing decisions.[21] As part of a crowdfunding signal mechanism, online transaction materials can help discover project managers' behavioral characteristics and provide reference material for the investment. More complex mechanisms rely on information on credibility from rating systems, which generally allow evaluation after transactions. For example, buyers can evaluate sellers on eBay. High-quality service results in positive evaluations, which then attract new customers. The literature confirms the importance of seller and customer evaluations on Internet platforms.[22] However, even a good producer is not likely to raise money repeatedly on crowdfunding platforms over a short time period. A potential solution is to divide a sizeable project into a series of smaller ones.

### 4.1.3 Trustworthy intermediaries

Quality signals provided by third-party intermediaries can promote trust among market participants. For example, Jin and Kato demonstrated the significance of third-party certification for the prosperity and collectibles markets.[23] Credit rating agencies should be able to provide an accurate and verifiable quality standard. On crowdfunding platforms, funders tend to use information posted on Facebook, Twitter, LinkedIn, and other large social networks to avoid moral hazard.

## 4.2 Rules and regulation

### 4.2.1 Platform rules

In order to maximize transaction scale, crowdfunding platforms modify their rules constantly based on user behavior. For example, Kickstarter added human and system resources to monitor the risk of fraud in 2013. Kickstarter managers believe that this reduces investment risk, protects funders, and encourages participation despite increasing cost. However, Kickstarter ultimately still relies on funders' own due diligence and must find a balance between many competing objectives.

### 4.2.2 Industry regulation

The US JOBS Act requires the SEC to establish industry rules for crowdfunding (see Chapter 10 for details). These rules are mainly for investor protection, but they will have a profound impact on the industry.

One of the regulatory areas includes risk exposure restrictions. According to crowdfunding law, such investments must not exceed 10% of an investor's annual income, net assets, or $100,000, whichever is smallest. In addition, if their incomes or net assets are less than $100,000, then the investment may not exceed the lesser of 5% of income/assets or $2,000.

Crowdfunding platforms need to register with the SEC, conduct investment risk education for investors, take measures to reduce fraud risk (e.g., check the history of directors and shareholders holding more than 20% of shares), and prove that the funders' investment on every platform is within the aforementioned limitations. It will also set a threshold to prevent producers from continually seeking financing if they fail to raise enough money within a certain time.

### *4.3 Group due diligence*

Crowdfunders are more vulnerable than traditional funders. They usually hold a very small stake and thus lack the incentive to conduct due diligence. This may lead them to "free ride" on due diligence done by others. However, a large number of funders means an examination of the project's prospects from many different angles, which together could lead to a unique sort of due diligence.

However, problems such as herding may reduce the effectiveness of collective due diligence. Research shows that crowdfunders regard accumulated capital as an important signal of quality. Project financing generally increases in accordance with the degree of difficulty (see Figure 9.1). In the initial phase, crowdfunders invest in projects sponsored by the project owner's relatives and friends, which stand in for quality and professional acceptance. Funders thus "herd" by choosing projects that are already funded. Besides, project managers may use prophase-financing data to attract funders. In extreme conditions, producers may take advantage of this by devoting much capital in early stages to then attract new funders, then withdraw the capital they invested earlier. Platform rules can work to prevent this from happening.

### *4.4 Provision point mechanisms*

Provision point mechanisms can help to solve the "the free rider" problem. For example, early funders can produce valuable signals for latecomers through due diligence and capital accumulation, thus creating an incentive for investors to wait. As for "free rider" problem, almost all crowdfunding platforms adopt some form of provision point mechanism. The mechanism requires producers to reach certain funding thresholds to continue financing. Projects that fall short must return all funds accumulated from investors and declare failure. In the provision of public goods and "free rider" problem, this particular type of contract is a classic coordination solution. Through the provision point mechanism, crowdfunding platforms can lower funders' risk and help to ensure that project managers do not engage in indefinite funding rounds.

## 5 Several open questions

Crowdfunding gets policy support because of its potential for societal benefit. Crowdfunding may improve the speed and direction of technological innovation. It may also help along the application of new technology to practical production. Although it is likely to improve overall social welfare, increase private returns, and generate positive externalities, crowdfunding may lead to greater financial risks. The way this is handled will have a strong influence on the future development of crowdfunding.

## 5.1 Social welfare

Crowdfunding creates two types of social welfare. Platforms create a win–win scenario by raising transaction revenue, while producers and funders obtain operating funds and equity transactions to meet their needs. This activity is also beneficial due to a positive spillover effect. In particular, crowdfunding focuses on enterprises in early stages, many of which may produce innovative products. The production this finances meets societal needs that may otherwise go unsatisfied.

Crowdfunding is, however, not perfect. It will definitely result in some social loss. For example, new forms of fraudulent activity and new securities sales methods could lead inexperienced or reckless individuals to make imprudent investment decisions. Regulation should be designed to minimize these effects while maximizing the positive aspects.

## 5.2 Technical innovation

Crowdfunding can affect the speed and direction of technological innovation. First, successful crowdfunding projects have generally already survived a public test. They are more innovative and in sync with societal needs. Projects with no practical value cannot succeed. Crowdfunding is essentially a mechanism for public screening of innovative projects. Traditional government support and bank loans cannot react in the differentiated manner required to effectively meet the needs of society through innovation. Second, creative productions and innovative business solutions cannot easily obtain operating funds through traditional financing channels. Crowdfunding helps them obtain funds to enter production as soon as possible, thus accelerating the pace of technological innovation.

## 5.3 Geographic distribution

Compared with conventional financing, crowdfunding makes it much easier to allocate capital globally. Traditional geographic restrictions will play a less important role in early stage investments as trading increasingly occurs on the Internet. For example, SellaBand's financing activities are almost completely unrestricted by geographical factors. Therefore, crowdfunding's capital has a completely different spatial distribution from that of the early traditional finance. Expect stepped up competition between traditional financing channels and crowdfunding in the future.

Finally, we believe that crowdfunding may develop into a "financing toolbox."[24] With sufficiently transparent information and low transaction costs, some companies (especially better qualified enterprises) will be able to raise money directly on crowdfunding platforms and integrate financing tools instead of operating only through the stock or bond markets. Companies will be able to issue stocks, bonds, or hybrid capital instruments dynamically according to their needs.

## Notes

1 Agrawal, Ajay K, Christian Catalini, and Avi Goldfarb. 2013. "Goldfarb Catalinimics of Crowdfunding," NBER Working Paper 19133. http://www.nber.org/papers/w19133.
2 Hardy, Wojciech. 2013. "How to Perfectly Discriminate in a Crowd? A Theoretical Model of Crowdfunding," *Working paper.* No. 16.
3 Wauters, Robin. 2009. " Kickstarter Launches Another Social Fundraising Platform."
4 Levy, Shawn. 2010. "Kickstarter Raises Money Online for Artistic Endeavors, Tapping into Portland Ethos."
5 Walker, Rob. 2011. "The Trivialities and Transcendence of Kickstarter," The New York Times Magazine, August 5.
6 Musgrove, Mike. 2010. "At Play: Kickstarter is a Web Site for the Starving Artist," The Washington Post, March 7.
7 Blattberg, Eric. 2012. "Kickstarter Bans Project Renderings, Adds 'Risks and Challenges' Section," Crowdsourcing.org.
8 Andrews, Robert. 2011. "Crowdfunding: How Does The Scene Stack Up?." http://paidcontent.org/table/crowdfunding. 1US$= 0.7057€.
9 Hemer, Joachim. 2011. "A Snapshot of Crowdfunding," Working Papers Firms and Region, No. R2/2011.
10 Andrews, Robert. 2011. "Crowdfunding: How Does The Scene Stack Up?" http://paidcontent.org/table/crowdfunding. 1US$= 0.7057€.
11 This section mainly refers to Hardy, Wojciech. 2013. "How to Perfectly Discriminate in a Crowd? A Theoretical Model of Crowdfunding," *Working paper.* No. 16.
12 Agrawal, Ajay K, Christian Catalini, and Avi Goldfarb. 2013. "Goldfarb Catalinimics of Crowdfunding," NBER Working Paper 19133. http://www.nber.org/papers/w19133.
13 Lauga, D, and E. Ofek. 2009. "Market Research and Innovation Strategy in Duopoly," Marketing Science, 28(2), 373–396.
14 Gubler, Z.J. 2013. "Inventive Funding Deserves Creative Regulation," Wall Street Journal, January 31, http://online.wsj.com/article/SB10001424127887323468604578251913868617572.
15 Cabral, L. 2012. "Reputation on the Internet," in Martin Peitz and Joel Waldfogel, eds. Ch. 13, The Oxford Handbook of the Digital Economy, pp. 343–354.
16 Waldfogel, J, and L. Chen. 2006. "Does Information Undermine Brand? Information Intermediary Use and Preference for Branded Web Retailers," Journal of Industrial Economics, 54(4), 425–449.
17 Lewis, G. 2011. "Asymmetric Information, Adverse Selection and Seller Disclosure: The Case of eBay Motors," American Economic Review, 101(4), 1535–1546.
18 Roberts, J. 2011. "Can Warranties Substitute for Reputations?" American Economic Journal, 3(3), 69–85.
19 Elfenbein, D.W, R. Fisman, B. McManus. 2012. "Charity as a Substitute for Reputation: Evidence from an Online Marketplace," Review of Economic Studies, 79(4), 1441–1468.
20 Hsu, D. 2007. "Experienced Entrepreneurial Founders, Organizational Capital, and Venture Capital Funding," Research Policy, 36(5), 722–741.
21 Tucker, C, and J. Zhang. 2011. "How Does Popularity Information Affect Choices? A Field Experiment," Management Science, 57(5), 828–842.
22 Cabral, L. 2012. "Reputation on the Internet," in Martin Peitz and Joel Waldfogel, eds. Ch. 13, The Oxford Handbook of the Digital Economy, pp. 343–354.
23 Jin, G. Z, and A. Kat. 2007. "Dividing Online and Online: A Case Study," Review of Economic Studies, 74(3), 981–1004.
24 This concept is similar to Internet Financing Trading Platform described in Chapter 3.

# 10 The regulation of Internet finance

Regulation of Internet finance remains an open question and mature regulations are not yet in place. Currently, governments are exploring possible regulation. This chapter discusses three issues. Whether it is necessary to supervise Internet finance, functional supervision of Internet finance, and organizational supervision of Internet finance.

## SECTION 1: SHOULD INTERNET FINANCE BE REGULATED?

After the most recent financial crisis, we believe that governments should regulate Internet finance. However, it is also necessary to take into account the special characteristics of Internet finance.

## 1 Necessities of regulation

When the market is efficient (the ideal case of Internet finance, see Chapter 1), market participants are rational and their self-interested behaviors make it possible to automatically achieve market equilibrium through the "invisible hand." The market both balances prices fully and accurately reflects all available information. When this point is reached, Internet finance regulation should follow the concept of "laissez-faire," the key objectives of which are to remove factors causing market inefficiencies and to allow the market mechanism to play a role with little or no regulation. We justify this assertion through three principal assumptions. First, the market price signals will be correct, so we can rely on market discipline to take effective control of harmful risk-taking behavior. Second, we make it possible for financial institutions to fail, thus achieving the survival of the fittest in a competitive market. Finally, it is not necessary to supervise financially innovative products. Unnecessary or non-value-creating innovations will be eliminated under market competition and discipline. Well-regulated financial institutions will not develop high-risk products, and consumers with full information will only choose products that meet their own needs. Additionally, in terms of determining whether the financial innovation is valuable or not, regulatory authorities may not take the best position. Instead, regulation may inhibit beneficial financial innovation. However, before reaching the ideal situation, non-effective factors like asymmetric information and transaction costs still exist, making the concept of laissez-faire regulation not applicable.

First of all, individuals may be irrational in Internet finance. For example, in P2P network loans, investors lend personal credit loans to borrowers. Even if the P2P platform accurately reveals the borrower's credit risk and the investment is diversified enough, it remains a high risk investment. Investors may not be able to fully understand the impact on individuals when the investment fails. Therefore, for P2P network loans, it is necessary to introduce regulation to protect investors.

Second, individual rationality does not necessarily imply that collective rationality is achieved. For example, in the "third-party-payments plus money market fund," exemplified by Yu'E Bao, investors buy fund shares in the money market (see Chapter 3). Investors can redeem their fund at any time, but money market fund positions generally have a longer maturity. This means one may be forced to sell at a discount in the secondary market, initiating problems like maturity mismatch or insufficient liquidity. If money market volatility occurs, investors may redeem their funds in order to control risks, which is absolutely rational from the individual's perspective. It is problematic that money market funds will encounter a run if there are large-scale redemptions, which is irrational from the collective point of view. In September 2008, one of the oldest US Money market funds, the Reserve Primary Fund, suffered this after the bankruptcy of Lehman Brothers. The Reserve Primary Fund was exposed to Lehman Brothers, and the writedowns on the Lehman commercial paper they held led them to "break the buck," or fall below a net asset value (NAV) of $1. Therefore, institutional investors scrambled to redeem their investments although the net loss was no more than 5%. Thus, the fund had to be liquidated. The whole money market fund industry then suffered the hit of redemptions overnight. The liquidity crunch had also spread to the entire financial system, and the central banks of related countries had to team up to launch massive liquidity support measures. Such collectively irrational behavior exhibited by institutional investors is entirely possible for individual investors as well.

Third, market discipline may not able to control harmful risk-taking behaviors. In China, there exist various implicit and explicit guarantees against investment risks (e.g. implicit deposit insurances, implicit promises from banks for financial products sold at their branches), and investors have become accustomed to "fixed pay-outs." This implies that risk-based pricing mechanisms have failed. In this environment, some Internet financial institutions have launched high-risk and high-yield products. They try to attract investors and achieve a large scale through expected high-returns. However, they may not truthfully reveal risks. There is a huge moral hazard.

Fourth, if Internet financial institutions involve in large number of users and reach a certain scale of funds, it is difficult to solve the problem by clearing the market in a crisis situation. If the institution provides payment, clearing, and other basic financial services, its bankruptcy may also damage the infrastructure of the financial system, posing a systemic risk. For instance, the scale of people involved and business funds are so large in Alipay and Yu'E Bao that they have reached systemic importance.

Fifth, Internet financial innovation may have major defects. For example, P2P network loans in China appear to be a mixed bag. In some P2P platforms, customer funds and platform funds are not effectively separated. There are thus situations in which platform managers escape with customer's money. Some P2P platforms have aggressive marketing strategies, selling high-risk products to people who do not have the capacity for risk identification and risk bearing (e.g. retired people). Some P2P platforms even breached the regulatory red line of illegal fund-raising and illegal deposits. Take Bitcoin as another example: because of the characteristic of anonymity, it is used in money laundering, drug trafficking and other illegal activities.

Sixth, there may be fraud and irrational behavior in the consumption of Internet financial products, finance institutions may develop or sell overly risky products, and consumers may buy products they do not understand. For example, when sold online, some products generally disclose their expected rate of return without explaining how they achieve it or the potential risk factors. Some products even use subsidies, guarantees, "loss leaders," and other ways to magnify gains, which are not pure market competitive behaviors. On the other hand, some consumers are even unclear on the differences between P2P network loans, deposits and bank financial products because of their limited financial knowledge and, expectation of "fixed-payouts."

Meanwhile, behavioral finance also supports the need for regulation of Internet finance. It studies the irrational behavior of individuals and problems with the market. On the one hand, psychological research on cognition and preferences are introduced, implying that individual behavior does not necessarily meet the description of the rational expectations hypothesis; on the other hand, it studies the limits of arbitrage, which can hinder the achievement of market equilibrium. Thus, it can prove that the efficient market hypothesis is not necessarily true. The revelation behavioral finance gives us when considering questions in Internet finance are as follows: first, we must curb excessive speculation. For instance, the deflationary effect of Bitcoin comes with serious problems of speculation (see Chapter 5). Second we should restrict market access. Internet financial institutions and investors are not completely rational, so certain markets or products should only open to those who satisfy certain conditions. Third, we should strengthen the supervision of Internet financial innovations and promptly correct any problems. Fourth, we must strengthen protection for financial consumers. Fifth, we need regulation that fits investor needs.

Therefore, for Internet finance, we cannot adopt the concept of laissez-faire because of its immaturity, instead we should promote it with regulation. We need to encourage limited, well-regulated innovation in Internet finance.

## 2 Specialties of regulation

Compared with traditional finance, Internet finance has two unique characteristics. These present several risks to which we should pay attention.

## 2.1 Information technology risks

Because of increased connectivity (see Chapter 1), IT risk becomes a problem in the Internet finance, such as computer viruses, computer hacking, insecure payments, online financial fraud, financial phishing sites, customer data leaks, illegal identity theft, or tampering. The Vice Chairman of the China Banking Regulatory Commission, Yan Qingmin, explained that information technology risk can be understood from three perspectives: exposure source, objects impacted, and the influence on responsible units.[1]

Sources of information technology risk are divided into four categories:

1  Risks based on natural factors
2  Systemic risks caused by related hardware and software defects in information systems. They include aging infrastructure and hardware devices, applications and systems software quality defects, etc.
3  Risks caused by management defects, mainly reflected by the lack necessary management systems, imperfect organizational structure, or inadequate management processes
4  Operational risks caused by intentionally or unintentionally illegal operations of personnel.

Objects of information technology can also be divided into three categories: Data risks, risks in information technology platforms, and risks posed by the physical environment. In information technology areas, financial services involve a great deal of data processing. Once mismanagement rears its head, data errors like customer information leaks and mistakenly allocated capital will easily appear. Data processing in financial services need a robust operation system. Inherent defects or mistaken management of hardware devices, networks, operating systems, databases, middleware, and operations systems will affect the quality of the information systems, giving rise to potential risks. As for risks in the physical environment, the security of information system operation platforms relies on a suitable physical environment. Earthquakes, thunderstorms, and equipment failures in engine rooms will affect the supply of electrical power, along with temperature and humidity of engine rooms, potentially causing equipment malfunctions.

The influence of informational risks to organizations are divided into four categories:

1  Security risks, such as information that has been tampered with, stolen or used by unauthorized organizations
2  Availability risks, which means information or applications are unavailable due to system failures or natural disasters
3  Performance risks, meaning that the poor performance of systems, applications, or personnel lead to low efficiency of transaction and operation, as well as value destruction
4  Compliance risks, including the handling and processing of information that does not meet the requirements of laws, regulations or policies made by

IT or financial institutions, which may damage the reputation of financial institutions

Regulatory approaches for information technology risks include[2] off-site operation (using regulatory compliance), on-site inspections, risk assessment and supervisory ratings, forward-looking risk control measures, and mathematical models for measuring IT risks (e.g. measurement methods based on the loss distribution).

### 2.2 *"Long Tail" risks*

As Internet finance expands the boundaries of transactions and serves a large part of the population that is not under the coverage of traditional finance (the so-called "long-tail" feature), Internet finance exhibits quite different risk characteristics than those of traditional finance. First, target groups for Internet finance know little about finance and have a poor ability to identify risk and risk-taking. They are especially vulnerable to misleading, deceptive, and unfair treatment. Second, their investments are small and scattered. For individuals, the costs of financial institution regulation far outweigh their benefits, thus the "free rider" problem is more prominent,[3] and Internet financial market discipline fails easily. Third, situations of individual and collective irrationality are more likely to appear. Fourth, once Internet risks break out, a large set of negative externalities will be unleashed on society (the specific meaning of externalities can be seen below) due to the population involved (while the funds involved may not). In general, because of the "long tail" risks of Internet finance, mandatory, professional, knowledge-based, and lasting financial regulation is indispensable, while financial consumer protection is particularly important.

### SECTION 2: FUNCTIONAL REGULATION OF INTERNET FINANCE

The core of functional regulation is to set regulation based on the business and risks of Internet finance. Internet finance should accept regulation consistent with that of traditional finance if its function is similar. Different Internet financial institutions should be subjected to the same regulation if they are engaged in the same business or are subject to the same risks, otherwise it is likely to cause regulatory arbitrage. This is not only harmful to fair competition in the market, but also gives rise to regulatory blind spots. Institutional regulation also corresponds with functional regulation. Although institutional regulation is clearer in regulatory issues, functional regulation involves more basic theories and methodology. It is necessary to discuss this before discussing institutional regulation.

Functional supervision mainly refers to supervision of risk. It is based on risk identification, measurement, prevention, early warning, and disposal. Like traditional finance, the risks of Internet finance mean the possibility of future loss. Conceptual and analytical frameworks of market risks,[4] credit risks,[5] liquidity risks,[6] operational risks,[7] reputational risks,[8] and legal compliance risks[9] are adaptable to Internet finance.[10] There also exist problems of misleading consumers, exaggerated marketing, fraud, etc. Therefore, there are no significant differences between conventional finance and Internet finance in the functional regulation area. They can be divided into three categories: prudential regulation, behavioral regulation, and protection for consumers of financial products (although specific measures may be different from traditional finance).

# 1 Prudential regulation

The goal of prudential regulation is to control the externalities of Internet finance and protect the public interest.[11] According to microeconomic theory, externalities refer to a situation in which the behavior of economic actors will directly affect the welfare of other consumers and the production capacity of other vendors. If additional restrictions are not imposed on the market, the equilibrium yield is lower than the socially optimal level when the externality is positive, while higher when the externality is negative (in general, the financial sector belongs to the latter case). The basic methodology of prudential supervision is to introduce a series of risk management tools based on risk identification (generally using methods of regulatory limits) to control risk-taking behaviors of Internet financial institutions and the negative externalities they produce for society. Therefore, the socially optimal level may be reached.

At the moment, the externalities of Internet finance revolve primarily around externalities of credit and liquidity risks. To deal with this, we can design practices of banking regulation according to the principle of "substance is over form," and design regulatory measures for Internet finance.[12]

## 1.1 Regulation of credit risk externalities

Some Internet financial institutions are engaged in credit intermediation. For example, in P2P network loans, some platforms are directly involved in the borrowing chain or provide guarantees for lending activities. Overall, they are taking credit and will bring credit risk externalities. If they go bankrupt, their creditors and counterparties are not the only one whose interests are going to be damaged, because creditors and counterparties of similar Internet financial institutions would also doubt the solvency of these institutions. This is a key component of financial contagion. According to the "notice on strengthening regulation of shadow banks and related issues" (i.e. "the 107th text") by the State Council, 2013, Internet financial institutions engaging in intermediation activities without financial licenses and unregulated are shadow banks, and the Chinese regulatory authorities should thus formulate regulatory measures for them.

We can refer to the practices of banks for the supervision of external credit risks. Under Basel II and III, banks need to provision for loss reserves and capital assets to remain as solvent "going concerns," even under the impact of credit risks. Among them, losses are divided into expected and unexpected categories. Expected losses are not real risks, rather they represent the mean of future possible losses and can be covered by asset reserves. Unexpected losses refer to fluctuations from the value of expected losses and are certainly real risks. They must therefore be covered by capital. Concrete manifestations include loan loss provision coverage, capital adequacy ratios, and other regulatory indicators.

For example, P2P platforms generally allocate part of their revenue to risk reserve pools (e.g. 2% of total loans) to offer capital protection for investors. Risk reserve pools are functionally consistent with bank reserves for asset losses. How do we determine the appropriate size of the risk reserve pool? The capital adequacy ratio for banks is 8%, calculated as the bank's capital divided by risk-weighted assets. The average risk weight is about 50%, thus bank capital assets must account for 4% of total assets. Correspondingly, the risk reserve pool of P2P platforms should be 4% of total loans. Of course this is just a simple calculation to illustrate the relevant regulatory logic. More specific standards for risk reserve pools should be determined according to risk measurement.

### 1.2 Regulation of liquidity risk externalities

Some Internet financial institutions undertake credit intermediation through maturity transformation and/or liquidity provision. This is exemplified in Yu'E Bao's "third party payment and money market fund" product, in which investors can always redeem their fund shares, but the duration of the fund may be longer. Such an Internet financial institution will bring about liquidity risk externalities. If they suffer from a liquidity crisis, creditors, and counterparties of similar Internet financial institutions will suspect the liquidity situations of their own, thus causing contagion. Moreover, when financial institutions suffer from a liquidity crisis, they usually recover their cash through the sale of assets to meet liquidity requirements. Large-scale asset sales in a short time (a "fire sale") will cause a decline in assets prices. Under a fair value accounting system, other financial institutions holding similar assets will also be harmed. In extreme cases, a vicious cycle of "asset prices fall, sales are triggered, asset prices fall further" may even appear.

We can also refer to bank practices for the supervision of external credit risks. Basel III introduces two regulatory liquidity indicators: the Liquidity Coverage Ratio (LCR) and Net Stable Funding Ratio (NSFR). Among them, the LCR has been implemented, requiring banks to set aside high-quality liquid asset reserves to deal with net cash outflows within thirty days in amounts estimated with liquidity pressure tests. The regulatory logic for the NSFR is similar.

For Yu'E Bao, we should estimate the volume of investor redemptions by taking stress tests in situations of large shopping seasons and money market volatility. We should then accordingly limit the position of money market funds to guarantee a sufficient proportion of high liquidity assets (this would of course sacrifice some profitability.)

## 2 Behavioral regulation

Behavioral regulation, including regulation of Internet financial infrastructure, financial institutions, and related behavior of participants, is aimed to make Internet finance transactions more secure, fair and effective. In a certain sense, behavioral regulation optimizes Internet finance operations.

We first emphasize regulation of the shareholders and managers of Internet financial institutions. The certification process should exclude those who are imprudent, lack requisite capacity, are dishonest, or have a poor record as shareholders and managers. On the other hand, once operations have started, regulators should strictly control transactions among shareholders, managers, and Internet financial institutions to prevent them from damaging the legal interests of Internet financial institutions and customers through means of asset expropriation and fraud, etc.

Second, behavioral regulation focuses on deposits, trusts, the trading and clearing system of funds, and securities related to Internet finance. On the one hand, we must improve the efficiency of Internet financial operations and control operation risks; on the other hand, platform-based Internet financial institutions must prevent misappropriation of client funds by clearly separating platform and customer's money, and taking measures against other potential malfeasance.

Third, Internet financial institutions are required to have a sound organizational structure, internal control system and risk management measures, business premise, IT infrastructure, and security arrangements.

## 3 Protection for consumers of financial products

Protection for consumers of financial products refers to protection of their interests in Internet finance transactions. Protection for consumers is closely related to behavioral regulation, but we list it separately because consumer protection is aimed to serve the "long tail" groups in financial services, while behavioral regulation is aimed at Internet financial institutions.

The background of consumer protection is the theory of consumer sovereignty and damages to interests of consumers from financial institutions under asymmetric information.[13] We must realize that interests of Internet financial institutions and consumers of financial institutions are not exactly consistent, so the sound development of Internet financial institutions cannot fully protect the interests of consumers.

In reality, due to the limitations of expertise, financial consumers cannot fully understand the costs, risks, and benefits of financial products as Internet financial institutions do. They are at a disadvantage and cannot afford the monitoring and due diligence required. The consequence is that Internet banking companies have the appearance of financial products and pricing information dominance, and they will consciously take advantage of the relatively weak information possessed by consumers. In economics, we call this the implicit fraud tendency (or quasi-fraudulent), but it is not necessarily equivalent to the legal definition of fraud. Moreover, there is a "lock-in effect" between Internet financial institutions and consumers of financial products, meaning that the fraud activities are generally subtle and cannot be eliminated by competition in the market (in another words, even if consumers have discovered that there is a fraud, they may not be able to choose another institution).

To protect consumers, we can use methods of self-regulation. However, if there are no appropriate, low-cost activist channels, or if financial institutions are too strong while the self-regulatory bodies lack effective measures, the aforementioned quasi-fraud activities are generally difficult to stop and punish. Many cannot even be disclosed. In this case, self-regulation will fail, and the government will take mandatory regulatory powers. The primary measures which must be taken are as follows:

First, we must require financial institutions to strengthen information disclosure. Terms and conditions of Internet financial products should be simple and clear, and the information must be transparent. Then, consumers of financial products can understand the relationship between risks and returns.

Second, we should give consumers their own advocacy channels. The first is a compensation mechanism. Just as those who buy electrical equipment are able to ask for compensation when encountering fake products, consumers of financial products should also be able to make a claim when they encounter situations of misleading or exaggerated marketing and fraud. The second requirement is an action mechanism. The original provisions of US law stipulated that class actions lawsuits are only available for stock investment. However, after this round of financial crisis, consumers are allowed to sue banks, insurance companies and securities companies if there is fraud, and sales agencies may also be forced to take joint responsibility. This mechanism can be used in consumer protection.

Third, we must be able to detect regulatory loopholes promptly by receiving complaints from consumers and taking swift action. At the moment, some quasi-fraudulent products are difficult to be discovered by regulators, but this must be improved.

Fourth, the Internet should be used as a platform to allow consumer complaints to be broadcast widely. When a consumer of financial products finds problems with products and publishes them online, other consumers can become "free riders." Protection thus expands to all consumers of the financial product. This is equivalent to the use of the principles of social networking and big data.

## SECTION 3: ORGANIZATIONAL REGULATION OF INTERNET FINANCE

Among the six major types of Internet finance listed in this book (see Chapter 1), P2P network loans and public financing loans most urgently require regulation. Other forms more or less already have an established regulatory framework. This section will focus on the regulation of P2P network and public financing loans.[14] Organizational regulation operates on the premise that similar institutions engage in similar businesses and produce similar risks. They should therefore be subject to similar regulation. However, there have been mixed results for this approach so far in Internet finance. In this case, we need to formulate regulatory measures from an organizational perspective according to specific businesses and risks of financial institutions. We must also coordinate supervision more effectively.

## 1 Current regulatory framework

Online banking, mobile banking, online securities companies, online insurance companies and online financial trading platforms (see Chapter 1) act as substitutes for traditional financial intermediaries such as banking, securities companies, insurance companies, and exchange institutions. The application of big data to credit assessment, network loans, securities investment, and actuarial services (see Chapters 7 and 12) mainly improves information processing chains in related financial activities. Although these Internet financial institutions are more transparent, have lower transaction costs, and allocate resources more efficiently, their financial capabilities and risk characteristics do not differ much from traditional financial intermediaries. Therefore, the regulatory frameworks for traditional financial intermediaries and markets are still applicable; we need only add regulation for information technology risks.[15] Relevant laws and regulatory frameworks for China are on the respective of the People's Bank of China, China Banking Regulatory Commission, China Securities Regulatory Commission, and China Insurance Regulatory Commission.

Second, China has established a comprehensive regulatory framework for mobile and third-party payments. The specific laws are too numerous to list here, but can be found on the website of the China Association for Payment and Clearing.

Third, protecting consumers' rights is the regulatory focus for online sales of financial products, which needs strict control over problems such as misleading buyers, exaggerated advertising and fraud. According to the CBRC's "Securities Investment Fund Sales Management" regulation, Article 35: "The fund publicity and promotion materials must be true, accurate, and consistent with its contract and prospectus. They may not contain false records, misleading statements, or major omissions; may not forecast the performance of the fund's securities investments; may not make a commitment of gain or loss; ....must avoid exaggerated or one-sided marketing; cannot use terms which imply that the investment is risk-free such as 'safe,' 'guarantee,' 'promise,' 'hedge,' 'secured,' 'high yield,' and 'no risk' or emphasize a time limit for collecting funds; and may not publish endorsements or recommendations from entities or individuals." The CBRC expressly forbids financial and trust products to promise yields or forecast returns. Marketers must repeatedly warn investors that investors are responsible for investment risk. In January 2014, the Zhejiang branch of the China Securities Regulatory Commission issued the first violation for Internet wealth management products. Shumi Fund (Fund123) was found to be using improper wordings like "maximum yield of 8.8%" in its materials and was required to correct them.

For cooperative products of "third party payment and money market funds" represented by Yu'E Bao, in view of the possible liquidity risks, we should refer to the US's regulatory measures for money market fund after the international financial crisis:

First, cooperative products of "third party payment and money market funds" are required to reveal risks to investors so as to avoid the incorrect assumption that there can be no loss in money market funds. Article 43 of "Measures for the Sale of Securities Investment Funds," stipulates that: the marketing and recommendation materials of a money market fund shall remind investors that their investment in the fund is not the same as a bank deposit, and the fund manager does not guarantee the profitability or minimum yield of the fund.

Second, cooperative products of "third party payments and money market fund" are required to fully disclose information of fund distribution (including security types, issuers, counterparties, amounts, duration, rating, and other dimensions) and redemption.[16]

Third, cooperative products of "third party payment and money market funds" should meet conditions like average duration, rating, and investment concentration to ensure that there are sufficient liquidity reserves to cope with large investor withdrawal under stress scenarios.

## 2 Regulation of P2P network loans

Theoretically, if the loans operate purely in a platform mode (neither bear credit risks associated with loans, nor conduct liquidity or maturity transformation), and investor risks are adequately diversified, a P2P platform itself does not require prudential supervision.

P2P network loans represented by Lending Club and Prosper have the following characteristics (see Chapter 8 for more details):

1  There is no direct credit and debt between investors and borrowers. Investors purchase bills (i.e. usufruct certificate) registered and issued by P2P platforms according to US Securities Law, while loans to borrowers are first offered by third-party banks, and then transferred to the P2P platform.
2  The relationship between bills and loans is like a mirror. Borrowers repay the loan principle and interest, and P2P platforms pay holders of corresponding bills in the same quantity.
3  If the borrower defaults on the loan, the holder of the corresponding notes will not receive payment from P2P platforms (i.e., P2P platforms do not offer guarantees for investors), but this does not constitute a breach of contract for the P2P platform itself.
4  Personal credit is highly developed (such as FICO credit score). P2P platforms do not have to carry out a much due diligence.

Under these circumstances, the regulation of the US Securities and Exchange Commission (SEC) focuses on information disclosure rather than the operation of P2P platforms. P2P platforms must constantly update information about each bill in issue instructions, including terms of corresponding loans and anonymous borrower information. We should pay particular attention to the flexibility of capital instruments provided by the US Securities Act; usufruct certificates are not only the core of P2P network operating framework, but also serve as the "starting point" for regulation of P2P network loans.

P2P network loans in China have some unique characteristics, including the following:

1 Online information is insufficient to meet credit assessment needs, therefore underlying due diligence investigation are generally carried out.
2 Investors are used to fixed payment schemes, so it is difficult to attract investors without this structure. P2P lending platforms generally allocate part of the revenue to risk reserve pools for the protection of investor principal.
3 The "professional lenders and debt transaction" model is aimed to better connect the financial needs of borrowers and demands for investor funds. It actively conducts business in large amounts rather than passively waiting for their match.
4 A large number of underlying promotional activities are carried out, so it is important to strengthen protection for consumers of financial products.

Overall, Chinese P2P network loans are more similar to private loans over the Internet. Currently, Chinese P2P network loans exceed other countries in terms of both the number of loan institutions and total loans issued. The "Chinese" process of P2P network loans has produced many unique business models, operating systems and potential risks. Some regulators have already expressed their concern with this growing business. The deputy governor of the People's Bank of China Liu Shiyu (also the group leader of "Development and Regulation of Internet Finance" in the State Council) stated on December 4, 2013 that central banks and financial regulatory authorities will cooperate with security organs and all levels of government to deal a "heavy blow" to violators in order to promote the healthy development of Internet finance. Illegal fund-raising and illegal deposits from the public are two red lines which cannot be crossed. Capital pools are thus unacceptable, especially for P2P platforms.

We believe that the regulation of P2P network loans should introduce the following measures, whose core idea is "open access, tracing activity, and post-issuance accountability."

### 2.1 Market access regulation

1 Establish basic entry criteria. Directors, supervisors, and senior executives should have certain financial knowledge and experience, which must be reviewed. P2P platforms should be subject to minimum operating conditions. For example, the IT infrastructure should safely store and manage customer information and transaction records, in addition to running a solid risk management system.
2 Establish the principle that "people who set and approve an institution are responsible for its supervision and risk evaluation." (this is also the spirit of the "*Notice on Issues of Strengthening the Regulation of Shadow Banking*" by the Chinese State Council, released in 2013.)

## 2.2 Operational regulation

P2P Platforms:

1   Should be limited to the financial information services business and establish directly corresponding relationships between investors and borrowers. However, P2P platforms cannot directly involve themselves in lending activities and are not allowed to go beyond a certain scope of operation even when technical means improve.
2   Must accept regulatory standards for non-performing assets and capital if they bear credit risks (such as through risk reserve pools). These are normally applied to banks to ensure that the risk reserve pool has adequate risk absorption capacity. The core objective of this requirement is to adapt the business scale of P2P platforms to their risk appetite, thus protecting the continued viability of the business.
3   Should strictly separate own funds and client funds. Client accounts should be managed by a third party fund (e.g. third-party payment agencies approved by the People's Bank of China). P2P platforms shall not appropriate client funds in any way.
4   Should know their customers and take effective means to identify and authenticate identities in order to prevent criminals from trading, fraud, finance scams, money laundering, and other illegal activities.
5   Should establish qualified investor systems to ensure that investors have sufficient financial knowledge, risk management capabilities, and financial capacity to invest in P2P network loans (e.g. investors must meet certain income and asset thresholds).
6   May not use false advertising.

## 2.3 Information regulation

P2P platforms should:

1   Save credit rating information (including application and credit assessment data), matching customer information from the lending and borrowing sides, repayment, and other transaction information.
2   Not tamper with lending information. If shareholders or staff of a P2P platform raise finance on their own platform, they need to truthfully disclose this to prevent conflicts of interest and related party transactions.
3   Fully fulfill the obligations to disclose risks to ensure that investors and borrowers clearly know their rights and obligations (including the loan amount, term, interest rates, service rates, repayment, etc.), and protect the customer's right to know and choose.
4   Truthfully disclose operating information, including corporate governance, platform operational model (such as assessment method, matching mechanism between lenders and borrowers, customer funds management system, and

guarantees), business data (such as transactions, the cumulative number of users, the average single loan amount, investor earnings, NPL indicators, etc.) for customer reference.

5   Protect the security of customers' information. They should not use this information for purposes not related to the lending or borrowing activity requested by the customer, and any such use should require customers' express authorization.

## 3 Public finance regulation

Because of current restrictions on the number of investors in the Securities Act (not more than 200), public finance is mainly confined to "charitable donation" of creative art projects, and does not extend to SMEs. They thus cannot set up platforms to link SMEs and capital markets. Doing so will not produce insurmountable financial risks. In the future, if China allows public finance to give investors returns in the form of equity financing, the securities regulatory framework will require some changes. In this regard, the US. JOBS Act is worth careful study. The bill is based on the US's developed capital markets and securities regulatory mechanisms. It allocates the rights and obligations between all participants in public finance in order to achieve a balance between investor protection and investment and financing promotion.

Finally, regulatory coordination for Internet finance is also an important issue. At present, China has adopted the framework of "separate operation, separate supervision" between banking, securities and insurance, while the regulatory authority is highly concentrated in the central government. This approach may not fit the Internet financial industry. For example, Internet sales of financial products, bank financial products, securities investment products, funds, insurance products, and trust products are sold at the same network platform. Yu'E Bao combines third-party payments and money market funds, and is also involved in broad money creation. In addition, large numbers of Internet financial institutions have emerged with small, scattered scale and a variety of business models that may defy the unified central financial regulation. Therefore, the allocation of responsibility for issuing licenses, daily supervision, and risk disposal of Internet financial institutions between different central government departments and between central and local governments is a very complicated question.

In August 2013, the State Council of China established the "financial supervisory coordination leading group" led by the People's Bank of China, whose responsibilities include the "coordination of cross-financial products and cross-marketing financial innovation." The Third Plenum document states a priority for "improving regulatory coordination mechanisms" and "defining the duties of financial regulation and responsibilities of risk disposal between central and local government." The Institutional framework for Internet financial supervision and coordination has thus already taken shape.

# Notes

1 Yan, Qingmin. 2013. "Research on Supervision over Information Technology Risks of Banking Financial Institutions," China Financial Publishing House.
2 For specific regulatory measures, interested readers can refer to the book written by Yan Qingmin mentioned on the previous page.
3 More discussion about "free-rider" issues can be found in Chapter 9.
4 Risks of losses caused by adverse changes of market prices.
5 Risks of losses caused by failure of debtors to fulfill debt obligations.
6 Risks of being unable to obtain sufficient funds timely or at reasonable cost to compensate for with asset growth or paying debts due.
7 Risks of losses caused by inadequate or failed internal processes, personnel and information technology systems, or external events.
8 Risks of negative evaluation for financial institutions from stakeholders caused by inappropriate management, administration, and other activities or external events.
9 Risks caused by financial institutions failing to comply with laws, regulations, regulatory requirements, rules made by self-regulatory organizations, or codes of conduct applicable to financial institutions in their business activities, and may be subject to legal sanctions or regulatory sanctions, material financial loss or loss of reputation.
10 This was discussed in more details in the section on IT risks.
11 Prudential regulation can be divided into two categories: microprudential supervision and macroprudential supervision. Microprudential supervision refers to regulation for safety and soundness of single Internet financial institutions; macroprudential supervision is aimed to the regulatory impact of the Internet for safety and soundness of the financial system and the real economy.
12 For more information about the banking regulatory measures involved, interested readers can refer to: Xie Ping, Zou Chuanwei. 2013. "Basic Theory of Macroprudential Supercision of Banks," China Financial Publishing House.
13 Xie Ping. 2010. "Consumer-Oriented Financial Regulation," New Century.
14 Chapter 5 discussed the currency regulation of Internet (especially Bitcoin).
15 China always has reservations about various of financial trading platforms hold by non-central-government institutions. In 2011, the State Council has made policies of "Decision on Straighten Out All Kinds of Trading Venues and Effectively Guard Against Financial Risks" (i.e. "No. 38").
16 Not necessarily the details of each position.

# 11 Internet exchange economy

The exchange economy is the economic concept that describes exchange after products are produced and find themselves in the hands of owners. The problem then becomes the allocation of these goods between different people. The exchange economy abstracts away the process of production and consumption from economic activities, and its foundation is the different resource endowments or division of work from person to person. It is essentially everywhere, from goods trade markets to art auctions. The Internet-based exchange economy is a concept we propose to highlight the influence that the Internet has on patterns of exchange, which represents both e-commerce and the sharing economy.

In this book on Internet finance, we discuss the Internet-based exchange economy in a single chapter because there is a close connection between two concepts. First, Internet finance can be regarded as a special case of the Internet-based exchange economy, and some perspectives in this chapter are actually complementary to Chapter 2. Second, Internet finance can quickly apply its innovations to the Internet-based economy, which also helps drive the development of Internet finance itself. We study the Internet-based exchange economy mainly by discussing some basic economic concepts in the context of the Internet: such as preference, utility, market, exchange, and resource allocation, which help us understand the mechanisms of Internet finance.

## SECTION 1: ANALYSIS OF THE SHARING ECONOMY

### 1 Definition of sharing economy

In this section, we focus on the sharing economy, another representation of the Internet-based exchange economy, since there has been a flood of literature on e-commerce. The sharing economy refers to an economy and social system where commodities, services, data, and intelligence can all be shared. Even though there are various forms of the sharing economy, one thing they have in common is the use of information technology. In the sharing economy, it is possible to share and reuse surplus or idle goods and services as long as market participants have the requisite information.

Rachel Botsman and Roo Rogers fully introduce the sharing economy in a 2010 monograph in which they classify the sharing economy into three types. The first is product service systems that focus on utilization of idle resources, which therefore pay more attention to resource accessibility than to ownership. Examples include Airbnb (an online platform for house rental) and ZipCar (an online platform for car rentals). The second is redistribution markets, which focus on the reuse or recycling of old commodities with environmental goals and a reduction in overconsumption. Examples include Freecycle, an online exchange platform of used commodities, and thredUP, an online exchange platform for used clothes. The third type is collaborative lifestyles, which focuses on trades between friends or neighbors with the abandonment of impersonal trade and the return to nature. Examples include TaskRabbit and Etsy, online distribution platforms for small tasks and self-produced goods. Additionally, R Botsman and R Rogers also consider P2P network loans and crowdfunding as a type of sharing economy.

## 2 Case analyses

We will primarily introduce four cases in this section, Airbnb, Zipcar, TaskRabbit, and BarterCard. From the logistics demands of exchanging, Airbnb, ZipCar, TaskRabbit just represent three different types. On Airbnb, houses (i.e. the exchangeable goods) cannot move. On TaskRabbit, little tasks can be delivered over the Internet. However, BarterCard represents bartering in the Internet era.

### 2.1 Airbnb

Airbnb, founded in 2008 and headquartered in San Francisco, focuses on home exchange. It offers an online service platform for homeowners to rent out unused living space (including the whole house, single rooms, beds, boats, and even tree rooms) over a short period to tourists who travel to cities in which the homeowners live. The business model of Airbnb is much more like the hotel industry than an ordinary housing rental intermediary. Moreover, landlords can benefit from otherwise idle residences through Airbnb while tenants can get a cheaper and more personalized housing experience than they can with hotels. By September 2013, users of Airbnb have come from 192 countries and 33,000 cities, with more than 500,000 total rentals.

Landlords and tenants need to register and create a profile on Airbnb.com. It encourages landlords and tenants to validate their identities and evaluate each other, so as to establish their reputations for the site. The identification process may be completed either by scanning ID cards or associating with websites such as Google, Facebook or LinkedIn. Additionally, landlords must supply basic information and photos of the housing. They can make the price flexible through negotiations with potential renters or reduce rates for longer leases.

Potential tenants search Airbnb by city, travel dates, and specific housing requirements (such as types of housing, prices, sizes, surroundings, facilities, and acceptance of pets.), Airbnb then returns the best match to potential tenants.

Airbnb also set a response rate index system for each supplier to measure their responsiveness to tenants' questions and booking applications.

### 2.2 ZipCar

ZipCar is an online car-sharing company founded in 2000 with business in cities and college campuses in the United States, Canada, Spain, Australia, and other countries.

ZipCar both manages and owns cars. People who want to rent cars must first become members of ZipCar, and then obtain membership cards with antenna chips embedded inside. As of July 2013, ZipCar has 10,000 cars and 810,000 members. Each ZipCar is equipped with Radio frequency identification (RDIF) transponders to connect membership cards. ZipCar's central system tracks car positions, members' rental periods and distances.

ZipCars are parked at special parking lots near residential areas. Members can reserve cars online or over the phone at any time in any participating city, either to use right now or up to one year later. After receiving the reservation, ZipCar offers car profiles and prices on the e-map for members to choose according to the distance between cars and members. Members obtain the cars from special parking lots. At the designated reservation time, membership cards will activate. This allows the member to enter and start the car. In order to protect members' privacy, ZipCar does not track cars during the rental period, but the car security systems remain activated. Members must return cars to the original parking places within the reservation time and lock them with their membership cards.

ZipCar's completely self-service rental model not only reduces labor costs, but also gives consumers more choice. The fee structure includes an application fee, an annual fee and a reservation fee, for each use. Cars are paid by the hour, including gas and insurance. Electronic bills are conveniently sent by ZipCar over the Internet and paid automatically.

### 2.3 TaskRabbit

TaskRabbit, founded in 2008, is an online post and claim tasks community with the concept of "Do More, Live More, Be More." The platform allows some users called TaskPosters to distribute small tasks to others called TaskRabbits. TaskRabbits are then paid after completing tasks from the TaskPosters. On the website of TaskRabbit, TaskPosters can solve many problems at low prices. On the other hand, TaskRabbits get opportunities to show their abilities. TaskRabbit's business is mainly located in big cities around the east and west coast of the US including Boston, Chicago, New York, San Francisco, Los Angeles. TaskPosters can post just about any task on TaskRabbit, including everything from installing furniture to dog walking. They just describe the tasks and set price caps based on the prices paid for similar ones.

The other side of the equation is the TaskRabbits, who offer help. They are mainly retirees or full-time parents who have the time and ability to fulfill tasks.

If one wants to become a TaskRabbit, he or she must apply on the website, including a video interview and criminal background check. Those who pass will be distributed to different communities depending on their location and skills.

TaskPosters select the most suitable TaskRabbit, depending on applicant skills, fee, and so on. After the tasks, TaskPosters evaluate the work of the TaskRabbit.

To motivate TaskRabbits, the website designs an incentive "point" mechanism. TaskRabbits are ranked by their points according to the accomplishment of tasks. The website displays a ranking list to show those TaskRabbits with the most points and best evaluations.

The website of TaskRabbit also provides a "Deliver Now" service. For example, if a TaskPoster needs someone to help buy some food or get clothes from the laundry immediately, the website will provide tools for the TaskPoster to help track the location of the TaskRabbit after a TaskRabbit claims the task. The website earns a 13%–30% referral commission for each completed task.

### *2.4 Bartercard*

Bartercard mainly operates in Australia, New Zealand, the United Kingdom, the United States, and Thailand. It currently has 55,000 cardholders throughout the world, who together trade in excess of US$60 million per month. Members earn Bartercard Trade Dollars for the goods and services they sell. This value is recorded electronically in the member's account database or goes toward repaying credit that the member may have used. Bartercard provides services like billing, matching, and providing monthly statements. It makes its money through service fees on transactions between its members.

There are three main reasons why barter exchanges like Bartercard can still thrive in modern society. First, the development of Internet technology expands the scope of barter and promotes the "double coincidence of wants" (see Section2 1.2 below). Second, Bartercard uses credit as a medium of exchange. In fact, the use of credit in barter has a very long history. For example, reciprocity among relatives and friends can be regarded as a form of barter. If Alice gives Bob a gift or does Bob a favor, Bob will not immediately pay Alice back with money. Instead, Bob will think of himself as owning Alice a favor. He will then give a gift to Alice or return Alice a favor afterward. Here the "favor" can be regarded as a kind of credit. Third, this Internet-based barter has a background in environmental protection and consumer culture.

## SECTION 2: PRINCIPLES OF THE INTERNET-BASED EXCHANGE ECONOMY

## 1 Basic framework

Combining e-commerce and the sharing economy, we consider three key elements of the Internet-based exchange economy: the exchanged commodity, the medium of exchange, and those who undertake the exchange.

### *1.1 Exchanged commodity*

The exchanged commodity is the commodity which is being exchanged. It can be one single item or multiple items. What is most important is the commodity's form of existence, its divisibility, the form of property transfer, and whether it is a public good or a private good.

#### *1.1.1 Form*

Exchanged commodities can be classified into four forms: The first is substantial and electronic goods, such as houses, cars, books, electronics, clothing, household goods, music, and videos. The second includes services such as health care, education, and tasks on TaskRabbit. The third is information, such as news and knowledge. The fourth includes rights, such as ownership, use rights, and operation rights. Because stocks, bonds, loans, and other financial instruments are in essence claims on an individual or an organization (see Chapter 1), they also count as rights.

#### *1.1.2 Divisibility*

According to the divisibility concept, exchanged commodities fall into two categories. The first is indivisible commodities, which must be exchanged as a whole. When merchandise is being exchanged, it is usually indivisible. The other type is composed of divisible commodities. When financial resources are being exchanged, they can be divided into a number of small and homogeneous shares. For example, the sale of financial products on the Internet (Chapter 3), notes of P2P loans (Chapter 8), and equities in crowdfunding (Chapter 9).

##### 1.1.2.1 FORM OF PROPERTY TRANSFER

The two main forms of property transfer are exchanges which are accompanied by the transfer of ownership, and exchanges in which rights to use or to operate are transferred but the ownership remains the same. In the sharing economy, most exchanged commodities belong to this category. For example, landlords on Airbnb own the houses and ZipCar owns the cars. Tenants on Airbnb and ZipCar members have only temporary access to the houses or the cars.

##### 1.1.2.2 PUBLIC OR PRIVATE GOODS

Public and private goods are two opposing concepts in economics. In simple terms, public goods can be used by a group of people, while private goods can only be used by one person at any time. A person can only consume items. To distinguish these two more rigorously, we need to introduce two concepts: exclusivity and rivalry. A good is called exclusive if it is possible to prevent other people from having access to it. A good is rivalrous if consumption by one consumer prevents simultaneous consumption by other consumers.

Thus, exchanged commodities include public goods that are both non-exclusive and non-rivalrous, such as national defense, television and radio broadcasting, and clean air. Public goods rarely become exchanged commodities. They also include private goods that are both exclusive and rivalrous. Most exchange commodities are private goods, such as commodities, financial resources, and health care. Additionally, many exchanged commodities fall between public goods and private goods. For example, some music, videos, information, educational resources, and so forth on the Internet are exclusive but non-rivalrous. These are called "club goods."

## 1.2 Medium of exchange

Most Internet-based economies need to use currency as the medium of exchange. Both fiat money issued by central banks and Internet currency may serve this function (see Chapter 5). This is, however, not always true. Some Internet-based economies reject this and use barter, thus taking up one of the earliest, pre-fiat money human means of exchange. This can be problematic and even break down unless both parties possess something the other desires, the so-called "double coincidence of wants."

Some online companies have used innovative approaches to overcome these issues. For example, websites such as YouTube offer free digital goods but insert advertisements into them. Each party has something the other wants, in this case digital goods and the attention of the viewer. These transactions flow effortlessly, with no exchange of money, by involving a third-party advertiser that provides funds.

## 1.3 Parties to the exchange

An Exchange requires a supplier and a consumer and can be classified into three types based on the quantity of each:

### 1.3.1 One-to-one

One-to-one means there is only one supplier and one demander. This type rarely occurs in the Internet exchange economy.

### 1.3.2 One-to-many

In this type, there can be either one supplier and many demanders or vice versa. This is a more common form of Internet-based exchange than one-to-one, but is less common than many-to-many.

### 1.3.3 Many-to-many

Most Internet-based economies thrive in this form. There are many suppliers and demanders interacting together in a market that can shift into one-to-many transactions. A P2P lending platform clearly illustrates this phenomenon. Multiple investors face multiple potential investment projects and are thus clearly many-to-many. From the perspective of a single project, it is one-to-many, with one project and many funders. From that of an individual investor, it is a many-to-one with one funder and many projects.

Different types of exchanges have very different modes of resource allocation. One-to-one functions like negotiation; one-to-many is similar to an auction; and for many-to-many, there are many different modes, such as the Edgeworth Box and stable matching. These forms involve very complex economic problems that we discussed in detail in a later section.

### 1.4 Three pillars of the Internet-based exchange economy

The Internet-based exchange economy is incredibly diverse. There are many different combinations of the exchanged commodity, the medium of exchange, and actors who undertake the exchange. Just like Internet finance, we believe this unique economy can be understood as standing on three pillars.

The first pillar is logistics and payment. This is the physical process of completing the exchange. The second pillar is information processing, including identification and selection of exchanged commodities (types and amounts) and the other participants. The third pillar is the allocation of resources. The core issue is to design a mechanism that is able to match supply and demand efficiently based on a comprehensive consideration of the participants' endowments, preferences, and utility.

## 2 Logistics and payment[1]

Logistics is to the Internet-based exchange economy as payment is to the Internet finance. Exchanged commodities in different forms have different logistical requirements. Some Internet-based exchange economies have little or non-existent logistic requirements. Electronic products, information, and financial products are transferred, paid for, and consumed online. Traditional logistics are unnecessary.

When services and rights are being exchanged, though the final consumption is physical, the logistics are mobile and are usually embedded in the exchange process. For example, the houses on Airbnb cannot be moved, but the arrangements can be done from anywhere with an Internet connection. These core processes of exchange are all online, so logistics costs are minimal.

However, in cases in which exchanged commodities are physical goods, logistics play a key role in delivery and cost. Chinese E–commerce is a perfect example. Alibaba has developed a symbiotic relationship with the logistics industry due to its massive employment of logistics resources to deliver products ordered on its sites. In 2013, Alibaba co-founded "CaiNiao," or Rookie Logistics, to create a massive open social logistics platform in five to eight years that can reach any place in China within 24 hours. In order to ensure its delivery speed and consumer experience, Jingdong Mall (JD.com) chose to build a logistics network itself. Another example is Amazon. Amazon started testing delivery with drones in late 2013. These drones can deliver packages up to 2.3 kilograms (86% of Amazon's packages would qualify) in half an hour door-to-door. These examples show how closely the e-commerce and logistics industry are connected. Logistics give rise to relatively large transaction costs for e-commerce, but new technology has the potential to significantly reduce these costs.

One of these new technologies is intelligent logistics, which uses sensor technologies like RDIF to track the location of every piece of merchandise in real time, feeding back information that includes aspects of the goods' location and status. Intelligent logistics reduce transaction costs by optimizing the geographical distribution of warehouses so as to better match customer needs. It can also save costs by optimizing warehouse management, minimizing inventory, using less capital, and increasing inbound, storage, and outbound efficiency. Optimization of the transportation routes with these methods can also reduce transportation time and cost.

The second technology is 3D printing, which allows for a new type of "additive" rather than "subtractive" manufacturing. It prints objects layer by layer using digital files as the model and powdered metal or plastic as the material. 3D printing digitalizes physical commodities, which allows the creation of more personalized and customized products. E-commerce of the future will allow consumers to purchase the plans for products, and then print them out nearby or even at home. 3D printing will make exchange of physical goods become like the exchange of electronic goods today. It can be carried out on the Internet, significantly reducing or even eliminating the demand for logistics. We can see that Intelligent logistics and 3D printing together will both lower costs and bring the exchange economy of physical commodities increasingly online.

## 3 Information processing

Just as we saw in Internet finance, big data is the core information processing technology in the Internet-based exchange economy. Since data usage makes no fundamental distinction between finance and real economy, both can use the same data analysis tools.

The Internet-based exchange economy generates large amounts of information. One key type of information involves preference and utility, two fundamental economic concepts. Preference shows how much consumers enjoy goods, mainly reflecting consumer priority when selecting among several goods. Utility is a quantification of preference that measures how consumption satisfies consumer needs and wants. We will illustrate these two concepts with some examples.

Investors allocate their funds, subject to a budget constraint, among various financial products, such as crowdfunding, P2P network loans, or traditional financial products. Their preferences are, however, not uniform For example, young people tend to select stocks due to their high expected return while the old prefer bonds because of the increased stability of payment and lower volatility. We can express their preferences with utility functions that describe the risk-return characteristics of financial products. The most important parameter is investor risk aversion.

In e-commerce, every consumer can choose between many goods. For instance, if one wants to buy a book on Internet finance online, he/she will make the purchasing decision based on the contents, authors, price, reviews, and many other factors. Websites like Amazon and Dangdang use browsing and purchasing histories to predict consumer preferences, according to which they recommend books (see Chapter 6).

We can similarly understand decision making in sharing economy. For example, Airbnb helps tenants and landlords select each other according to certain preferences. ZipCar lets members select cars according to distance, price, and model. The ultimate goal of information processing is to discover preference and increase the utility of exchanges. The essential problem is information asymmetry.[2] For instance, the realized return for financial products is not knowable ex-ante. Book customers are not usually able to read the whole book themselves before purchase. Property owners on Airbnb cannot be sure how well prospective tenants will take care of their property. Such examples abound in all exchanges, online and off, meaning that virtually all decisions are made in the presence of asymmetric information. Mitigating asymmetric information can thus reduce non-beneficial exchanges and provide more efficient resource allocations.

## 4 Resource allocation

The core of resource allocation is to increase utility by matching demand and supply. First, it is important to design a matching mechanism based on the set of transactors. Generally, more transactors lead to a more efficient allocation of resources through a diversification of supply and demand. Following the logic outlined in Chapter 2, we can prove that the set of possible exchanges will increase as transaction cost and/or information asymmetry decline. For instance, strangers are able to lend to each other through P2P network loans because of the innovative credit evaluation system. It is possible now to stay in strangers' homes because of the trust we place in the evaluation system provided by Airbnb. These examples show that the Internet exchange economy expands the range of possible transactions by making it possible to accept recommendations from people other than friends and family. Below we introduce four representative supply and demand matching mechanisms.

### 4.1 Auction[3]

The auction is one of the oldest market mechanisms. Auctions differ based on two main parameters: open- vs. sealed-bid and ascending vs. descending price. In a sealed bid auction, bidders submit their prices simultaneously without knowledge of others' bid amounts. In an open auction, bidders bid directly against each other until the final sale price is reached with the highest bid. In ascending-price auctions, the auctioneer continues raising the price until the highest bid emerges and the sale concludes. In a descending-price auction, the auctioneer begins with a high asking price. This price is then lowered until a participant is willing to accept the auctioneer's price.

There are four primary forms of auction used today. English auctions, the most common form of auction, are open ascending-price auctions. Companies such as eBay use this form. Dutch auctions are open, descending-price auctions. TaskRabbit takes this form, as TaskPosters select the lowest price among TaskRabbits with the same skills. In a first-price sealed auction, all bidders simultaneously submit sealed bids. The highest bidder wins and pays the price they submitted. A second-price sealed or "Vickery auction" is identical to the first-price sealed auction except that the winning bidder needs to pay the second highest bid.

Bidders offer prices based on their valuation of the good, which in turn is a function of the utility they expect to gain from its ownership. If a bidder knows his/her expected value, the auction is termed "private value." In this case, a bidder is not able to accurately know or influence others' valuations. Most Internet-based exchange auctions are in the private value category. Another kind of auction is common value auction, which means that the item's value is the same to all the bidders, but the bidders are unsure of the value. For example, in an offshore oil-license auction, bidders have different valuations based on their exploration, but no matter who the winner is, the oil license has the same market value because oil reserves are certain.

### 4.2 Edgeworth box[4]

The Edgeworth Box applies to multiple, separable, many-to-many exchanges, such as Bartercard. Each transactor has an endowment of certain consumer goods. Each exchanger has individual preference for the consumption group, and he only cares about his own utility. Every exchanger can choose to consume by himself or volunteer to exchange with others. This kind of trade is the only way to reallocate the initial resource endowment. The Edgeworth box results correspond to a Pareto efficient equilibrium resource allocation.[5]

We generally develop an Edgeworth box with two exchangers and two types of exchange. Here we use "A" and "B" to denote exchangers and "x" and "y" to denote two items for exchange. At first, A's initial endowment is $(\omega_A^x, \omega_A^y)$,[6] and B's initial endowment is $(\omega_B^x, \omega_B^y)$. Thus, their total endowment is $(\omega_A^x + \omega_B^x, \omega_A^y + \omega_B^y)$, which is marked with a blue star in Figure 11.1.

In Figure 11.1, the horizontal axis represents the quantity of x with length of $\omega_A^x + \omega_B^x$, while the vertical axis represents y with length of $\omega_A^y + \omega_B^y$. Exchanger A's original state is on the lower left of the box, from which the distance upward shows his endowment or consumption of "x." Exchanger B's original state is on the top right corner, from which the distance downward represents his endowment or consumption of y. The beauty of the Edgeworth box is that no matter how they exchange, the total consumption of two exchanged items equals their total endowment $(\omega_A^x + \omega_B^x, \omega_A^y + \omega_B^y)$, therefore the exchange between the two people can always be reflected by points in Edgeworth box.

In an Edgeworth box, individual utility is depicted with indifference curves. Under the classical assumption of utility in economics, indifference curves are

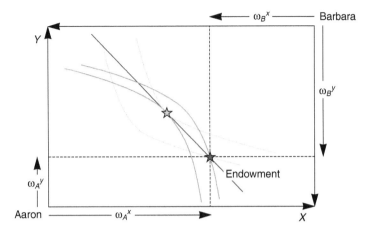

*Figure 11.1* Edgeworth box.[7]

convex to the origin. The utility declines when indifference curves get further away from the origin. Our two exchangers correspond to two sets of indifference curves.

The equilibrium resource allocation is marked with a red star in the Figure 11.1. Three lines are tangent at this point: the line from the red-star point to the initial endowment point (blue line in Figure 11.1), A's indifference curve and B's indifference curve. It is Pareto efficient because A and B's indifference curves are tangential at this location. At any place other than this point, possible exchanges lower either A's utility or B's utility or both. Therefore, each exchanger achieves maximum utility. The slope of the blue line also shows the equilibrium price for the two items.

### 4.3 Stable matching

Stable matching applies to the Internet-based exchange economy in the context of two-way choices. For example, at Airbnb.com, landlords and tenants both make choices. Now we explain the concept and mechanism of stable matching through the lens of Airbnb.

We assume that the quantity of landlords and tenants are the same. Every landlord can sort tenants according to his preference and vice versa. To simplify the problem, let us suppose that landlords believe it is better to rent out their houses rather than leave them idle, no matter to whom they rent. Also, tenants believe it is better for them to have a room to rent than no place to live, no matter who provides the room.

There is then a one-to-one correspondence between landlords and tenants. This kind of correspondence is called matching. Stable matching means that both the landlords and the tenants believe that the combinations between them are the best under the present conditions, and are thus Pareto efficient.

Stable matching exists all the time as long as certain assumptions are made. The most famous matching mechanism is the deferred acceptance algorithm, as shown in the following steps:

1 Each tenant applies to his favorite landlord for a reservation.
2 Each landlord examines the reservations he has received. Some may receive more than one application while some may receive none.
3 Those landlords who have received reservations select their favorite tenants and reject others. These landlords then no longer accept reservation applications.
4 The rejected tenants apply to their second-choice landlords for reservations according to their own preferences.
5 Steps 2–4 repeat until all landlords and tenants find a match.

In the deferred acceptance algorithm, the power of the initial choice first influences both the final matching results and the welfare effects.

### 4.4 Markowitz mean-variance model[8]

Investors build portfolios by allocating funds between financial products to maximize their expected utility. The most important asset allocation model is the Markowitz mean-variance model, in which fund allocation depends on the expected rate of return and volatility. It assumes investors' utility functions are quadratic, or the rates of return for financial products are normally distributed.

Suppose there are n types of financial products $A_1, A_2, \ldots, A_n$ (excluding risk-free assets). Within the given investment horizon, the rate of return of $A_i$ has random variance $r_i$. The Markowitz mean-variance model solves the following problem: if the expected rate of return of portfolio $\bar{\mu}$ is given, find the weight of each financial product $w = (w_1, w_2, \ldots, w_n)'$ to minimum the variance of the rate of return $\sigma_w^2$.

Assume that the rate of return and the covariance of financial products are $\mu = (\mu_1, \mu_2, \ldots, \mu_n)'$, $\Sigma = (\sigma_{ij})_{i,j=1,2,\ldots,n}$, in which $\mu_i = E(r_i)$, $\sigma_{ij} = \mathrm{cov}(r_i, r_j)$. The optimization problem becomes:

$$\min_{w} \quad \sigma_w^2 = w'\Sigma w = \sum_{i,j=1}^{n} \sigma_{ij} w_i w_j$$

$$s.t. \quad w'e = \sum_{i=1}^{n} w_i = 1, w'\mu = \sum_{i=1}^{n} w_i \mu_i = \bar{\mu}$$

(11.1)

in which $e = (1,1,\ldots,1)'$.

We can prove that if the expected rates of return for n kinds of financial products $\mu_i$ are all different, then the covariance matrix $\Sigma$ is positive definite. If the expected rate of return of portfolio $\bar{\mu}$ is given, then Equation (11.1) has a unique solution:

$$\bar{w} = \Sigma^{-1}(\mu, e) A^{-1} \begin{pmatrix} \bar{\mu} \\ 1 \end{pmatrix}$$

(11.2)

in which $A = \left(\mu, e\right)' \Sigma^{-1} \left(\mu, e\right)$.

Denote $A = \begin{pmatrix} a & b \\ b & c \end{pmatrix} = \begin{pmatrix} \mu' \Sigma^{-1} \mu & e' \Sigma^{-1} \mu \\ e' \Sigma^{-1} \mu & e' \Sigma^{-1} e \end{pmatrix}$, then the expected rate of

return of the portfolio $\overline{\mu}$ and the minimum variance $\overline{\sigma}^2$ satisfy:

$$\overline{\sigma}^2 = \frac{a - 2b\overline{\mu} + c\overline{\mu}^2}{ac - b^2} \tag{11.3}$$

With risk on the horizontal axis and the rate of return on the vertical axis, we draw the graph of $\overline{\sigma}$ and $\overline{\mu}$ (Figure 11.2) to obtain the portfolio frontier, here expressed by the right branch of the hyperbola. The hyperbola's apex corresponds to the minimum variance portfolio $w_G = \dfrac{\Sigma^{-1} e}{e^T \Sigma^{-1} e}$, whose expected rate of return is $\mu_G = \dfrac{e^T \Sigma^{-1} \mu}{e^T \Sigma^{-1} e}$, and whose standard deviation is $\sigma_G = \dfrac{1}{\sqrt{e^T \Sigma^{-1} e}}$. The upper half of the hyperbola is called the efficient frontier, and each point on it constitutes a portfolio, which is called an efficient portfolio. The bottom half of the hyperbola is the inefficient frontier.

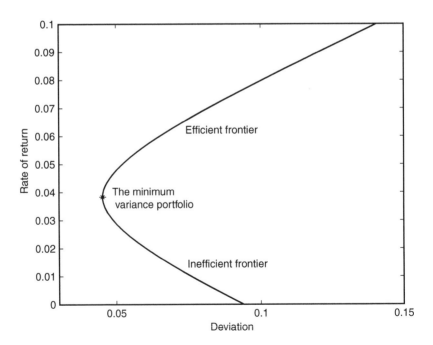

*Figure 11.2* Markowitz mean-variance model.[9]

## SECTION 3: THE RELATIONSHIP BETWEEN THE INTERNET-BASED EXCHANGE ECONOMY AND INTERNET FINANCE

### 1 Internet finance: a special case

Internet finance is in essence the exchange of financial resources between individuals or organizations. It is within the realm of the exchange economy because it does not refer to specific production and consumption processes. The Internet-based exchange economy and Internet finance reflect the impact of the Internet on real economic and financial activities, particularly in three areas: physical exchange (logistics and payment), the processing of exchange-relevant information, and resource allocation mechanisms. Thus, we can apply the same analytical framework to both the Internet-based exchange economy and Internet finance.

Internet finance has unique characteristics. One of them is that the financial resources are claims on an individual or an organization and thus do not require any attached physical objects or logistics. Second, it can be broken down into small, homogeneous shares. Third, the transfer of ownership usually accompanies the exchange. Last, financial resources are private goods.

It is not an exaggeration to say that the impact of the Internet is all encompassing. It has already disrupted telecommunications, journalism, book publishing, broadcasting, music, and retail businesses. In the future, we may see its disruptive impact on more industries such as cinema, education, and advertising. These complex phenomena share the logic inherent to the Internet-based exchange economy.

### 2 Internet finance derives from the Internet-based exchange economy

E-commerce exemplifies the derivation of Internet finance. For example, in order to promote online shopping and improve the consumer experience, Alibaba developed Alipay to solve the payments problem (see Chapter 4), and then opened up a microfinance business with the data it accumulated online (see Chapter 7). It finally developed Yu'E Bao (see Chapter 3) to make use of Alipay account balances and meet consumers' financial needs. Yu'E Bao is successful because it connects financial products and payment instruments, improving capital efficiency without affecting payment efficiency. Alibaba's financial innovation shows that the real economy is the foundation of Internet finance. Without the real economy, Internet finance is like a fish out of water.

Internet finance has even more potential as the Internet-based exchange economy develops. Internet finance can then promote the Internet-based exchange economy and form a virtuous circle through deep integration.

### 3 The Internet-based exchange economy serves Internet finance

Credit collection and Internet lending based on big data (see Chapter 7) use the records of the Internet-based exchange economy (such as e-commerce) to assess creditworthiness. The core here is the application of behavioral data.

Traditional credit quality assessment is based on financial statement analysis, mainly focusing on the gearing ratio, debt-to-income ratio, ratio of interest income, and a few other indicators. This assumes that a default is triggered by insolvency, income insufficient to repay the debt, and other situations. The basis of this approach is that credit risks have a clearly identified causal chain.

However, in many real cases, the causal chain of credit risks is not so clear (especially ex-ante). Also, in a rapidly changing market, causal analysis is not conducive to capturing changes in credit risks. More importantly, financial statements only reflect a small portion of an individual or an organization's information, while a large amount of their behavioral information on the Internet remains unused. Sometimes it is hard to see if there is a causal relationship between behavioral information and credit risks. The key of behavioral information application is to predict, and these predictions are based on correlation, not causation (see Chapter 6). Therefore, as long as the behavioral information on credit risks has predictive abilities, the behavioral information is certainly valuable to the pragmatic evaluator.

In credit risk management, analysis methods based on causality are called structural approaches, represented by the Merton model. Analysis methods based on behavioral information are called simple approaches, such as the credit default swap (CDS) model, the Logit model, the Bayesian Criterion (see Chapter 7), and the default density model (introduced in Chapter 12). Simple approaches turn out to be superior to structured approaches when applied in practice, and are thus becoming more mainstream.[10]

## Notes

1 Since Chapter 4 is devoted to payments, so we will not repeat the discussions here.
2 Information asymmetry typically arises when the buyer is unable to obtain all relevant information about the product he is buying, which can lead to situations in which the seller takes advantage of this informational advantage.
3 Data sources: (a) Varian, Hal R. 2009. "Intermediate Microeconomics: A Modern Approach," 8th ed., W. W. Norton & Company, Inc.; (b) Wolfstetter, Elmar. 1999. "Topics in Microeconomics: Industrial Organization, Auctions and Incentives," Cambridge University Press.
4 Data sources: (a) Ping, Xinqiao. 2001. "Eighteen Lessons of Microeconomics," Peking University Press. (b) Varian, Hal R. 2009. "Intermediate Microeconomics: A Modern Approach," 8th ed., W. W. Norton & Company, Inc.
5 Pareto optimality implies a state in which no party can be made better off without making another worse off.
6 A has x of $\omega_A^x$ unit and y of $\omega_A^y$ unit.
7 The graph is selected from a public lecture of Hal R. Varian.
8 Huang, Chi-fu, and Robert H. Litzenberger. 1988. "Foundations for Financial Economics," Elsevier Science Publishing Co., Inc.
9 Figures in the graph are for demonstration purposes only.
10 See Duffie, Darrell, and Kenneth Singleton. 2003. "Credit Risk: Pricing, Measurement, and Management," Princeton University Press.

# 12 Issues requiring further research

In this book, we have already outlined the principles and basic types of Internet finance. However, much of Internet finance is still open. There are many undeveloped areas and unanswered questions that deserve thorough discussion. In this chapter, we focus on big data's utilization in two areas: securities investment and actuarial science. We both share our understanding on these two questions and welcome interested readers to undertake further research that could lead to future breakthroughs.

## SECTION 1: UTILIZING BIG DATA FOR SECURITIES INVESTMENT

Utilizing big data in securities investment has always been a sensitive topic. If the securities market is fully functional, then the price should fully reflect all information available to investors. In this case, choosing any security would only yield a gain equal to the investment risk. In reality, however, investors seeking excess returns (alpha), tend to perform active portfolio management and diverge from the benchmark index. This indicates that investors do not believe the securities market is fully efficient. Investors create value by conducting market studies to form distinctive judgments and decisions. Insider information, however, is not part of big data. Utilizing big data in securities investment is very different from insider trading.

We will start by introducing two famous models in active portfolio management—the Black–Litterman model and the fundamental law of active management to show how information affects decision-making. Afterwards, we will discuss how big data plays an important role in securities investment.

## 1 The Black–Litterman model

The Black–Litterman model was first proposed in 1992 by Fisher Black and Robert Litterman. Fisher Black was renowned for his Black—Scholes formula, while Robert Litterman was working at Goldman Sachs Asset Management.

The Black–Litterman model improved on several shortcomings of the Markowitz mean-variance model (See Chapter 11). The Markowitz mean-variance model has three main weaknesses: the portfolio is often non-intuitive or highly concentrated, the model is very sensitive to the change of variable inputs, and the parameter estimation error is often magnified (estimation error maximization). The Black–Litterman model uses a Bayesian method to combine the market's equilibrium return on assets (ROA) and the investors' subject view of the ROA. The resulting estimation of the ROA is used to construct the optimal portfolio. The Black–Litterman model is now increasingly accepted on Wall Street.

## 1.1 Reverse optimization

In the Black–Litterman model, the optimal portfolio is the result of the following optimization problem[1].

$$\max_{w} w'\mu - \lambda w'\Sigma w/2 \tag{12.1}$$

With $w$ being the weight of the assets, $\mu$ being the expected excess return on assets over the risk-free rate, $\Sigma$ being the covariance matrix of the excess return, $\lambda$ being the coefficient of absolute risk aversion.

Without any constraints, when solving for $w$, we obtain:

$$w = \frac{1}{\lambda}\Sigma^{-1}\mu \tag{12.2}$$

The Black–Litterman model considers the opposite scenario: given the weight of each asset in the portfolio, what would be the expected excess return on assets? The solution to this reverse optimization problem is:

$$\mu = \lambda\Sigma w \tag{12.3}$$

The Black–Litterman model inherited Fischer Black's view on universal hedging. $w_{mkt}$ marks the weight of the portfolio where each asset is weighted according to its market capitalization (The Market Benchmark Index). The Black–Litterman model states that the reverse optimization problem has a special connotation, that the resulting expectation of the excess return on assets can clear the market. This is called the implied excess equilibrium return.

$$\Pi = \lambda\Sigma w_{mkt} \tag{12.4}$$

The implied excess equilibrium return $\Pi$ is the starting point of the Black–Litterman model.

## 1.2 Investor views

Investors often form distinctive views on the amount of a particular asset's excess return. These views are different from the implied excess equilibrium return. In the

Black–Litterman model, these views are categorized into the absolute view and relative view. Confidence levels are used to measure them: a 100% confidence level indicates that the investor is absolutely certain, while a 0% confidence level indicates that the investor rejects the view completely. The Black–Litterman model assumes that the views are independent of each other.

The absolute view involves judgment on the ROA of a single asset, for example:

– **View 1:** The excess return on the housing market is 0.5% (25% confidence level). The relative view, on the other hand, involves comparing the ROA of multiple assets, for example:
– **View 2:** The ROA of the global stock market will be 2% higher than that of the global bond market (65% confidence level).
– **View 3:** The ROA of the Chinese stock market will be 3.5% higher than that of the other emerging markets (50% confidence level).

A key question to the Black–Litterman model is: how do you quantify the investors' views? We will use the three views mentioned above as examples. Assuming there are nine types of assets, as shown in Table 12.1[2]:

Set the excess return of the nine assets as $r = \left( r_C, r_{US}, r_{DE}, r_{EE}, r_{GFI}, r_{HY}, r_{PE}, r_{RE}, r_{HF} \right)'$.

View 1 only involves Real Estate (RE) and can be expressed as $r_{RE} = 0.5\% + \varepsilon_1$, where $\varepsilon_1$ follows a normal distribution $N(0, \omega_1)$, which reflects the uncertainty of the view. A greater value of $\omega_1$ translates to a higher level of uncertainty (lower confidence level). Next, we will discuss the method of setting the value of $\omega_1$ relative to the confidence level.

View 2 involves the global stock market, which includes Chinese stocks (C), US stocks (US), stocks of developed (Non-US) economies (DE), and stocks of

Table 12.1 Asset types and symbols

| Asset type | Symbol |
|---|---|
| Chinese stocks | C |
| US stocks | US |
| Stocks of developed (Non-US) economies | DE |
| Stocks of emerging (Non-Chinese) economies | EE |
| Global fixed income | GFI |
| High yield | HY |
| Private equity | PE |
| Real estates | RE |
| Hedge fund | HF |

emerging (Non-Chinese) economies (EE). It also involves the global bond market, which includes global fixed income (GFI) and high yield (HY).

As shown by View 2, relative views always have two elements: a set of outperforming assets and a set of underperforming assets. The relative view implies the existence of a portfolio with both a long and short side—going long outperforming assets and shorting underperforming assets. There is no guidebook when it comes to the asset allocation, so we can allocate them evenly or according to their market cap. We will choose the former in this example.

View 2 can be expressed by the following equation: $0.25r_C + 0.25r_{US} + 0.25r_{DE} + 0.25r_{EE} - 0.5r_{GFI} - 0.5r_{HY} = 2\% + \varepsilon_2$, where $\varepsilon_2$ follows a normal distribution $N(0, \omega_2)$. Similarly, view 3 can be expressed as $r_C - r_{EE} = 3.5\% + \varepsilon_3$, where $\varepsilon_3$ follows the normal distribution $N(0, \omega_3)$. The implication of $\omega_2$ and $\omega_3$ are the same as before.

We introduce the following symbols:

$$p_1 = (0,0,0,0,0,0,0,1,0), q_1 = 0.5\%$$

$$p_2 = (0.25,0.25,0.25,0.25,-0.5,-0.5,0,0,0), q_2 = 2\%$$

$$p_3 = (1,0,0,-1,0,0,0,0,0), q_3 = 3.5\%$$

$$P = \begin{pmatrix} p_1 \\ p_2 \\ p_3 \end{pmatrix}, Q = \begin{pmatrix} q_1 \\ q_2 \\ q_3 \end{pmatrix}, \varepsilon = \begin{pmatrix} \varepsilon_1 \\ \varepsilon_2 \\ \varepsilon_3 \end{pmatrix}, \Omega = \begin{pmatrix} \omega_1 & 0 & 0 \\ 0 & \omega_2 & 0 \\ 0 & 0 & \omega_3 \end{pmatrix}$$

Then, views 1–3 can be expressed as the following:
$$P \cdot r = Q + \varepsilon, \text{ where } \varepsilon \text{ follows the normal distribution } N(0, \Omega). \qquad (12.5)$$

Equation (12.5) has a general connotation. Assuming there are $n$ types of assets and $m$ mutually independent views, then $P$ is the matrix created by $m \times n$, $Q$ is the magnitude of $m \times 1$ and $\Omega$ is the diagonal matrix created by $m \times m$. We mark row $k$ of $P$ as $p_k$, element number $k$ of $Q$ as $q_k$, element number $k$ on the diagonal $\Omega$ as $\omega_k$, as a result, view $k$ can be expressed as:
$$p_k \cdot r = q_k + \varepsilon_k, \varepsilon_k \text{ follows the normal distribution } N(0, \omega_k)$$
Where $p_k \cdot r$ can be viewed as a portfolio, $q_k + \varepsilon_k$ is the investor's view on the excess return of the portfolio, and $\omega_k$ reflects the uncertainty of the view.

### 1.3 The Bayesian method

Under the equilibrium approach of the Black–Litterman model, the excess return $r$ follows the normal distribution $N(\Pi, \tau\Sigma)$, where $\Pi$, the implied excess equilibrium return, is provided by Equation (12.4). $\tau$ is a scaling factor. The reason we introduce $\tau$ is that the covariance matrix of the excess return $\Sigma$ is usually estimated with historical data. Any covariance matrix with a value higher than the excess return under market equilibrium must be adjusted using $\tau$. The distribution $N(\Pi, \tau\Sigma)$ is equivalent to the prior distribution.

The investor views essentially create $m$ portfolios $P \cdot r$, while these portfolios follow a normal distribution $N(Q,\Omega)$, and are equivalent to new information.

Using the Bayesian method, we can calculate the posterior distribution of the excess return.

$$r \sim N\left(\left[(\tau\Sigma)^{-1} + P'^{T}\Omega^{-1}P\right]^{-1}\left[(\tau\Sigma)^{-1}\Pi + P'\Omega^{-1}Q\right], \left[(\tau\Sigma)^{-1} + P'\Omega^{-1}P\right]^{-1}\right) \quad (12.6)$$

### 1.4 Asset allocation

According to Equations (12.1) and (12.6), the asset allocation given by the Black–Litterman model is:

$$w_{BL} = (\lambda\Sigma)^{-1}\left[(\tau\Sigma)^{-1} + P'\Omega^{-1}P\right]^{-1}\left[(\tau\Sigma)^{-1}\mu + P'\Omega^{-1}Q\right] \quad (12.7)$$

We have already explained how to set parameters $\Sigma, \Pi, P, Q, \tau$ in Equation (12.7) and will now introduce the method of setting parameters $\lambda, \Omega$. The method of setting $\Omega$ is especially important.

To estimate the coefficient of risk aversion $\lambda$, we use the following formula:

$$\lambda = \frac{E\left(r_{mkt} - r_{rf}\right)}{\sigma^2} \quad (12.8)$$

Where $E\left(r_{mkt}\right)$ is the expected return of the market portfolio, $r_{rf}$ is the risk-free rate, $\sigma^2 = w'_{mkt}\Sigma w_{mkt}$ is the variance of the excess return on the market portfolio.

Thomas Idzorek[3] has proposed a calculation for $\Omega$. The logic behind his calculation is that for every view, if the confidence level of that view is 100%, then a strategy for asset allocation can be determined. If the confidence level of that view is 0%, then the assets should be allocated according to their market capitalization, which is $w_{mkt}$. If the confidence level of the view is between 0% and 100%, then the allocation strategy should be based on $w_{mkt}$ (the asset allocation strategy for a 0% confidence level), and tilt toward the asset allocation strategy for a 100% confidence level.

We use view $k$, $p_k \cdot r = q_k + \varepsilon_k$ as an example. If the confidence level of this view is $c_k$ ($c_k$ is between 0% and 100%), we can introduce a indicative vector $index_k$: if a certain element of $p_k$ is not 0, then the respective element of $index_k$ equals 1. On the other hand, if an element of $p_k$ is equal to 0, then the respective element of $index_k$ equals 0. In short, $index_k$ shows the non-zero elements in $p_k$, which is the asset mentioned in view $k$. Idzorek's calculation follows the following six steps.

Step 1: if the confidence level is 100%, the expected posterior distribution of the excess return can be calculated using the following formula:

$$E\left(r_{k,100\%}\right) = \Pi + \tau\Sigma p'_k\left(p_k\tau\Sigma p'_k\right)^{-1}\left(q_k - p_k\Pi\right) \quad (12.9)$$

Step 2: calculating the asset allocation strategy at a 100% confidence level:

$$w_{k,100\%} = (\lambda\Sigma)^{-1} E(r_{k,100\%})$$  (12.10)

Step 3: calculating the difference between the asset allocation strategy at a 100% confidence level and $w_{mkt}$:

$$D_{k,100\%} = w_{k,100\%} - w_{mkt}$$  (12.11)

Step 4: calculating the tilt:

$$\text{Tilt}_k = D_{k,100\%} \,.\, * \,\text{index}_k * c_k$$  (12.12)

Where . * represents the pair-wise multiplication, the above formula shows that the calculation of tilt involves only the assets mentioned in view $k$, as the confidence level $c_k$ rises, the tilt also steepens.

Step 5: calculating the asset allocation strategy resulted from the tilt method:

$$w_{k,c_k} = w_{mkt} + \text{Tilt}_k$$  (12.13)

Step 6: solving the optimization problem involving $\omega_k$:

$$\max_{\omega_k > 0} \left(w_{k,c_k} - w_k\right)' \left(w_{k,c_k} - w_k\right)$$  (12.14)

$$s.t. \quad w_k = (\lambda\Sigma)^{-1}\left[(\tau\Sigma)^{-1} + p'_k p_k \,/\, \omega_k\right]^{-1}\left[(\tau\Sigma)^{-1}\Pi + p'_k q_k \,/\, \omega_k\right]$$

For every view, we use the six steps listed above to calculate $\omega_k, k = 1, 2, ..., m$, the result is the following: $\Omega = \begin{pmatrix} \omega_1 & 0 & ... & 0 \\ 0 & \omega_2 & ... & 0 \\ \vdots & \vdots & \ddots & \vdots \\ 0 & 0 & ... & \omega_m \end{pmatrix}.$

## 2 The fundamental law of active management

Richard Grinold and Ronald Kahn first introduced the fundamental law of active management.[4] It explained the source of excess return alpha and the composition of information ratio. We will present the relevant hypothesis as we discuss this law further.

### 2.1 Information model

**Hypothesis 1:** Suppose there are $N$ types of securities available for investment. We use the $N \times 1$ random variable $r$ to demonstrate their expected returns (discounted by the risk free rate, similarly hereafter). The random variable $r_B$ represents the expected return of the market benchmark index. If the allocation ratio of the securities in the market benchmark index is $N \times 1$ vector $h_B$, then $r_B = h_B' \cdot r$. $N \times 1$ vector $\beta$ demonstrates the beta coefficient of the $N$ securities relative to the market benchmark index.

Then the following must be true:

$$r = \beta \cdot r_B + \theta \qquad (12.15)$$

Where $N \times 1$ vector $\theta$ demonstrates the residual return of the $N$ securities relative to the market benchmark index, and $h_B' \cdot \beta = 1, h_B' \cdot \theta = 0$.

**Hypothesis 2**: The statistical characteristic of the residual return $\theta$ is $E(\theta) = 0, \mathrm{var}(\theta) = \Sigma_\theta$.

Typically, the components of $\theta$ are correlated, for example, $\Sigma_\theta$ is not a diagonal matrix. We can prove that there exists a $N \times 1$ random variable $x$ and a $N \times N$ matrix $A$ where:

1  $\theta = A \cdot x$
2  The components of $x$ are not correlated; their expected values are 0, and their standard deviations are 1
3  $\Sigma_\theta = A \cdot A'$

**Hypothesis 3:** We use BR $\times 1$ vector $z$ to demonstrate BR units of signals (earnings forecasts, price trends, analyst opinions, etc.). Suppose the statistical characteristics of $z$ are $E(z) = 0, \mathrm{var}(z) = \Sigma_z$.

Typically, these BR units of signals are correlated, for example $\Sigma_z$ is not a diagonal matrix. Like $\theta$, there exists a BR $\times 1$ random vector $y$ and a BR $\times$ BR matrix $B$ where:

1  $z = B \cdot y$
2  The components of $y$ are uncorrelated; their expected values are 0, and their standard deviations are 1
3  $\Sigma_z = B \cdot B'$.

We use $N \times$ BR matrix $Q$ to demonstrate the covariance matrix of residual return $\theta$ and signal $z$, $Q = \mathrm{cov}(\theta, z)$.

We use $N \times$ BR matrix $P$ to demonstrate the correlation coefficient matrix of $\theta$ and $z$, $P = \mathrm{corr}(\theta, z) = \mathrm{cov}(x, y) = (\rho_{n,b})_{1 \leq n \leq N, 1 \leq b \leq BR}$, where $\rho_{n,b} = \mathrm{corr}(\theta_n, z_b)$.

The correlation between $Q$ and $P$ is: $Q = A \cdot P \cdot B'$.

After acquiring signal $z$, the investors renew their expectations of the residual return $\theta$, which is demonstrated in the form of the conditional expectation and conditional variance of $\theta$ (We introduce symbol $D = B^{-1}$, where $I$ represents the $N \times N$ identity matrix):

$$a(z) = E(\theta \mid z) = A \cdot P \cdot D \cdot z \qquad (12.16)$$

$$C = \mathrm{var}(\theta \mid z) = A \cdot (I - P \cdot P')A' \qquad (12.17)$$

## 2.2 Investment target

We use $N \times 1$ vector $h_p$ to demonstrate the allocation ratio of the securities, $N \times 1$ vector $h = h_P - h_B$, which demonstrates the active positions relative to the market benchmark index, where the projected rate of return for investors is:

$$r_P = h'_P \cdot r = h'_P \cdot \beta \cdot r_B + h' \cdot \theta \tag{12.18}$$

Where $h'_P \cdot \beta$ is the beta coefficient of the investors relative to the market benchmark index, and $h' \cdot \theta$ is the active return of the investors relative to the market benchmark index. The volatility of $h' \cdot \theta$ is called the tracking error, which demonstrates the active risk of investors who deviate from the market benchmark index.

Given active position $h$ and signal $z$, the expected active return of the investors can be written as $E(h' \cdot \theta \mid z) = h' \cdot \alpha(z)$, and the active risk squared is $\mathrm{var}(h' \cdot \theta \mid z) = h' \cdot C \cdot h$.

**Hypothesis 4**: Investor utility is expressed as a quadratic function with avoidance level of active risk $\lambda$.

Thus, with signal $z$ already provided, the utility function of the investors is

$$h' \cdot \alpha(z) - \lambda \cdot h' \cdot C \cdot h \tag{12.19}$$

## 2.3 The optimal active position

Using $h(z)$ to demonstrate the optimal active position given signal $z$. $h(z)$ can be determined by the following optimization equations:

$$h(z) = \arg\max_h h' \cdot \alpha(z) - \lambda \cdot h' \cdot C \cdot h \tag{12.20}$$

The first order condition is: $\alpha(z) = 2\lambda \cdot C \cdot h(z)$. Plugging in the expression of $\alpha(z)$ and $C$ $(E = (I - P \cdot P')^{-1})$, then the first order condition can be simplified as:

$$A' \cdot h(z) = \frac{1}{2\lambda} \cdot E \cdot P \cdot D \cdot Z \tag{12.21}$$

## 2.4 Information ratio

The information ratio is equal to the annual active return divided by active risk, which reflects the risk-adjusted rate of active management.

On the optimal active position $h(z)$, the conditional information ratio of the investors $\mathrm{IR}(z)$ satisfies the following equation: $\mathrm{IR}^2(z) = Z' \cdot D' \cdot P' \cdot E' \cdot P \cdot D \cdot z = y' \cdot P' \cdot E' \cdot P \cdot y$, and the information ratio squared is:

$$\mathrm{IR}^2 = E[\mathrm{IR}^2(z)] = Trace(P' \cdot E' \cdot P) \tag{12.22}$$

Where $Trace(\cdot)$ indicates the trace of the matrix (sum of the elements on the diagonal line).

Through a series of approximation, the following can be proved[5]

$$IR^2 \approx \text{Trace}(P' \cdot P) = \sum_{n=1}^{N} \sum_{b=1}^{BR} \rho_{n,b}^2 \tag{12.23}$$

We use $\xi_b^2 = \sum_{n=1}^{N} \rho_{n,b}^2$ to demonstrate the sum of squares of each correlation coefficient within signal $z_b$ and residual return $\theta$; this reflects the value of signal $z_b$. Therefore,

$$IR^2 = \sum_{b=1}^{BR} \xi_b^2 \tag{12.24}$$

**Hypothesis 5:** All signals have the same connotation, for every $b$, the following is true $\zeta_b^2 = IC^2$.

Under hypothesis 5, the fundamental law of active management can express the information ratio:

$$IR = IC \cdot \sqrt{BR} \tag{12.25}$$

BR is called the breadth. It is equivalent to the number of independent signals acquired by investors. Each independent signal represents a forecast by the investor and results in an active position or active investment strategy. This process is called an active bet. Consequently, the breadth BR reflects the number of independent bets placed by the investor.

IC is called the information coefficient; it demonstrates the level of correlation between the forecast (signal $z$) and the actual result (the residual return $\theta$).

The fundamental law of active management denotes the following:

1 Active management is essentially a forecast.
2 The consensus forecast will lead to passive investment based on the market benchmark index.
3 To outperform the market benchmark index, an investor must make different forecasts and create an active position based on this forecast.
4 To achieve a high information ratio, either the breadth BR must be large (making a large number of forecasts) or the information coefficient IC must be high (making accurate forecasts).

## 3 How is big data implemented?

The Black–Litterman model is different from the fundamental law of active management, yet they are closely connected. The Black–Litterman model is more practical, and the fundamental law of active management is useful in discussing general trends. Both of the models, however, argue that:

1 The market benchmark index is the starting point of investment activities and the default portfolio. This means that to some extent, the models imply a belief in market efficiency.

2  Investors can only deviate from the market benchmark index if they decide to make forecasts that differ from the average market forecast. Of course, they would have to evaluate the validity of their forecasts. In the models, this is reflected by the confidence level parameter in the Black–Litterman model and the information coefficient in the fundamental law of active management.

3  Integrating the two models, we can conclude that active management can be generalized to the following five steps: gather valuable signals from data, make distinct forecasts, form strategies based on forecasts, evaluate the strategies by observing results or performing back tests, and finally evaluate the validity of the forecasts based on their results and make corrections (Figure 12.1).

Big data analysis is mostly used in step 1 and step 2. These two steps are typically taken together. Investors can extract signals by using economic principles or data mining. The basic principle is that the signals must be useful to improve the forecasts, otherwise they are just noise. Richard Grinold and Ronald Kahn have established the following formula for the basic forecast:

$$\phi = E(r \mid g) - E(r) = \text{cov}(r,g) \cdot \text{var}^{-1}(g) \cdot (g - E(g)) \tag{12.26}$$

Where $r$ is the return of the security, $g$ is the signal, $E(r)$ represents the average market forecast, and $E(r \mid g)$ represents the forecast based on signals. Equation (12.26) is the general form of Equation (12.16).

If $r$ and $g$ are both random variables and not random vectors, then Equation (12.26) can be simplified as:

$$\phi = \text{corr}(r,g) \cdot \text{std}(r) \cdot \frac{g - E(g)}{\text{std}(g)} \tag{12.27}$$

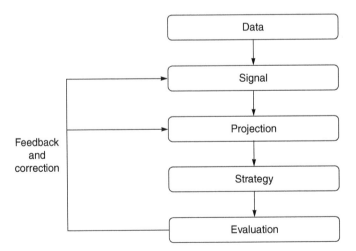

*Figure 12.1* The general steps of active management.

Where $\text{std}(\cdot)$ is the standard deviation of the random variable, $\text{corr}(r,g)$ is the information coefficient IC, and $\dfrac{g - E(g)}{\text{std}(g)}$ demonstrates the number of standard deviations the signal deviates from the average, we call it the z-score. The connotation of Equation (12.27) is:

$$\text{Forecast} = \text{Information coefficient} * \text{volatility} * Z-\text{score of signal} \qquad (12.28)$$

We will use the article written by Hristidis *et al.* to exemplify how big data is used by securities investors. This article focused on correlation between information on Twitter and stock prices. They started by analyzing all the data on Twitter about one stock, and designed several quantitative indexes to measure its activity on Twitter. The result showed that some indices were significant correlated with the trade volume of the stock in the next 1–3 days, as well as with the rate of return. The above demonstrated the first step—extracting signals from data.

Next, they created a Twitter-augmented regression on the rate of return using the aforementioned Twitter activity indexes. This model used vector auto-regression (VAR) with the rate of return of the stocks as the dependent variable, while the independent variables included the historical rate of return of the stocks as well as the Twitter activeness indexes. This is step 2—forming forecasts based on signals.

Step 3 was the formulation of strategy based on forecasts. This was done by investing in the stocks with the highest projected rate of return based on the Twitter-augmented regression.

At last, they used back tests to compare the result of their strategy with other strategies. The following were used in this comparison: (a) a portfolio that passively invested only in the market benchmark index; (b) a randomly selected stock; (c) a portfolio whose stocks were selected based on market cap, size, total liability, and so on; (d) a portfolio that invested in several stocks with the highest projected rate of return provided by the auto regression. Essentially this was very similar to the Twitter strategy, except that it did not include the Twitter activity indices.

In the end, they found out that the Twitter-based strategy had the best result. This proved that information on Twitter can actually be used in security investment. The above summarized steps 4 and 5—evaluation, feedback, and correction.

We would like to suggest that in Internet finance, the securities market may possess characteristics described in both behavioral finance and the efficient markets hypothesis. Investors affect each other in decision-making thanks to the prevalence of social networks, which means that their behavior will be similar to that described in behavioral finance. For example, they may exhibit a greater level of conformity, which could affect a particular security or even the entire securities market. On the other hand, big data is closing the gap in obtaining information. Securities pricing, which used to require complex calculations, is now made simple by apps. Pricing efficiency is becoming extremely high. As a consequence, the behavior of securities markets may be similar to the efficient markets hypothesis.

## SECTION 2: BIG DATA IN ACTUARIAL SCIENCE

The essence of insurance is to provide financial compensation to the insured. Risk events that require compensation can be either personal or property. The two major types of insurance, personal insurance and property insurance, are the result. Actuarial science analyzes future risk events and calculates their potential consequences. These calculations help to set the premium and margin. It is also divided into two categories, life contingencies and non-life contingencies. Though the fundamentals of the two categories are the same, the methods they implement diverge greatly.

We will provide a brief summary of life contingencies and non-life contingencies with a special focus on contingency rate setting. Afterwards, we will discuss how big data can be used in actuarial science.

## 1 An introduction to life contingency[6]

### 1.1 Basic concepts

Life contingency focuses on mortality risks. If $X$ is the life expectancy for a 0-year-old infant, then $X$ is a random variable between $(0, \omega]$, where $\omega$ is called the limiting age, usually 105 or 110. We plug in the following functions to track the distribution of variable $X$.

The accumulated distribution function of longevity is:

$$F(x) = \Pr(X \leq x), x \geq 0 \qquad (12.29)$$

$F(x)$ is the probability of the person dying before age $x$. $F(x)$ increases monotonically in interval $(0, \omega]$, and satisfies $F(0) = 0, F(\omega) = 1$.

The survival function of longevity:

$$S(x) = \Pr(X > x), x \geq 0 \qquad (12.30)$$

$S(x)$ is the probability of the person surviving beyond age $x$. $S(x)$ and $F(x)$ satisfy the following: $S(x) = 1 - F(x)$.

Mark a person $x$ years old as $(x)$. The years left for $(x)$ until death is called $(x)$'s time until death, or $T(x)$. The accumulated distribution function of $(x)$'s time until death is marked $_tq_x$, which is the probability of a person $x$ years old dying in the next $t$ years is:

$$_tq_x = \Pr(T(x) \leq t) = \Pr(X \leq x + t \mid X > x) = \frac{S(x) - S(x + t)}{S(x)} \qquad (12.31)$$

The survival function of $(x)$'s time until death is marked $_tp_x$, which is the probability of a person at the age of $x$ living beyond $x + t$ years old:

$$_tp_x = \Pr(T(x) > t) = \Pr(x > x + t \mid X > x) = \frac{S(x + t)}{S(x)} \qquad (12.32)$$

The force of mortality at the age of $x$ is $\mu_x$, which means that a person can live to $x$ years old, and dies right after that moment:

$$\mu_x = \lim_{\Delta x \to 0} \frac{\Pr(x \le X \le x + \Delta x \mid X > x)}{\Delta x} = -\frac{S'(x)}{S(x)} \tag{12.33}$$

The correlation between the force of mortality and the survival function is demonstrated in the follow equation:

$$S(x) = \exp\left(-\int_0^x \mu_s \, ds\right), \ _tp_x = \frac{S(x+t)}{S(x)} = \exp\left(-\int_x^{x+t} \mu_s ds\right) \tag{12.34}$$

The density function of the remaining life duration $T(x)$ is $f_T(t) = \dfrac{d}{dt} {}_t q_x$, thus

$$f_T(t) = -\frac{\dfrac{d}{dt} S(x+t)}{S(x)} = \mu_{x+t} \cdot {}_t p_x \ f_T(t) = -\frac{\dfrac{d}{dt} S(x+t)}{S(x)} = \mu_{x+t} \cdot {}_t p_x \tag{12.35}$$

Generally speaking, the curve of the force of mortality is bowl shaped. Infants have high forces of mortality, while the forces of mortality are lowest during youth. The forces of mortality then gradually increase as people grow older. Some of the most famous models for the force of mortality are: the De Moivre model, the Gompertz model, the Makeham model, and the Weibull model.

### 1.2 Setting net premiums

To demonstrate the core skills of life contingency, we will set the net premium of a single payment and build its actuarial models. The net premium covers only the cost of risk, not operating costs and other profits. A single premium is a payment plan in which all the charges are paid with one payment.

To set a net premium, we must follow the net equilibrium theory. This implies that the net premium is equal to the sum of future insurance payments. The net equilibrium theory is an underlying principle of the insurance industry, in that it is a guideline every type of insurance follows in setting net premiums.

There are two assumptions in setting net premiums. First, the residual life data sets of a group of policyholders who share the same age, gender, and starting date are independently, identically distributed. Second, the insurance company can forecast the investment rate. With these two assumptions, we can convert individual risk events to a sum of homogeneous risk events. On an individual basis, one policyholder cannot predict the time he will encounter a risk event, nor the amount that he will be compensated. However, in total, the pattern for residual life is very clear statistically.

As mentioned before, $T(x)$ is the residual life variable of a group of policyholders who share the same age, gender, and policy start date. If a mortality event occurs after $t$ units of time, the compensation is payable at the moment of death, the amount of compensation is $b_t$, and the discount function at this point is $v_t$. The present value function of compensation is then:

$$z_t = b_t \cdot v_t \tag{12.36}$$

The density function at the moment of payment is $f_T(t)$, and the expected compensation function is:

$$E(Z_t) = \int z_t f_T(t)\, dt \tag{12.37}$$

The individuals do not necessarily receive compensation equal to their payments. Rather, we view the entire body of policyholders with the same risks as one entity, and balance achieved on a larger scale. Equation (12.37) is very universal. The structure of the model remains the same despite different insurance types. The differences lay only in the function format of $b_t$, $v_t$, $f_T(t)$.

Take whole life insurance as an example. Whole life insurance is insurance that covers any applicable mortality event. If $(x)$ applies a whole life insurance policy with the coverage of \$1, where $b_t = 1$, $t \in (0, \omega]$, and the annual compound rate is $v$, then $v_t = v^t$, $t \in (0, \omega]$. The present compensation value function is $z_t = v^t$, $t \in (0, \omega]$. The net insurance amount is:

$$E(z_t) = \int_0^w z_t \cdot f_T(t)\,dt = \int_0^w v^t \cdot {}_t p_x \cdot \mu_{x+t}\,dt \tag{12.38}$$

### *1.3 The life table*

Though the force of mortality models demonstrated the longevity variable by using extremely simple models and equations, the actual distribution of life expectancy is complex. To avoid errors, life contingency often implements life tables to approach the distribution of longevity.

The life table describes the mortality patterns of a closed population from birth to death, supposing that there is no mobility or reproduction, and that the only factor able to reach the population is death. Assuming that the population is consisted of $n$ individuals, observation shows that $k_n$ people within the group die at the age of $x$, then $\frac{k_n}{n}$ is the mortality probability at age $x$. $\frac{k_n}{n}$ is an empirical estimation of $F(x)$. The theories of big data dictate that, if $n$ is large enough, $\frac{k_n}{n}$ converges to $F(x)$.

Official life tables often use a number of 100,000 or 1,000,000 as the surviving population at age $0(l_0)$. Life tables are divided into different age groups (from $x$ to $x + t$). Except for infants, whose data is often measured in days or weeks, the other age groups usually use years as inspectional units. For every age group from $x$ to $x + t$, the life table provides the following statistics:

1  Initial surviving number $l_x = l_0 \cdot S(x)$
2  Mortality rate ${}_t q_x$
3  Number of mortality ${}_t d_x = l_x \cdot {}_t q_x$
4  Number of years where $l_0$ units of newborns survive in their age groups
$${}_t L_x = \int_0^t l_{x+s}\,ds$$

5 The total amount of residual life of all individuals who will live to age $x$.
$$T_x = \int_0^{\omega-x} l_{x+t} dt$$

6 The average residual life of individuals who will live to age $x$. $e_x^0 = \dfrac{T_x}{l_x}$

The life table provides the life distribution in whole numbers. In practice, the survival rate of the integer years is often used to estimate the probability of survival and mortality between the integer years. This is basically an interpolation problem. Provided $(x, l_x)$ and $(x+1, l_{x+1})$, estimate one point between the integer years $(x+t, l_{x+t})$, $0 < t < 1$. Three approaches are used to solve this problem. The first uses linear interpolation in between the integer years. The second uses geometrical interpolation, and the last is harmonic interpolation.

## 2 An introduction to non–life contingency[7]

### 2.1 The compound risk model

Non-life contingency analyzes risk on property and obligation. The compound risk model is a key tool in non-life contingency.

Suppose non-negative random variable sequences $\{X_i, i \geq 1\}$ are mutually independent. $N$ is a non-negative whole number, and $\{X_i, i \geq 1\}$ and $N$ are mutually independent given $\sum_{i=1}^{0} X_i = 0$.

$$S = \sum_{i=1}^{N} X_i \tag{12.39}$$

In reality, the compound risk model is used to plot the total loss of one policy or policy set over a period of time:

1 A model for one policy: assuming that one policy will encounter $N$ losses within a certain period, and $X_i$ represents the amount of loss of $i$, the total policy loss of is $\sum_{i=1}^{N} X_i$.

2 A model of a set of policies: assuming that $N$ policies within the policy set will encounter losses within a certain period, and $X_i$ is the amount of loss incurred by policy $i$, the total loss of the set is $\sum_{i=1}^{N} X_i$.

In the mixed risk model $S = \sum_{i=1}^{N} X_i$, $X_t$ is called the individual loss, and its distribution is called the individual loss distribution or the loss distribution. Some common examples include: normal distribution, logarithmic normal distribution, $\Gamma$ distribution, B distribution, and Pareto distribution.

$N$ is the number of claims, and its expectation $E(N)$ is called the claim frequency. Common distributions of $N$ include: the Poisson, binomial, and negative binomial distributions.

In the compound risk model, the following is true:

$$E(S) = E(N) \cdot E(X_i) \tag{12.40}$$

Therefore, the expected loss of the model is equal to the product of claim frequency and individual loss. This is the theoretical basis of non–life contingency setting.

### 2.2 Setting risk premiums

The amount and period of coverage often differ for the same type of insurance. Thus, the risk or exposure unit is introduced as the basic unit for plotting the amount of risk. The risk unit must be able to quantify risk, easy for insurance companies to measure, easy to understand, hard to manipulate, and easy to manage. The sum of risk units in a policy is called the risk amount. For example, the risk unit for vehicle insurance is usually one vehicle-year. If two vehicles both have a coverage period of half year, then the total risk amount is 1.

The risk premium is the main component of non–life contingency. The process to set risk premiums has three steps. The first step is to estimate the claim frequency $N$ and the expected individual payment $X_i$ per risk unit. In a statistical sense, this step solves for the parameter values of distribution $N$ and $X_i$. Methods that are commonly used in this step include the moment estimation method and maximum likelihood method. (See Chapter 6)

We then implement net equilibrium theory (Equation 12.40) for the next step. The resulting formula for the risk unit policy is the following:

The risk premium of the risk unit policy = The claim frequency of the risk unit policy
* The average coverage of each payment

$$\tag{12.41}$$

The third step is to find the formula for calculating the risk premium:

The risk premium of the policy = The risk premium of the risk unit policy
* The risk amount of the policy    (12.42)

### 2.3 The experience rating

The Experience Rating Method is a quantification method designed to eliminate the heterogeneity of risks. This method enables insurance companies to modify premiums based on historical data. The basic logic is that if one policy is outperforming its original projection, then the policyholder may ask for lower payments. From the perspective of the insurance company, the reliability of its own data must be considered carefully. Moreover, the company needs to judge the risk based on the performance of one policy versus other policies in the same category. The experience rating method includes complete credibility, partial credibility, and greatest accuracy credibility. For clarification, we will use the Bühlmann model from the greatest accuracy credibility theory as an example.

The Bühlmann model focuses on the following problem: for a risk unit policy, if the compensations of the past $n$ years are $X_1, X_2, \ldots, X_n$, how do we determine the risk premium $X_{m+1}$ for the next year?

Suppose that $X_1, X_2, \ldots, X_n$ share the same type of distribution and the distribution parameter $\Theta$ is a random variable. If $X_1, X_2, \ldots, X_n$ are independent under the conditions provided by distribution parameter $\Theta$, and they have the same conditional expectation and conditional variance so that $\mu(\Theta) = E[X_i \mid \Theta], v(\Theta) = \mathrm{var}[X_i \mid \Theta]. \mu = E[\mu(\Theta)]$ is the rate in the premium chart or the estimated value of compensation based on analyses of similar policies.

The fundamental idea of the Bühlmann model is to estimate $X_{n+1}$ using the linear combination of historical compensations:

$$\min_{\alpha_0, \alpha_1, \ldots, \alpha_n} E\left[X_{n+1} - \alpha_0 - \sum_{i=1}^{n} \alpha_i x_i\right]^2 \tag{12.43}$$

The solution of optimization problem (Equation 12.43) is the credibility premium:

$$Z \cdot \overline{X} + (1 - z) \cdot \mu \tag{12.44}$$

Where $\overline{X} = \dfrac{\sum_{i=1}^{n} X_i}{n}$, credibility factor $z = \dfrac{n}{n + k}$ $\left(k = \dfrac{E[v(\Theta)]}{\mathrm{var}(\mu(\Theta))}\right)$.

The credibility factor $z$ illustrates the reliability of future risk premiums on historical data. When $z = 1$, the future risk premium relies completely on its own historical data $\overline{X}$. This is called complete credibility. When $0 < z < 1$, the future risk premium relies on both $\overline{X}$ and $\mu$, the weight of $\mu$ is less than 1. This is called partial credibility.

## 3 How is big data implemented?

### 3.1 The core variable of actuarial insurance

Force of Mortality $\mu_x$ is the core variable of actuarial science's application to life insurance. If $\mu_x$ is known, then we can calculate the cumulative distribution function of life span $F(x)$, survival function $S(x)$, and the survival function of residual life ${}_t q_x$. Since the life variable $X$ represents the time point of mortality events, $X$ is the stopping time in the probability theory, and $\mu_x = \lim_{\Delta x \to 0} \dfrac{\Pr(x \le X \le x + \Delta x \mid X > x)}{\Delta x}$ marks the intensity of mortality events.

The claim frequency $E(N)$ in non-insurance actuarial science is one of the two core variables. The claim frequency is essentially a counting process. Assuming we have a counter that starts from 0, and we raise the number every time the insurance policy suffers a loss (if we assume the duration is $T$), then the last reading is $N(T)$. More precisely, $T_k$ represents the time interval between loss number

$k$ and loss number $k + 1$ $(k = 0,1,2,...)$. The time point of loss number $k$ is $S_k = T_0 + T_1 + ... + T_{k-1}$, and the claim frequency $N(T)$ can be expressed as:

$$N(T) = \sum_{k=0}^{\infty} 1_{\{S_k \le T\}} \tag{12.45}$$

Where $1_{\{\cdot\}}$ represents the indicative function, the value is 1 if the logic in the parenthesis is true, 0 in all other cases.

The time point of loss also involves the stopping time concept. If we look forward from $S_k$, the occurrence of loss number $k$, we can describe the duration of time before loss $k + 1$ by using the intensity of loss event:

$$\lambda(t) = \lim_{\Delta x \to 0} \frac{\Pr(t \le T_k \le t + \Delta t \mid T_k > t)}{\Delta t} \tag{12.46}$$

$\lambda(t)$ fully describes the distribution of claim frequency $N(T)$.

Consequently, the force of mortality $\mu_x$ and the occurrence of loss have the same statistical connotation in reaching intensity $\lambda(t)$.

### 3.2 Responsiveness of actuarial science to individual heterogeneity

Technically, the force of mortality is applicable to everyone, and the intensity of loss events are applicable to every vehicle, apartment, or other non-life objects. Therefore, these two variables can be used to create models and perform projections on an individual level. Based on this, actuarial science can reflect differences between individuals, which may lead to the creation of a personalized premium rate. To some extent, the current trend of actuarial science reflects this logic.

In life contingency, the life table is categorized into male, female, and general life tables. Other categories include smoking and non-smoking life tables, national life tables targeting national citizens, as well as experience life tables that target only the policyholders of the insurance company.

Many types of insurance require the applicants to pass certain health requirements, and only those who pass may enter the plan. The health exam is like a doorstep of selection, only admitting people in a superior health condition. This is called selection bias. In order to assign risks fairly, the mortality rate of these new applicants is very low. However, this effect does not last forever. Within 2–3 years, their health condition would be indistinguishable from the rest. The select-and-ultimate tables are designed specifically for this. Within the selection period, life tables with smaller mortality rates are used. After the selection period, the ultimate table, or life table with normal mortality rates, is used. These adjustments to the life tables are essentially setting differentiated force of mortality based on individual cases.

In non-life contingency, the experience rating method adjusts future payments based on historical experience such as historical compensation. If each compensation is consistent with the rest, the experience rating method would essentially be forecasting the future value based on the historical values of the intensity of loss events.

Overall, actuarial science does not reflect individual characteristics adequately. There are countless factors that could affect one's risk, such as his genes, inheritance, habits, occupation, climate, and pollution. The life table is still lacking in inclusion of these factors for analysis. In non-life contingency, aside from historical compensation, cross sections of the policyholder and macroeconomic variables can also be included in actuarial science.

### 3.3 Thoughts on using big data in actuarial science

In actuarial science, we believe that big data analysis, instead of rules of thumb, can be used to build a connection between force of mortality and intensity of loss events. A related field—credit risk management has been explored with big data. There is much that actuaries can learn from this field.

We will focus on the simplicity method for risk management (See Chapter 7). The simplicity method does not discuss why a default may happen. Rather, it views default as a random event that could happen at any time. Hazard ratios and default intensity are used to plot the default rate. If $\tau$ is the time point for the occurrence of a credit event, then risk rate means that:

$$h(t) = \lim_{\Delta x \to 0} \frac{\Pr\left(\tau \leq t + \Delta t \mid \tau > t\right)}{\Delta t} \tag{12.47}$$

Comparing Equations (12.33), (12.46), and (12.47), we can tell that the risk rate has the same connotation as in force of mortality and in intensity of loss events. In credit risk management, there are many interesting methods to build models. For more information, you can refer to the book by Darrell Duffie and Kenneth Singleton.[8] These models are designed to compare the force of mortality and the intensity of loss events. Here we will use the corporate credit risk model by Sudheer Chava and Robert Jarrow.[9]

Suppose that there are $n$ policyholders. For each policyholder, a one-time risk event may occur—personal or property. For policyholder $i$, we use $\tau_i$ to represent the points in time when his risk events happen. $\tau_i$ also demonstrates the stopping time concept.

For a set of scattered time points $t = 0,1,2,...,T$, we know that $X_{it}$ is the basic information of the policyholders at time point $t$ regarding policyholder $i$. We use $N_{it}$ to determine that there are no risk events at time point $t$. $N_{it}$ is a variable that ranges from 0 to 1. We assign the values in the following manner:

$$N_{it} = \begin{cases} 0 & t < \tau_i \\ 1 & t \geq \tau_i \end{cases} \tag{12.48}$$

For each $i$, $N_{i0} = 0$.

Risk event $\lambda_{it} = \lim_{\Delta x \to 0} \dfrac{\Pr\left(\tau_i \leq t + \Delta t \mid \tau_i > t\right)}{\Delta t}$ represents the intensity of risk event at time point $t$ for policyholder $i$. Since the data points are scattered, a more convenient analysis is the conditional probability of default (equivalent to $\lambda_{it}$).

If no risk event has happened at time point $t$, then the probability of a risk event occurring before time point $t + 1$ is:

$$p_{it} = \Pr\left(\tau_i \leq t + 1 \mid \tau_i > t, X_{it}\right) \tag{12.49}$$

Assuming that there is a functional relationship between $p_{it}$ and $X_{it}$:

$$p_{it} = \frac{\exp\left(\alpha + \beta' X_{it}\right)}{1 + \exp\left(\alpha + \beta' X_{it}\right)} \tag{12.50}$$

Next, we will estimate $\alpha$ and $\beta$ in Equation (12.50) based on the observation $\{(X_{it}, N_{it}) : i = 1, 2, \ldots, n, t = 1, 2, \ldots, T\}$.

$N_{iT} = 0$ means that until reaching time point $T$, the beneficiary $i$ does not experience a risk event, where $\tau_i > T$. $N_{iT} = 1$ means that the beneficiary $i$ experienced risk events before reaching $T$. In this case, data after $\tau_i$ has no significance. Consequently, we define $D_i = \min(\tau_i, T)$.

For the following equations

$$L\left[N_{iD_i} \mid X_{it}, 1 \leq t \leq D_i\right] = \begin{cases} \Pr\left(\tau_i = D_i\right) & N_{iD_i} = 1 \\ \Pr\left(\tau_i > D_i\right) & N_{iD_i} = 0 \end{cases} \tag{12.51}$$

$$= \Pr\left(\tau_i = D_i\right)^{N_{iD_i}} \Pr\left(\tau_i > D_i\right)^{1 - N_{iD_i}}$$

Where $\Pr\left(\tau_i = D_i\right) = p_{iD_i - 1} \prod_{t=0}^{D_i - 2}\left(1 - p_{it}\right)$, $\Pr(\tau_i > D_i) = \prod_{t=0}^{D_i - 1}\left(1 - p_{it}\right)$.

We define the likelihood function as:

$$L\left[\alpha, \beta \mid (X_{it}, N_{it}) : i = 1, 2, \ldots, n, t = 1, 2, \ldots, T\right] = \prod_{i=1}^{n}\left[N_{iD} \mid X_{it}, 1 \leq t \leq D_i\right]$$

The log-likelihood function is equal to:

$$LL(\alpha, \beta) = \sum_{i=1}^{n} N_{iD_i} \log \frac{p_{iD_i - 1}}{1 - p_{iD_i - 1}} + \sum_{i=1}^{n} \sum_{t=0}^{D_i - 1} \log\left(1 - p_{it}\right) \tag{12.52}$$

Optimizing Equation (12.52), we obtain estimates on parameters $\alpha$ and $\beta$. Consequently Equation (12.50) can be used to assess the risk of the policyholders.

Looking at the current trend, there has been some big data utilization in non-life contingency. Usage-based insurance could be a good example. This type of insurance sets its rate based on vehicle usage. The insurance requires the installation of a GPS, a velometer, and a radio device. All data collected by the insurance company can help to set the rate. Another benefit is that claims are easier to settle once the company obtains information about the vehicle and the driver.

At last, it is important to point out that the insurance component of Internet finance is an extremely interesting topic. We have already stated that the essence of insurance is financial compensation, which means that using theories of big data, the insurance companies would provide financial compensation for unexpected losses. In this process, the insurance payments of the policyholders who do not experience unexpected losses would pay for those who incur losses. In a perfectly competitive environment, the total amount of all insurance payments should be equal to the total amount of the unexpected losses (the net equilibrium theory), while the insurance company oversees the insurance payment transfer. Of course, it is impossible to foretell which policyholders will experience losses and which will not, thus it is impossible to predict the direction in which payments will flow. Therefore, we can conclude that the risking sharing with insurance is different from the risk shifting of usual derivatives (options, futures, swaps, etc.). The former is a group contract and the latter is a bilateral contract. In Internet finance, even if the level of information asymmetry and the transaction costs are low, the core characteristic of insurance being a group contract will not change.[10] While the business model of insurance remains the same, the specific organizational structures are subject to change. For example, a group of individuals with similar risk level can sign a contract through the Internet stating that if one of them suffers unexpected losses, the rest will be obligated to provide compensation. Once this group reaches a certain size, it could replace insurance companies.

## Notes

1  This is different from the mean-variance optimization problem (Equation 11.1). However, it can be proven that if a utility function is quadratic, or if the excess return is normally distributed, then we can conclude that this problem is equivalent to the mean-variance optimization.
2  This is designed solely for demonstrational purposes and does not necessarily reflect reality.
3  Idzorek, Thomas. 2004. "A Step-by-Step Guide to the Black-Litterman Model: Incorporating User-Specified Confidence Levels."
4  Grinold, Richard, and Ronald Kahn. 1999. "Active Portfolio Management: A Quantitative Approach for Providing Superior Returns and Controlling Risk," 2nd edition, McGraw-Hill.
5  We can decompose $E = \left(I - P \cdot P'\right)^{-1}$ to $E = I + P \cdot P' + P \cdot P' \cdot P \cdot P' + \dots$. Therefore $P' \cdot E' \cdot P$ can be decomposed to $P' \cdot E' \cdot P = P' \cdot P + P' \cdot P \cdot P' \cdot P + \dots$. Since the elements within $P$ are correlated coefficients, we can neglect the higher-order terms to get $P' \cdot E' \cdot P \approx P' \cdot P$.
6  Wang, Yan. 2008. "Life Contingency," China Renmin University Press.
7  Yang, Jingping. 2008. "Non-Life Contingency," Peking University Press.
8  Duffie, Darrell, and Kenneth Singleton. 2003. "Credit Risk: Pricing, Measurement, and Management," Princeton University Press.
9  A fundamental model for risk management company Kamakura Corporation.
10  As we pointed out in chapter 1, the terms of financial contracts remain the same in Internet finance.

# Appendix 1

## Overview of SFI

Founded on July 14, 2011, the Shanghai Finance Institute (SFI) is a leading non-governmental, non-profit institute dedicated to professional academic financial research. SFI is operated by the China Finance 40 Forum (CF40) and has a strategic cooperation with the Shanghai Huangpu District government. The Shanghai Financial Services Office is SFI's regulator, and SFI is registered with the Shanghai Administration of Social Organizations.

The mission of SFI is to explore new trends in the global financial market, pursue solutions to novel problems associated with China's financial development, and support the development of Shanghai as an international financial center.

Known for its professionalism and openness, SFI is an independent think tank dedicated to promote academic exchange. It conducts high-level research activities to provide first-class research products.

SFI hosts events such as closed-door seminars, the Shanghai Annual Conference of New Finance, and the Bund Forum of Internet Finance. It also conducts research projects and is responsible for the publication of the New Finance Review, the New Finance Book Series, various academic journals and articles, and media columns.

The China Finance 40 Forum (CF40) is a non-government, non–profit, and independent think tank dedicated to policy research on economics and finance. CF40 was founded on April 12, 2008, and operates as a "40 × 40 club" that consists of forty influential experts around 40 years old. CF40 aims to enhance the academic foundation of China's finance, provide high-quality research on emerging financial issues, and promote financial reform and development.

# Appendix 2

## Organizational structure

### Members of SFI Advisory Committee:

| | |
|---|---|
| FANG Xinghai | Director, International Economic Bureau, Office of the Central Leading Group for Financial and Economic Affairs |
| HU Huaibang | Chairman, China Development Bank |
| JIANG Yang | Vice Chairman, China Securities Regulatory Commission |
| TU Guangshao | Executive Vice Mayor of Shanghai |
| WANG Jiang | Professor of Finance, MIT Sloan School of Management |
| Weng Zuliang | Secretary of CPC Huangpu District Committee, Shanghai |
| WU Xiaoling | Vice Chairman, the Financial and Economic Affairs Committee, the National People's Congress of the People's Republic of China |
| YAN Qingming | Vice Mayor, Tianjin |
| YI Gang | Deputy Governor, the People's Bank of China; and Chief Administrator, State Administration of Foreign Exchange |
| YUAN Li | Vice President, China Development Bank |

### The Chairman of SFI Executive Council:

| | |
|---|---|
| WAN Jianhua | Chairman, E-Capital Transfer Co., Ltd |

### The Vice-Chairmen of SFI Executive Council:

| | |
|---|---|
| ZHENG Yang | Director, Shanghai Financial Services Office |
| TANG Zhiping | Governor of Huangpu District, Shanghai |
| WANG Haiming | Secretary-General, China Finance 40 Forum |

### Members of SFI Executive Council:

| | |
|---|---|
| CHEN Jiwu | Principal Partner and Chairman. Shanghai VStone Asset Management Co., Ltd |
| GAO Keqin | President, ABC Financial Leasing Co., Ltd |
| Gregory D Gibb | Chairman, Lufax |
| KWAN Tatcheong | Executive Director & Chief Executive, The Bank of East Asia (China) |

| HOU Fu'ning | President, Shanghai Rural Commercial Bank |
| LAN Rong | Chairman, Industrial Securities Co., Ltd |
| LI Jianguo | Vice President, Shanghai Bank |
| LI Lin | Head of Strategic Development Department, Shanghai Pudong Development Bank |
| LING Tao | Chairman, Shanghai Huarui Bank |
| LI Xunlei | Vice President & Chief Economist, Haitong Securities |
| LIAN Ping | Chief Economist, Bank of Communications |
| PAN Weidong | Chairman, Shanghai International Trust Co., Ltd |
| PAN Xinjun | Chairman, Orient Securities Co., Ltd |
| PENG Lei | CEO, Zhejiang Ant Small & Micro Financial Services Group |
| QIU Guogen | Chairman, Shanghai Chongyang Investment Management Co., Ltd. |
| Wang Song | President, Guotai Junan Securities |
| XU Luode | Chairman, Shanghai Gold Exchange |
| XU Zhen | Chairman, Shanghai Clearing House |
| YANG Huahui | Chairman, China Industrial International Trust Limited |
| YAO Wenping | Chairman, Tebon Securities Co., Ltd |
| ZHAO Linghuan | Chief Executive Officer, Hony Capital |
| ZHOU Xiong | President, Zhongtai Trust Co., Ltd. |
| ZHOU Ye | President, China PnR |

**Member of SFI Council:**

| GUO Yuhang | Co-CEO & Founding Partner of DianRong |
| LI Guohong | Chairman & President, Shangdong Gold Financial Holding Capital Management Co., Ltd. |
| SHENG Jia | CEO, Net Credit Finance Group |
| TANG Ning | CEO & Founder, CreditEase |
| Yang Yifu | Chairman, Renrendai.com |
| YAO Naisheng | Vice CEO, JD Finance |
| ZHANG Jialin | Chairman, Beijing Zipeiyi Investment Management Co., Ltd. |

**Members:**

CHINA RAPID FINANCE

| HUCHEN | Investment |
| HUAHUI | Fortune |
| NI WO DAI | |
| YIBank | |
| TAIRAN | Internet Finance |
| | 100credit.com |

**Chairman of SFI Academic Committee:**

| QIAN Yingyi | Dean, School of Economics and Management, Tsinghua University |

**SFI Academic Committee Members:**

| | |
|---|---|
| LI Xunlei | Vice President & Chief Economist, Haitong Securities |
| LIAN Ping | Chief Economist, Bank of Communications |
| LIAO Min | Director, Shanghai Office, China Banking Regulatory Commission |
| MIAO Jianmin | President, China Life Insurance (Group) Company |
| WANG Qing | President, Shanghai Chongyang Investment Management Co., Ltd |
| ZHANG Chun | Executive Dean, Shanghai Advanced Institute of Finance, Shanghai Jiaotong University |
| ZHENG Yang | Director, Shanghai Financial Services Office |
| ZHONG Wei | Director, Finance Research Center, Beijing Normal University |

**The Chairman of SFI Supervisory Committee:**

| | |
|---|---|
| XU Zhen | Chairman, Shanghai Clearing House |

**SFI Supervisors:**

| | |
|---|---|
| GUAN Tao | Senior Fellow, China Finance 40 Forum |
| WU Cheng | Deputy Governor, Huangpu District, Shanghai |

**The Director of SFI:**

| | |
|---|---|
| QIAN Yingyi | Dean, School of Economics and Management, Tsinghua University |

**The Deputy Director of SFI:**

| | |
|---|---|
| ZHONG Wei | Director, Finance Research Center, Beijing Normal University |

**The Executive Deputy Director of SFI:**

| | |
|---|---|
| WANG Haiming | Secretary-General, China Finance 40 Forum |

For Product Safety Concerns and Information please contact our EU
representative GPSR@taylorandfrancis.com
Taylor & Francis Verlag GmbH, Kaufingerstraße 24, 80331 München, Germany

www.ingramcontent.com/pod-product-compliance
Ingram Content Group UK Ltd.
Pitfield, Milton Keynes, MK11 3LW, UK
UKHW021611240425
457818UK00018B/504